Sams'

Teach

Yourself

THE
INTERNET
STARTER KIT

in 24 Hours

Sams'

Teach Yourself

THE
INTERNET
STARTER KIT

Ned Snell

in 24 Hours

SAMS
PUBLISHING

201 West 103rd Street
Indianapolis, Indiana 46290

For my family.

Copyright © 1998 by Sams Publishing

SECOND EDITION

International Standard Book Number: 1-57521-402-4

Library of Congress Catalog Number: 98-84263

2001   2000   99

Interpretation of the printing code: the rightmost double-digit number is the year of the book's printing; the rightmost single digit, the number of the book's printing. For example, a printing code of 98-1 shows that the first printing of the book occurred in 1998.

Composed in AGaramond and MCPdigital by Macmillan Computer Publishing

Printed in the United States of America

Trademarks

Publisher   John Pierce
Executive Editor   Karen Reinisch
Managing Editor   Thomas F. Hayes

Acquisitions Editor
Don Essig

Development Editor
Melanie Palaisa

Copy Editor
Julie McNamee

Indexer
Craig Small

Technical Reviewers
Bill Bruns
John Purdum

Editorial Coordinator
Mandie Rowell

Cover Designers
Gary Adair
Karen Ruggles

Book Designer
Gary Adair

Cover Production
Aren Howell

Production Team Supervisor
Andrew Stone

Production
Jeanne Clark
Heather Howell
Christy M. Lemasters
Julie Searls
Sossity Smith

Overview

Contents

Acknowledgments

I sat down and wrote a book very much like this one, but that's not the book you're holding.

The book you're holding is a better book, in which my work has been guided and shaped by the good folks at Sams, especially Melanie Palaisa, John Purdum, and Don Essig.

If you like this book, you owe them thanks, as I do.

—Ned Snell

About the Author

Ned Snell has been making technology make sense since 1986, when he began writing beginners' documentation for one of the world's largest software companies. After writing manuals and training materials for several major companies, Snell switched sides and became a computer journalist, serving as a writer and eventually as an editor for two national magazines, *Edge* and *Art & Design News*.

A freelance writer since 1991, Snell has written 10 computer books and hundreds of articles and is the courseware critic for *Inside Technology Training* magazine. Between books, Snell works as a professional actor in regional theater, commercials, and industrial films. He lives with his wife and two sons in Florida.

Tell Us What You Think!

As a reader, you are the most important critic and commentator of our books. We value your opinion and want to know what we're doing right, what we could do better, what areas you'd like to see us publish in, and any other words of wisdom you're willing to pass our way. You can help us make strong books that meet your needs and give you the computer guidance you require.

Check out our World Wide Web site at http://www.mcp.com.

JUST A MINUTE

If you need assistance with the information provided in this product, please feel free to access our web site at http://www.mcp.com/info.

Here you can enter the ISBN number and view a product information page that will include any available downloads or updates. Our Technical Support department can also be reached at support@mcp.com or via telephone at 317-581-3833.

As the Executive Editor of the group that created this book, I welcome your comments. You can fax, email, or write me directly to let me know what you did or didn't like about this book—as well as what we can do to make our books stronger. Here's the information:

Fax: 317-581-4669

Email: kreinisch@mcp.com

Mail: Karen Reinisch
          Comments Department
          Sams Publishing
          201 W. 103rd Street
          Indianapolis, IN 46290

Introduction

Hello? *Helloooo?* Is anybody there? Nobody reads introductions. I don't know why I bother.

Oh well, looks like it's just you and me. So welcome to *Teach Yourself the Internet in 24 Hours Starter Kit*, the book that gets you into and all around the Internet in a single day's worth of easy lessons. Each of the 24 chapters in this book is called an "Hour," and is designed to endow you with new Internet skills in one hour or less.

Who I Wrote This Thing For

Here's what you're in for. We've designed this book for people who

☐ Are absolutely new to the Internet

☐ Want a quick, easy, common-sense way to learn how to use it

☐ Don't appreciate being treated like morons

(By the way, being new to the Internet doesn't mean you're an idiot or dummy. You just have other priorities. Good for you.)

This book is *system neutral*, which is another way of saying you can use this book no matter what kind of computer you have. As you'll see, using the Internet is pretty much the same no matter what computer you use it from. Setting up each type of computer for the Internet is a little different, however, so I show you how to set up a PC or a Mac for the Internet in Hour 4.

You do not need to know a thing about the Internet, computer networks, or any of that stuff to get started with this book. However, you do need to know your way around your own computer. With a basic, everyday ability to operate the type of computer from which you will use the Internet, you're ready to begin. I'll take you the rest of the way.

Don't have a computer yet? In Hour 2, I'll help you choose one that's properly equipped for the Internet.

> At the very back of this book, you'll find the part that puts the start in Starter Kit: a CD-ROM packed with all the Internet software you need, and even a few things you may not need, just for fun.

How This Book Is Organized

This book is divided into six parts, each four hours long:

☐ **Part I** introduces you to the Internet and the many different things you can do there, and shows how to get yourself and your computer set up for it.

- [ ] **Part II** takes you onto the World Wide Web—the fun, graphical, incredibly useful part of the Internet that everybody's talking about.
- [ ] **Part III** shows you how to find anything and everything on the Internet, including people, products, news, reference information, good advice, bad advice, and so on.
- [ ] **Part IV** covers exchanging messages with anyone on the Internet, first through email and then through topical discussions called *newsgroups*.
- [ ] **Part V** is a grab bag of all the valuable stuff you can do on the Internet that's not covered in other parts: Having a live online chat or voice/video conference, running programs on distant computers, and much more.
- [ ] **Part VI** lets you put your accumulated skills to new and powerful uses, such as making the Internet safe for family viewing, doing business on the net, and even creating your own Web pages that anyone on the Internet can visit.

After Hour 24, you'll discover some terrific resources for your Internet travels:

Appendix A tells you what to do when (if) your Net travels don't go the way you expect them to.

Appendix B offers the *New Riders Yellow Pages* Preview, a terrific compendium of Web sites culled from the popular directory, organized by subject.

Appendix C supplies the *Internet Business Guide* Preview, with still more great Web sites—all about and for business.

What's on the CD? tells you what's included on the Starter Kit CD-ROM.

Things You'd Probably Figure Out by Yourself

There's a long tradition in computer books of using the introduction to explain the little tip boxes and other elements that are absolutely self-explanatory to any reader over the age of six. Just call me "Keeper of the Flame."

Instructions, Tips, and Terms

Here and there, I use step-by-step instructions to show you exactly how to do something. I will always explain how to do that thing in the text that precedes the steps, so feel free to skip them when you want to. However, anytime you feel like you don't completely understand something, follow the steps, and you'll probably get the picture before you're done. Sometimes we learn only by doing.

I call attention to important new terms by tagging them with a New Term icon. It won't happen often, but when it does, it'll help you remember the terms that will help you learn the Internet.

You'll also see three different kinds of tips set off in boxes:

TIME SAVER

A Time Saver box points out a faster, easier way to do something, or a way to use the Internet to get something done quickly, or a way to save time by not doing something. These boxes are completely optional.

JUST A MINUTE

A Just a Minute box highlights an important consideration, tip, or interesting tidbit related to the topic at hand. They're optional, too, but always worth reading (otherwise, I wouldn't interrupt).

CAUTION

A Caution box alerts you to actions and situations where something bad could happen, such as accidentally deleting an important file. Because there's very little you can do on the Internet that's in any way dangerous, you'll see very few Cautions. So when you see them, take them seriously.

At the end of every hour is an easy, fun Workshop designed to reinforce the most important skills and concepts covered in the hour. Each Workshop contains the following:

☐ A **Q&A** session contains a few quick questions and answers explaining interesting stuff that wasn't included in the hour because it doesn't directly contribute to teaching yourself the Internet (even though it's interesting).

☐ A **Quiz** contains three or four multiple-choice questions that help you recall important points and also provide me with a good place for jokes I couldn't work into the book elsewhere.

☐ An **Activity** is something you can do to practice what you learned in the hour or to prepare for the hour that follows.

One More Thing...

Actually, no more things. Start the clock, and hit Hour 1. Twenty-four working hours from now, you'll know the Internet inside-out.

PART
I

Getting Started

Hour

Hour 1

What Is the Internet and What Can You Do There?

You probably think you already know what the Internet is, and you're probably 90 percent right, for all practical purposes. But by developing just a little better understanding of what the Internet is all about, you'll find learning to use it much easier.

Don't get me wrong; this hour is *not* about the tiny, techy details of how the Internet works. You don't need to know exactly how the Internet works to use it, any more than you need to know the mechanics of an engine to drive a car. Rather, this hour is designed to give you some helpful background—and perhaps dispel a few myths and misconceptions—so you can jump confidently into the stuff coming up in later hours.

At the end of the hour, you'll be able to answer the following questions:

- [ ] What *exactly* is the Internet?
- [ ] Where did the Internet come from, and where is it going?
- [ ] What are clients and servers, and how do they determine what you can do on the net?
- [ ] What types of activities can you perform on the net, given the right hardware and software?

Understanding the Net (the Easy Version)

No doubt you've heard of a *computer network*, a group of computers that are wired together so they can communicate with one another. When computers are hooked together in a network, users of those computers can send each other messages and share computer files and programs.

Computer networks today can be as small as two PCs hooked together in an office or as big as thousands of computers of all different types spread all over the world and connected to one another not just by wires, but through telephone lines and even via satellite.

To build a really big network, you need to build lots of little networks and then hook the little networks to each other, creating an *internetwork*. That's all the Internet really is: The world's largest internetwork (hence its name). In homes, businesses, schools, and government offices all over the world, millions of computers of all different types—PCs, Macintoshes, big corporate mainframes, and others—are connected together in networks, and those networks are connected to one another to form the Internet. Because everything is connected, any computer on the Internet can communicate with any other computer on the Internet (see Figure 1.1).

How It All Began

In the late 1960s, the U.S. Department of Defense (DoD) recognized how dependent the U.S. Government had become on its national computer network, and asked, "What would happen if an enemy knocked down our network? Could we respond without access to our computers?"

In those days, if one network in an internetwork failed, the whole internetwork collapsed. If defense computers in Washington were disabled by a bomb, a power failure, a disgruntled programmer, or a spilled Pepsi, defense computing in Colorado or California could be compromised. The whole system depended on every part operating properly.

1

Figure 1.1.

The Internet is a global internetwork, a huge collection of computers and networks intercon- nected so they can exchange information.

So the DoD designed a new kind of internetwork that could still function when part of the network died. The linchpin of the whole system was a set of communications rules, or protocols, called TCP/IP (Transmission Control Protocol/Internet Protocol). In general, any network communicating with TCP/IP can communicate with any other network communicating with TCP/IP. And, if any part of a TCP/IP internetwork fails, the rest of the internetwork can keep running.

TCP/IP worked so reliably that other government (and government-related) agencies began to apply it in their own networks, even those with no defense role. By the late 1970s, most large computer networks used by the government, defense contractors, large universities, and major scientific and research organizations were using TCP/IP for internetworking. (Most still use it today.)

Because all these internetworks communicated in the same way, they could communicate with one another, too. The government, defense contractors, and scientists often needed to communicate with one another and share information, so they hooked all their computers and networks into one big TCP/IP internetwork. This larger internetwork became the infant Internet.

JUST A MINUTE

When you use a computer that's connected to the Internet, you can communicate with any other computer on the Internet.

That, however, doesn't mean you can access *everything* that's stored on the other computers. Obviously, the government, university, and corporate computers on the Internet have the capability to make certain kinds of information on their computers accessible through the Internet and to restrict access to other information so only authorized people can see it.

Similarly, when you're on the Internet, any other computer on the net can communicate with yours. That does not mean, however, that someone can reach through the net into your computer and steal your resume or recipes. As you'll learn in later hours, you control what others can learn about you through the net.

What the Net Became

The first great thing about the Internet's design is that it's open to all types of computers. Virtually any computer—from a palmtop PC to a supercomputer—can be equipped with TCP/IP so it can get on the net. Even when a computer doesn't use TCP/IP, it also can access information on the net using other technologies, basically "back doors" to the net.

The other important thing about the Internet is that it allows the use of a wide range of *communications media*—ways computers can communicate. The "wires" that interconnect the millions of computers on the Internet include the wires that hook together the small networks in offices, private data lines, local telephone lines, national telephone networks (which carry signals via wire, microwave, and satellite), and international telephone carriers.

It is this wide range of hardware and communications options, and the universal availability of TCP/IP, that has enabled the Internet to grow so large, encompassing over 35 million users on every continent (yes, even Antarctica). That's why you can get on the Internet from your home or office, right through the same telephone line you use to call out for pizza. It's a crazy world.

The flexibility of the technology set the stage for the Internet's explosion, but didn't cause it. The boom came about this way: In the early 1990s, the business community recognized that the Internet was becoming a market. Not only that, but it was untapped because of anti-advertising policies left over from the Internet's days as a research tool. In 1995, the Internet was fully privatized, opening the door to any and all commercial opportunities.

At roughly the same time, consumer interest in the Internet took off, in part because the World Wide Web had evolved to make the Internet both easier to use and more fun to look at, and also because PCs were becoming more powerful and cheaper, just in time for Christmas.

Soon, a vicious cycle began: Organizations began making their Internet sites more fun and useful to entice folks to visit, which made the Internet more appealing, which inspired more people to go online, which inspired more organizations to establish an Internet presence to tap the growing market, which forced the organizations online to make their sites more fun and useful to compete for attention, which enticed more folks onto the Internet…and the beat goes on.

Still, few organizations really make any money online today. An Internet presence today is an affordable way for organizations to distribute information and to gain visibility. For you, that means there's a lot to see, do, and learn online that doesn't cost you a dime beyond whatever you pay for your Internet connection, which can be very little.

NEW TERM Any time your computer has a live, open connection to the Internet, you and your computer are said to be *online*. When the Internet connection is closed (because your computer is off or for any other reason), you're *offline*.

The idea is easier to grasp if you think in telephone terms: When you're in a call (even if nobody's talking), you're online; when the phone's in its cradle, you're offline.

Making the Net Work: Clients and Servers

The key to doing anything on the Internet is understanding two words: client and server. Figure 1.2 illustrates the relationship between clients and servers.

Figure 1.2.

From your computer, you use a set of client programs, each of which accesses a different type of server computer on the Internet.

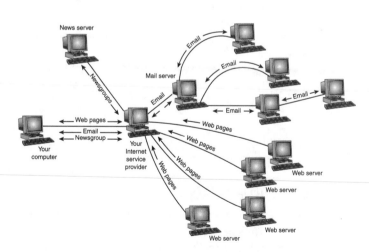

Most of the information you will access through the Internet is stored on computers called servers. A *server* can be any type of computer; what makes it a server is the role it plays. It stores information for use by clients.

A *client* is a computer—or, more accurately, a particular computer program—that knows how to communicate with a particular type of server to use the information stored on that server (or to put information there). For example, when you surf the web, you use a client program called a web browser to communicate with a computer where web pages are stored—a web server.

 NEW TERM A *web browser* is a program that lets a computer communicate with web servers and display the information stored there. You'll learn much more about web browsers and other client programs as your 24 hours tick by.

In general, each type of Internet activity involves a different type of client and server. To use the web, you need a web client to communicate with web servers. To use email, you need an email client to communicate with email servers.

This client/server business shows what the Internet really is: Just a communications medium, a virtual wire through which computers communicate. It's the different kinds of clients and servers—not the Internet itself—that enable you to perform various activities. Because new kinds of clients and servers can be invented, new types of activities can be added to the Internet at any time.

What Can You Do Through the Net?

I've known people who have gone out and bought a PC, signed up for an Internet account, and then called me to say, "Okay, so I'm on the Internet. Now what am I supposed to do there?"

That's backwards. I think the marketers and the press have pushed so hard that some folks simply think they *must* be on the Internet, without knowing why—sort of the way everybody thinks they need a beeper. Unless there's something on the net you want or need to use, you really don't need the net. You wouldn't buy a rice steamer unless you liked rice. You don't need a beeper if you never leave the house. In other words, don't let Madison Avenue and Microsoft push you around.

So here's a good place to get a feel for what you can actually do on the Internet. If nothing here interests you, please give this book to a friend or to your local library. You can check out the net again in a year or two to see whether it offers anything new.

Browse the Web

It's likely that your interest in the Internet was sparked by the World Wide Web, even if you don't know it. When you see news stories about the Internet showing someone looking at a cool, colorful screen full of things to see and do, that person is looking at the World Wide Web, most commonly referred to as "the web," or occasionally as "WWW."

1

The web is used so often by the media to describe and illustrate the Internet, many folks think the web *is* the Internet. But it's not; it's just a part of the net, or rather one of many Internet-based activities. The web gets the most attention because it's the fastest-growing, easiest-to-use part of the net.

All those funky-looking Internet addresses you see in ads today—www.pepsi.com and so forth—are the addresses you use to visit those companies on the web. With an Internet connection and a web browser on your computer, you can type an address to visit a particular web site and read the web pages stored there. Figure 1.3 shows a web page, viewed through a web browser.

Figure 1.3.

Seen through a web browser, a web page is a file of information stored on a web server.

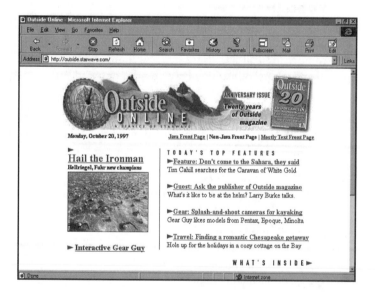

NEW TERM   The terms *web site* and *web page* are used rather flexibly, but in general, a *web site* is a particular web server or a part of a web server, where information about a particular organization or subject is stored.

When you use your *web browser* to contact a web site, the information on the server is displayed on your computer screen. The particular screenful of information you view is described as a web page, but it's really just a computer file stored on the server.

By browsing the web, you can do a staggering number of different things, including all the activities described in the following sections.

Visit Companies, Governments, Museums, Schools...

Just about any large organization has it own web site these days. Many smaller organizations also have their own sites or are discussed in pages stored on other's sites. You can visit these sites to learn more about products you want to buy, school or government policies, and much more.

For example, I belong to an HMO for medical coverage. I can visit my HMO's web site to find and choose a new doctor, review policy restrictions, and much more. I can do this any day, any time, without waiting on hold for the "next available operator."

Just as easily, I can check out tax rules or order forms on the Internal Revenue Service web site, view paintings in museums all over the world, or find out when the next Parent's Night is at the local elementary school.

Read the News

CNN has its own web site, as do the *New York Times*, the *Wall Street Journal*, and dozens of other media outlets ranging from major print magazines to fly-by-night rags spreading rumors, to small sites featuring news about any imaginable topic. You'll also find a number of great news sources that have no print or broadcast counterpart—they're exclusive to the web.

Whatever kind of news you want, you can find it on the web. Often, the news online is more up-to-the-minute than any print counterpart, and unlike broadcast news, you can look at it any time you find convenient.

Explore Libraries

Increasingly, libraries large and small are making their catalogs available online. That means you can find out which library has the book you need, without spending a day driving to each one. Some libraries even allow you to borrow online; you choose a book from the catalog of a library across the state from you, and in a few days you can pick it up at a library closer to you or right from your mailbox.

Read

Books are published right on the web, including classics (such as Shakespeare and Dickens) and new works. You can read them right on your screen or print them out to read later on the bus. (*Please* don't read while you drive. I *hate* that.) The web has even initiated its own kind of literature, *collaborative fiction*, in which visitors to a web site can read—and contribute to—a story in progress.

Get Software

Because computer software can travel through the Internet, you can actually get software right through the web and use it on your PC. Some of the software is free, some isn't. But it's all there, whenever you need it—no box, no disc, no pushy guy saying, "Ya want a cell phone with that?"

1

Shop

One of the fastest-growing, and most controversial, web activities is shopping. Right on the web, you can browse an online catalog, choose merchandise, type in a credit card number and shipping address, and receive your merchandise in a few days, postage paid. Besides merchandise, you can buy just about anything else on the web: stocks, legal services, you name it. Everything but surgery, and I'm sure that's only a matter of time.

The controversy arises from the fact that sending your credit card number and other private information through the Internet exposes you to abuse of that information by anyone clever enough to cull it from the din of web traffic. That risk factor, however, is rapidly shrinking as the web develops improved security. (You'll learn about web security in Hour 7, "Protecting Your Privacy (and Other Security Stuff).") By shopping from your PC, you can't get mugged in the mall parking lot.

Play Games, Watch Videos, Get a Degree, Waste Time...

Have I left anything out? There's too much on the web to cover with the limited space I have here, but I hope you get the idea. The web is where it's at. In fact, there are many folks on the Internet who use the web and nothing else. Unfortunately, those folks are missing out...read on.

JUST A MINUTE

> There's one more thing you can do on the web: publish. Just as you can access any web server, you can publish your own web pages on a web server, so anyone on the Internet with a web browser can read them.
>
> You can publish web pages to promote your business or cause, to tell others about a project or hobby that's your passion, or just to let the world know you're you. You'll learn how in Hour 23, "Creating Web Pages and Multimedia Messages."

Exchange Messages

Email, in case you didn't know, is a message sent as an electronic file from one computer to another. Using Internet email, you can type a message on your computer and send it to anyone else on the Internet.

Each user on the Internet has a unique email address; if your email address is suzyq@netknow.com, you're the only person in the world with that email address (isn't that nice?). So if anyone, anywhere in the world, sends a message to that address, it reaches you and you alone. As mentioned earlier, to use email, you need an email client program, which interacts with the email servers that store and send email around the world.

Email is great for simple messages, but these days, it can do more. You can attach computer files to email messages to send them to others, broadcast a message to two or a hundred recipients at once, and even create cool, colorful messages with graphics and sound. (You'll learn how in Hour 23.)

Have a Discussion

Using your email client, you can join mailing lists related to topics that interest you. Members of a mailing list automatically receive news and other information—in the form of email messages—related to the list's topic. Often, members can send their own news and comments to the list, and those messages are passed on to all members.

But the Internet's principal discussion venue is the *newsgroup*, a sort of public bulletin board. Thousands of newsgroups exist, each centering on a particular topic—everything from music to politics, from addiction recovery to TV shows. Newsgroup messages are stored on news servers. To read the messages and post your own messages, you need a client called a newsreader.

Visitors to a newsgroup post messages that any other visitor can read. When reading a message, you can quickly compose and post a reply to that message, to add information to the message, or to argue with it. (You know how much folks like to argue.) As the replies are followed by replies to the replies, a sort of free-form discussion evolves.

By following (and participating in) a newsgroup discussion, you can learn a lot about a topic and pick up a lot of rumor, gossip, and unsubstantiated opinion (depending on who's doing the talking).

JUST A MINUTE

You may have heard that you can pick up a lot of unreliable information on the Internet, and indeed, that's true. As when absorbing information from any communications medium—print, broadcast, Internet, water cooler, back fence—you must always consider the source, and take much of what you learn with a grain of salt.

You must also trust that, just as the Internet offers a forum to nutballs with axes to grind, it also offers an incredible wealth of authoritative, accurate information that's often difficult to find elsewhere. It's just like newspapers: You can read the *Wall Street Journal*, or you can read the *Star*. If you choose the latter, you can't blame your paper for misinforming you.

As you move through this book, I'll help you learn how to verify the source of what you learn online, so you can make informed choices about what to doubt, what to believe, and what to keep an open mind about.

1

1

Chat

Exchanging messages through email and newsgroups is great, but it's not very interactive. You type a message, send it, and wait hours or days for a reply. Sometimes, you want to communicate in a more immediate, interactive, "live" way. That's where Internet Relay Chat, also known as IRC or just Chat, comes in.

Using chat client programs, folks from all over the world contact chat servers and join one another in live discussions. Each discussion takes place in a separate chat "room" or "channel" reserved for discussion of a particular topic. The discussion is carried out through a series of typed messages; each participant types his or her contributions, and anything anyone in the room types shows up on the screen of everyone in the chat room.

JUST A MINUTE

In addition to chat, there are other ways to have a live conversation over the Internet. As you learn in Hour 17, "Voice and Video Conferencing," you can hold voice and video conferences through the Internet, wherein you can see and hear your partners, and they can see and hear you.

Run Programs on Other Computers

Not everything on the Internet sits on a web server, email server, news server, or chat server. There are other kinds of computers and servers connected to the Internet—ones you can use, if you know how, through a client called Telnet. When you use a distant computer through Telnet, you can run programs on it and access its data as if you were there.

JUST A MINUTE

Telnet is one of the original Internet tools, used among our Internet forebears to share one another's computers. It's also the tool the infamous hackers once deployed to break into distant systems to make mischief (remember the movie *Wargames*?).

Telnet still works today, but computers are better protected than they used to be. In general, if you can successfully enter a remote computer through Telnet, you're welcome there. You won't accidentally start a global thermonuclear war just by poking around with Telnet.

There's so much on web and news servers these days that you may never want or need to journey beyond them. But for the adventurous, Telnet offers access to information you can't get any other way. In Hour 19, "Using Old-Fashioned Hacker's Tools: FTP, Gopher, and Telnet," you'll discover Telnet and a few other advanced tools for exploiting the Internet beyond the confines of the web and newsgroups.

Summary

The Internet is a huge, and growing, internetwork that nobody really planned but happened anyway. Your job is not really to understand it, but to enjoy it and to use it in whatever way you find valuable or entertaining.

The value and entertainment are stored all over the world on a vast array of servers; to tap the benefits of the Internet, you deploy a family of client programs that knows how to talk to the servers. In a way, most of this book is really about choosing and using client programs to make the most of the Internet's servers.

Workshop

Q&A

Q If the Internet "just happened," who's in charge? What keeps it going?

A That's one of the really neat things about the Internet: Nobody's in charge. (Microsoft and America Online *want* to be in charge, but that's different.) There are volunteer committees that handle such things as making sure every computer gets its own, unique Internet ID (which is essential to the workings of the Internet) and approving the *standards* for such things as the way web browsers communicate with web servers. However, nobody really controls the Internet, and nobody owns it.

It's the standards that keep the Internet going. The Internet is made of privately owned computers and networking equipment, whose owners have put it on the Internet for their own reasons. But because that hardware is part of the Internet and obeys its standards, you get to use it, too. It's really a big fat co-op, an amazing example of how independent parties collaborating for their own self-interest can inadvertently create a public good.

As you'll learn in Hour 3, "Internet Service Provider, AOL, or Other: Who's Best for You?," you generally pay a subscription fee to an Internet provider to use the Internet, but that fee covers the provider's costs (plus profit) in maintaining its service. You're not paying the Internet a dime because there's no actual organization to collect your money. In principle (if not always in practice), the Internet is free.

Q You just mentioned America Online. Isn't that the same thing as the Internet?

A No, no, no. As you'll learn in Hour 3, America Online (AOL) is a commercial online service. It provides its subscribers with a range of information and services that are not on the Internet, and it also provides those subscribers with access to the Internet, just like any other Internet service provider. But only a small fraction of the folks on the Internet use AOL. There are many other choices.

Q I have this funny rash on my elbow. Is it psoriasis?

A Stick to the subject. Or, better yet, learn to search for information on the web (as you will in Part III, "Finding What You're Looking For"), and you can find out everything you ever wanted to know about rashes.

In the meantime, dab on some cortizone cream, don't walk on it for a few days, and call me if it gets worse.

Quiz

Take the following quiz to see how much you've learned.

Questions

1. TCP/IP, the communications protocol that ties the Internet together, was created in the late 1960s by which arm of the U.S. Government, and for what purpose?

    a. The White House, to be able to locate Spiro Agnew quickly, anywhere in the world, in the event of an emergency requiring the vice president. (Status: Still in operation, never used.)

    b. The CIA, to spy on those Commie-Hippie-Liberals in higher education. (Status: Records vanished, 1976.)

    c. The FDA, to test the feasibility of transmitting cheese by phone. (Status: Still trying.)

    d. The DoD, to build a better defense network. (Status: They think it works, but nobody's attacked yet.)

2. To access information stored on the Internet in a server computer, you need a computer, an Internet connection, and

    a. The right client program for accessing the particular type of server.

    b. A Nintendo system, some wire, and a 9-volt battery.

    c. Guts.

    d. Matthew Broderick.

3. A *browser* is a client program that displays the _____ stored on the Internet on _____.

    a. truth   Macintoshes

    b. web pages   web servers

    c. monkeys   trees

    d. pantsuits   layaway

Answers

1. (d) The DoD (Department of Defense) planted the seeds of the Internet by developing TCP/IP. The other choices had nothing to do with TCP/IP, but I swear they're true otherwise.

2. (a) Each type of server is built to be accessed by a particular type of client program.

3. (b) Browsers are for getting web pages from web servers.

Activity

Because you'll be surfing the web very soon, start paying more attention to web site addresses when you see them.

For example, whenever you see an ad for something that interests you, and that ad shows an address (such as www.toyota.com or http://CNN.com), jot down the address or save the ad. Find out whether your company, school, or church has a web page and make a note of its address. You'll often find web addresses listed not only in ads, but on stationery, business cards, billing statements, billboards, and other highly visible spots. You'll soon have the tools to visit those sites.

1

Hour 2

What Hardware and Software Do You Need?

Got a computer made within the last 10 years? Then odds are you can get it onto the Internet. The power of your hardware doesn't have that much to do with whether you can get *on* the Internet, but it has everything to do with what you can *do* there.

In this hour, you'll discover the hardware required to use the Internet, and explore the available options and the pros and cons of each. After you've settled on a computer (or the pseudocomputer alternative, such as a WebTV terminal), you'll need to know which client programs and other software your Internet travels will demand.

At the end of the hour, you'll be able to answer the following questions:

☐ What kinds of computers can I use to surf the Internet, and how should they be equipped?

☐ How fast a modem do I need?

☐ What's WebTV and how is it different from surfing the Internet through a computer?

☐ What software do I need to get started, and where can I get it?

Modems—Wherein the *Lack* of Speed Kills

There are ways to connect to the Internet without a modem, but such options (which you'll discover at the end of this chapter) are wildly costly and complex today. Odds are that you will use an ordinary modem and telephone line for your Internet connection, so you must consider the capabilities of your modem in choosing or upgrading your computer for Internet access.

NEW TERM A *modem* is a device that enables two computers to communicate with one another through phone lines. Using a modem (installed inside or connected to your computer), you can communicate through your regular home or business phone lines with the modem at your Internet provider. That's how you connect to the Internet.

Although modem most often refers to the type just described, there are special types of modems designed not for use over phone lines, but for use over two-way cable TV connections (in the few areas where such lines exist), high-speed private data lines, and cellular/satellite networks. Such modems are expensive and require all sorts of costly equipment and software, and, as such, are not a reasonable option for someone just beginning to explore the Internet.

It doesn't really matter what brand of modem you buy, or whether it's an internal modem (plugged inside your computer's case), an external one (outside the computer, connected to it by a cable), or even one on a PCMCIA card inserted in a notebook PC.

What does matter is the modem's rated speed. That speed is usually expressed in *bits per second* (bps) or sometimes as a *baud rate*. Where choosing a modem is concerned, bps and baud rate are essentially the same thing. (There is a technical difference that matters to computer experts, but it's not a difference that matters to a typical user. A 9,600bps modem is the same device as a 9,600 baud modem.)

The higher the number of bps, the faster the modem. The faster your modem is, the more quickly web pages appear on your screen, which makes web surfing more fun and productive. A number of other Internet activities also run quicker and smoother over a faster modem. (Note, however, that the faster the modem, the more you'll pay for it.)

2

JUST A MINUTE

For modems rated at speeds above 9,600bps, the term bps is usually replaced by *kilobits per second* (Kbps), which equals 1,000bps. That way, a modem that runs at, oh, 28,800bps can be described as a 28.8Kbps modem, or even just 28.8K.

Modems for use with regular telephone lines are rated at the following speeds:

- ☐ 9,600bps (9.6K)
- ☐ 14,400bps (14.4K)
- ☐ 28,800bps (28.8K)
- ☐ 33,600bps (33.6K)
- ☐ 56,000bps (56K)

The practical minimum modem speed for Internet cruising (including web browsing) is 14.4K, although at that speed, you'll often face long waits for web pages to appear. Today, you'll find the best balance of speed and affordability in 28.8K modems, which provide decent (if not blazing) Internet performance at a reasonable price.

Faster modems may deliver performance superior to 28.8K modems, but not always perceptibly so. A number of factors—such as the reliability and noise level in your phone line, the speed supported by your Internet provider, and the responsiveness of the servers you contact—may cause these more costly modems to perform no better than a 28.8K modem, much of the time. Also, some Internet providers charge more to customers using 33.6K and 56K modems.

The capability for extra speed never hurts, so there's no reason not to go with the fastest modem you can afford. However, don't spend a month's rent on a hotrod modem on the assumption that you're guaranteed faster online performance.

JUST A MINUTE

Just because you have a fast modem doesn't mean you can use the Internet at the modem's rated speed. For example, if your Internet provider supports only 28.8K Internet access, and you have a 33.6K modem, your speedy modem will automatically slow down to 28.8K or slower to communicate with your Internet provider.

Also, although it's the most important factor, modem speed is not the only thing that governs the apparent speed with which things spring onto your screen. If it takes your computer a long time to process and display the information it receives through the Internet, you'll see some delays that have nothing to do with modem speed. A fast computer is almost as important as a fast modem—it's a team effort.

Choosing a Computer

I've told you that almost any computer—even an older one—can be used to get on the Internet, and that's true. But to take full advantage of what the Internet offers, you need a top-of-the-line computer, or pretty close to it.

You see, some Internet tasks (such as email) demand little processing power from a computer and don't require a really fast Internet connection; they're neither processor-intensive nor communications-intensive. However, the main thing most newcomers to the net want is the web, and browsing the web is just about the most processor-intensive, communications-intensive thing a computer can do.

To take full advantage of the web, a computer must be able to display and play multimedia content—graphics, animation, video, and sound—that's increasingly built into web pages. Such tasks require a fast processor and plenty of memory. In fact, a web browser capable of supporting this multimedia is about the most demanding application you can put on a PC or Mac, requiring more processing power and memory than any word processor or spreadsheet on the market.

In addition to the multimedia, more and more web pages feature Java programs, which enable all sorts of advanced web activities (see Figure 2.1). To run the Java programs in web pages, your computer must use a fast 32-bit processor (such as a 486) and operating system (such as Windows 95), which have been available in PCs and Macs for only the last few years. As a rule, a PC that can't run Windows 95, and a Mac that can't run System 7.5, can't run Java programs or the browsers that support Java.

Figure 2.1.

To enjoy the multimedia and Java content built into many web pages like these, you need a powerful, well-equipped computer and a fast modem.

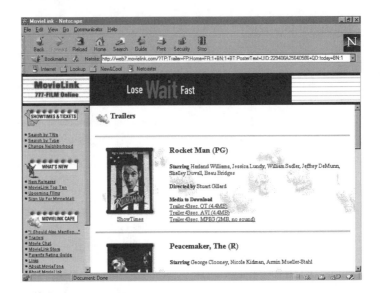

2

New Term *Java* is a programming language specially designed for use in computer networks, such as the Internet. On the web, programmers add Java programs to web pages to enable the page to do things it couldn't do otherwise, such as collect and process order information for an online store or make images dance around the page.

Java makes the web more powerful and interactive, but also more complex and demanding. You'll learn more about Java in Hours 7, "Protecting Your Privacy (and Other Security Stuff)," and 8, "Plug-ins, Helpers, and Other Ways to Do More Online."

Just a Minute

> What about notebooks and other portable computers? No problem. Notebook PCs, PowerBooks, and other portables make perfectly good Internet computers, as long as they meet the same general requirements (processor, modem speed, and so on) that a desktop computer must meet, as described later in this hour.
>
> Note, however, that a portable computer always costs much more than a desktop computer with the same specifications. Also, some portables with otherwise acceptable specifications may have screens that are too small for comfortable web browsing; any screen that measures less than 10 inches diagonally is probably too small, unless you have really, really, really good glasses.
>
> Any size screen is fine, however, for email and other text-based, off-the-web Internet activities.

Finally, newer, more powerful computers are required to run the newest, most advanced operating systems, such as Windows 95 (or the next version of Windows, scheduled for release sometime in 1998) on the PC or OS8 on the Macintosh. These operating systems have been designed with the Internet in mind, making setting up your computer for the Internet much quicker and easier.

Again, you can get a lot out of the Internet on a less capable computer—you just won't see or hear what your computer can't handle. The bottom line is this: Most of the exciting innovations on the Internet, now and in the future, are designed for use by the newest, most powerful computers. So if you're shopping, aim high. If you're standing still now with an older machine, forge ahead with the understanding that your Internet experience is not going to be all that it might be.

A PC for the Internet

To make the most of today's Internet, the minimum reasonable PC would be equipped as follows:

☐ **Processor**—A Pentium processor (or its cloned equivalent) is recommended for its capability to support the preferred operating systems listed next. Look for a Pentium rated at 166 MHz or faster. A 486 DX2 or 486 DX4 processor makes a workable, budget-minded alternative, provided that the PC also contains sufficient memory. (Even then, however, a 486 may struggle with Java, online video, and other processor-intensive activities.)

☐ **Operating System**—Windows 95 and Windows NT are good choices. If you are going to purchase a computer in the near future, or if your current computer is properly equipped, consider using the next release of Microsoft Windows. This newest version may be the best choice for many because it features a built-in web browser (Internet Explorer) and an easy-to-use program for setting up your Internet connection. For more information on the web browser, see Hour 3, "Internet Service Provider, AOL, or Other: Who's Best for You?"

The next version of Windows, however, will make greater memory demands on your PC than Windows 95; if your PC has less than 24MB of RAM (and you can't add more memory), you ought to stick with Windows 95. Windows NT is more costly and complex than either of its siblings, so Windows NT should be selected only when the PC will also be used for other tasks where Windows NT has an edge, such as company networking.

JUST A MINUTE

> What if you have a PC that only supports Windows 3.1? How do you get online?
>
> It can be done. First, you need to install and configure TCP/IP communications software in Windows 3.1; a popular program called Trumpet Winsock, available from most Internet providers, works great. You also need to find client software that runs in Windows 3.1, which you may also be able to get from your Internet provider.
>
> Note that both of the most popular web browsers—Internet Explorer and Netscape Navigator—are available for Windows 3.1, but those programs require a 486 or faster processor and 8MB of memory. Many Windows 3.1 PCs can't meet these requirements. If yours can't, you'll only be able to use older, less full-featured client programs, which will not support such recent innovations as Java.
>
> If you really can't upgrade to a more capable computer, you might consider a shell account (see Hour 3) as a way to get an older PC online. Heck, with a shell account, you can get a decade-old DOS PC onto the Internet!

2

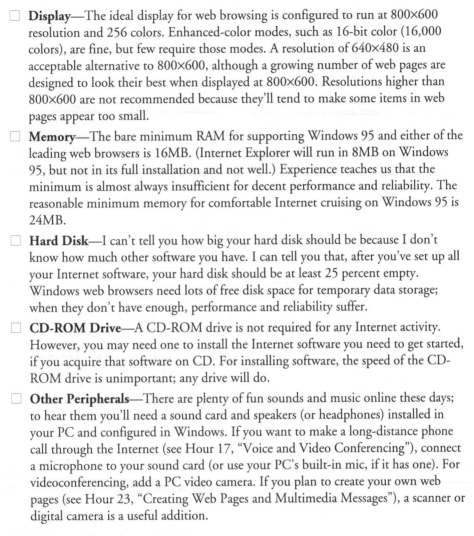

- **Display**—The ideal display for web browsing is configured to run at 800×600 resolution and 256 colors. Enhanced-color modes, such as 16-bit color (16,000 colors), are fine, but few require those modes. A resolution of 640×480 is an acceptable alternative to 800×600, although a growing number of web pages are designed to look their best when displayed at 800×600. Resolutions higher than 800×600 are not recommended because they'll tend to make some items in web pages appear too small.

- **Memory**—The bare minimum RAM for supporting Windows 95 and either of the leading web browsers is 16MB. (Internet Explorer will run in 8MB on Windows 95, but not in its full installation and not well.) Experience teaches us that the minimum is almost always insufficient for decent performance and reliability. The reasonable minimum memory for comfortable Internet cruising on Windows 95 is 24MB.

- **Hard Disk**—I can't tell you how big your hard disk should be because I don't know how much other software you have. I can tell you that, after you've set up all your Internet software, your hard disk should be at least 25 percent empty. Windows web browsers need lots of free disk space for temporary data storage; when they don't have enough, performance and reliability suffer.

- **CD-ROM Drive**—A CD-ROM drive is not required for any Internet activity. However, you may need one to install the Internet software you need to get started, if you acquire that software on CD. For installing software, the speed of the CD-ROM drive is unimportant; any drive will do.

- **Other Peripherals**—There are plenty of fun sounds and music online these days; to hear them you'll need a sound card and speakers (or headphones) installed in your PC and configured in Windows. If you want to make a long-distance phone call through the Internet (see Hour 17, "Voice and Video Conferencing"), connect a microphone to your sound card (or use your PC's built-in mic, if it has one). For videoconferencing, add a PC video camera. If you plan to create your own web pages (see Hour 23, "Creating Web Pages and Multimedia Messages"), a scanner or digital camera is a useful addition.

A Mac for the Internet

To make the most of today's Internet, the minimum reasonable Macintosh system would be equipped as follows:

- **Processor**—A 68040- or PowerPC-based Mac or Mac clone is recommended. A 68030-based system is a budget alternative, but it cannot support the Mac OS8 operating system and may struggle with Java processing.

☐ **Operating System**—System 7 or OS8 is necessary. If your Mac supports it, I strongly recommend OS8, which has a built-in, easy-to-use routine for setting up your Internet connection, built-in Java processing, and a complete set of Internet client programs.

☐ **Display**—The ideal display for web browsing is configured to run at 800×600 resolution and 256 colors. Enhanced color modes, such as 16-bit color (16,000 colors), are fine, but you'll see little content online that requires those modes. A resolution of 640×480 is an acceptable alternative to 800×600, although a growing number of web pages are designed to look their best when displayed at 800×600. Resolutions higher than 800×600 are not recommended because they'll tend to make some items in web pages appear too small.

☐ **Memory**—Consider 16MB as the workable minimum for web browsing on any Mac. If you use OS8, 16MB will do, but 24MB is recommended.

☐ **Hard Disk**—Your hard disk should be large enough to leave 25 percent of free space after you have installed all your software.

☐ **CD-ROM Drive**—A CD-ROM drive is not required for any Internet activity. However, you may need one to install the Internet software you need to get started if you acquire that software on CD. For installing software, the speed of the CD-ROM drive is unimportant; any drive will do.

☐ **Other Peripherals**—If you want to make a long-distance phone call through the Internet (see Hour 17), you'll need a microphone hooked to your Mac. If you want to have a voice conference call, you'll need a Mac-compatible video camera. If you plan to create your own web pages (see Hour 23), a scanner or digital camera can be handy.

Other Internet Options

The overwhelming majority of folks just getting online now are doing so through their personal Mac or PC at home or at work. That's the main scenario, and that's the main focus of this book.

However, I should point out that there are many people online that are not using PCs or Macs, or are not even using their own computers or signing up with an Internet provider. Here are a few ideas for getting online without buying a computer:

☐ **School or Company Computer**—If the company you work for or school you attend has an Internet account, you may be permitted to use the organization's computers to explore the net (usually within strict guidelines). Locate and speak to a person called the network administrator or system administrator; he or she holds the keys to the computer system and is responsible for telling you whether you may use the system, and how and when you're permitted to use it.

2

☐ **Public Library**—Many public libraries have Internet terminals set up for use by patrons. You may use these terminals to do quick research on the web or newsgroups. As a rule, you cannot use them for email because you won't have your own email address, and library machines are never equipped for chat. Even if they were, it's not polite to hog a library PC (as many evil people do) for a long, chatty Internet session.

☐ **Cyber Café**—In all cool cities, you can find *cyber cafés*, coffeehouses equipped with Internet-connected computers so patrons can hang out, eat, drink, and surf (see Figure 2.2). Some cyber cafés let you have an email address (for a fee), so you can send and receive email. Still, there may not always be a computer available when you need one, and you could probably afford your own computer with what you'll spend on Hawaiian Mocha and scones.

In general, the compromises you must make to enjoy these alternatives makes them poor long-term substitutes for having your own computer and Internet account. However, these are great ways to get a taste of the net and reap some of its benefits, if you're still trying to decide about the Internet or are still saving up for that new computer.

Figure 2.2.

The web page of a cyber café in New York City's Greenwich Village.

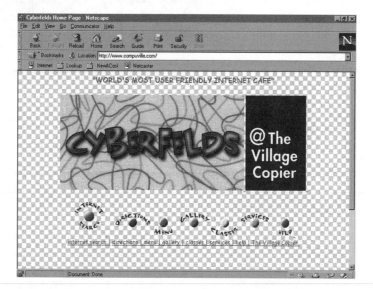

What About WebTV?

WebTV is a new product based on the premise that there are people who want to use the Internet but don't want a computer. Figure 2.3 shows WebTV's promotional web site.

Instead of buying a PC or Mac, all you need for WebTV is a WebTV terminal (a VCR-sized box) and a subscription to the WebTV Internet service. The terminal uses your TV as a display, and you navigate the Internet through the terminal's wireless remote control or an optional wireless keyboard. It uses your telephone line to connect to the Internet, just as a computer would.

Figure 2.3.

The web site of WebTV, where the Internet meets your home video appliance.

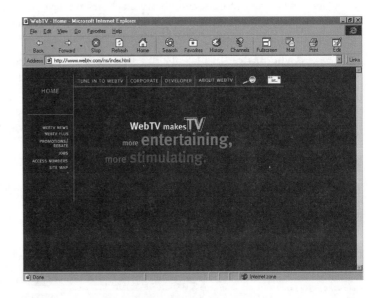

TIME SAVER

You can find WebTV terminals at electronics and appliance stores—anywhere that TVs and VCRs are sold. Models are available from Philips/Magnavox and from Sony, so shop around and compare.

Note, too, that there are two types: A WebTV terminal and a WebTV Plus terminal. The Plus version is more expensive, but it adds a number of new features. Most of the new features, however, work only if you use the WebTV network as your Internet provider.

The WebTV scenario has a few advantages: First and foremost, it's cheap (less than $300 for the terminal, versus $1,200 and up for a decent PC or Mac). WebTV is also comparatively easy to set up and use if you use the WebTV Network Internet service, which is priced comparably with most other Internet providers. At last report, you can also use a WebTV terminal with almost any Internet provider; however, setup is more difficult and you lose a number of special WebTV features (unless you pay an extra $9.95 over your regular Internet charges for access to the WebTV Network *through* your other Internet provider).

WebTV enables you not only to browse the Internet, but also to jump easily between TV shows and related information. While watching *Seinfeld*, you can display a *Seinfeld* web page in a picture-in-picture window on your screen or call up an online TV guide. (By touting this capability, the WebTV people have changed their pitch lately. Instead of selling the system as an alternative to a computer, they're pitching it as a way to enhance your TV viewing. It's high-end TV, not low-end Internet.)

The system also has some major drawbacks. The investment you make in a full computer buys you not only an Internet machine, but also one you can use to write letters, pay bills, do your taxes, play games, listen to CDs, teach your kids Spanish, and much more. A WebTV terminal, although technically a computer on the inside, is a single-purpose machine: You can use it for the Internet and nothing else.

WebTV cannot access all the Internet activities a computer can. You can't use it to get software online, to run Java programs, or to chat. You can send and receive email and newsgroup messages, but you must do so while online (using a real computer, you can do much of this offline). And of course, you can't choose your client software.

Beyond all that is the somewhat fuzzy question of whether the Internet is easier and more fun to use from a little screen on a desktop or a big TV in the living room. Some say it's more fun in the living room; some say web pages and email text are hard to read and navigate from a TV screen. No one can predict the long-term viability of WebTV, but it recently got an important vote of confidence: Microsoft bought the company and operates it as a subsidiary.

I'm not against WebTV, but I just want to make sure you understand that you get what you pay for. For a quarter of the cost of a decent PC, you get one-tenth the utility, and at that, you still don't get complete Internet functionality. As long as you understand that, if you think WebTV is right for you, go get it. You're the boss.

Getting Internet Software

Getting Internet software is like borrowing money: It's only difficult when you really need it. If you already have money (or Internet software), getting more is easy. So the trick is getting started.

You see, after you go online, you can search for, find, and download all the software you want—some of it for free, most at least cheap. You'll learn all about downloading software in Hours 5, "Browsing the Web," and 11, "Finding Programs and Files."

NEW TERM   To *download* is to copy a file—through a network—from another computer into your own. When you get software online, you copy that software from a server somewhere, through the Internet, to your computer, and store it on your hard disk.

What Do You Need?

To figure out what Internet software you need to get started, you must begin by looking at what your computer already has. Recall from Hour 1, "What Is the Internet and What Can You Do There?" that you need two types of software:

☐ Communications software to establish the TCP/IP connection between your computer and your Internet provider

☐ Client software for each activity you want to perform through the net, using the web browser, email client, newsreader, and so on

Table 2.1 shows what each popular operating system (PC and Mac) includes.

Table 2.1. Required Internet software each system features and lacks.

Operating System	Internet Software Included	You Still Need
PC		
Windows 95	Communications software. (A few clients are included, such as email, Telnet, and FTP, but these are not designed as beginner's clients, and no web browser is included.)	Client software.
Windows 3.1	None.	Communications software (such as Trumpet Winsock, supplied by most Internet providers to Windows 3.1 customers) and client software.
Mac		
OS8	Communications software, plus clients for web browsing, email, newsgroups, and more.	None.
OS7 (System 7)	Communications software.	Client software.

2

You needn't feel that you have to get all your client software right away. At first, all you'll really want or need is your web browser and maybe an email program.

You'll need no client other than your web browser for the first half of this book—all the way through Hour 12, "Finding People." If you want to, you can simply set yourself up for web browsing now and forget about all the other software until you need it. You learn more about each of the other clients—including how to get some of the more popular options—in the hours where those clients are introduced.

Where Can You Get It?

The best place to get your startup Internet software is from your Internet provider (which you'll learn to select in Hour 3).

Why? Again, after you're online, you can easily acquire any software you want. All you need from your startup software is a way to begin. Whatever your Internet provider offers is usually given free of charge, and may include an easy-to-use setup routine, specially designed for your Internet provider, that makes setting up your connection easier.

For example, Figure 2.4 shows a web page at Microsoft listing major Internet service providers who can supply a customized copy of Microsoft's Internet Explorer client software suite. If you sign up with any of these providers, you'll be provided with a copy of Internet Explorer that's preconfigured to make signing up with the provider as easy as possible.

TIME SAVER

At the back of this book, you'll find the Starter Kit CD-ROM, a disc loaded with all the Internet software you need to get up and running fast.

If you haven't installed the Starter Kit CD-ROM yet, now is a good time: You can check out what's available from the CD now, while you're thinking about what software you'll use.

You'll find instructions for installing the CD right next to it.

Figure 2.4.

A web page on Microsoft's web site introduces Internet providers who can supply their own customized version of Internet Explorer to subscribers.

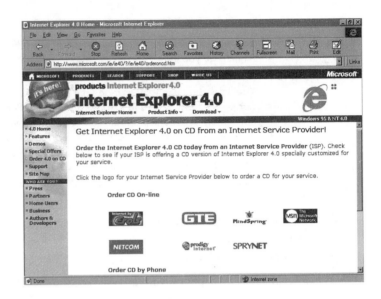

As an alternative to using the software your provider supplies, you can walk into a software store and buy commercial Internet software right off the shelf. Most prepackaged Internet software is inexpensive ($5 to $50), and often comes with setup programs to conveniently sign you up for one or more Internet providers. Be careful, though, not to pick up a box that is designed to sign you up with one (and only one) Internet provider, unless it happens to be the one you already plan to use.

Both of the two major Internet client suites—described next—are available on CD-ROM at any software store.

About the Suites: Internet Explorer 4 and Netscape Communicator

In just the last year or so, the two major suppliers of web browsing software—Microsoft and Netscape—have recognized that it's confusing for Internet users to have to go out and pick separate client software for each Internet activity.

So both companies have developed *Internet suites*, or bundles that include a whole family of Internet clients that install together and work together well. Within each suite, you can jump from any client program to any other in the suite simply by clicking a button or choosing from a menu. For example, you can conveniently jump from cruising the web to checking your email to opening a newsgroup, all within a few clicks.

Both suites include a web browser, email client, newsgroup client, and voice/video conferencing software. Both also include a web authoring tool for creating your own web pages (see Hour 23). To all that, Microsoft's suite adds a chat program.

You can buy either suite on CD at any software store or order the CD directly from the developer. You may also be able to get a copy from your Internet provider. Of course, after you're online, you can download the latest version of either program.

JUST A MINUTE

> If you follow the news, you've heard about the "Browser Wars," the fight between Microsoft and Netscape for supremacy of the browser world. So you may wonder: Which is the best browser?
>
> It really doesn't matter. The latest versions of Netscape and Internet Explorer are strikingly similar in almost every respect. For the purposes of a newcomer to the net, the two may as well be identical. As you begin to explore more advanced activities, you'll discover some small, technical differences that may or may not matter to you. But truthfully, you can flip a coin and wind up with a good browser either way.

Netscape Communicator

The Communicator suite, sometimes called Netscape 4 or Navigator 4, is available for Windows 95/NT, Mac System 7/OS8, many UNIX versions, and Windows 3.1/Windows for Workgroups. (Note that Windows 3.1 and Windows for Workgroups versions require a PC capable of running Windows 95, with 16MB of memory.)

The voice number for information or ordering is (650) 937-3777.

The Communicator suite includes

- ☐ **Navigator**—As the latest version of the most popular web browser, Navigator combines an easy-to-use web browsing interface with state-of-the-art support for advanced web features such as all multimedia types, frames, Java, enhanced security, and more (see Figure 2.5).

- ☐ **Messenger**—Messenger is a full-featured Internet email, including an address book (which makes recalling and using email addresses easier), support for messages containing multimedia (see Hour 23), and tools for organizing messages.

- ☐ **Collabra**—Collabra is a solid, easy-to-use newsreader program that also enables you to create your own, private newsgroups.

☐ **Conference**—Conference offers voice/video conferencing software that enables you to have a live conversation with anyone else on the Internet who also uses Netscape Conference.

☐ **Page Composer**—A web page editing environment, Page Composer enables you to create and publish your own web pages, almost as easily as creating a document in a word processor.

Figure 2.5.

Netscape's home page on the web, seen through Navigator, the web-browsing component of Netscape Communicator.

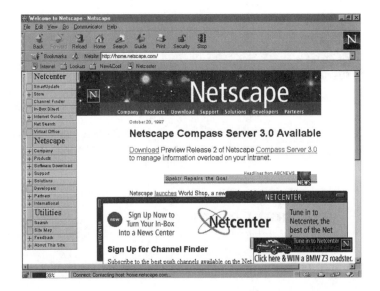

JUST A MINUTE

Although the suites cover all the client bases most users want or need, it's important to understand that they do not prevent you from using other client software.

You can use Netscape's suite and get a separate chat program from anywhere to fill the gap. You can install and use Microsoft's suite, but opt to use a different email program than the one Microsoft provides. You can even install more than one suite or more than one email program or more than one chat program and so on—and on any given day use the one you feel like using. (However, you may not be permitted this flexibility if you use an online service as your Internet provider; see Hour 3.)

Also, you don't have to install or use the whole suite. For example, you have the option to use only the web browser from a suite, and pick and choose other programs for other activities.

Microsoft Internet Explorer 4

Internet Explorer 4, sometimes called IE4, is available for Windows 95/NT, Mac OS7/OS8, UNIX, and Windows 3.1/Windows for Workgroups. (Note that the Windows 3.1 and Windows for Workgroups versions require a PC capable of running Windows 95.)

JUST A MINUTE

> At press time, the versions for Windows 3.1, Macintosh, and UNIX were in testing and not yet released. They should be available by the time you read this.

The voice number for information or ordering is (800) 485-2048.

The Internet Explorer suite includes

- ☐ **Internet Explorer Browser**—The latest version of the number two browser (second only to Navigator, and by a narrowing margin) features an easy-to-use web browsing interface with state-of-the-art support for advanced web features such as all multimedia types, frames, Java, enhanced security, and more (see Figure 2.6).

- ☐ **Outlook Express**—Many of the activities you perform in email and newsgroups are the same; in both, you compose, send, read, and organize messages. So Microsoft has combined email and newsreading into one client program, Outlook Express. (The name is borrowed from Office 97's Outlook program, which is a far more powerful program that handles email, scheduling, and contact management.) The combination works well, as both halves of Outlook Express supply all the email and newsgroup functionality anybody could want.

- ☐ **NetMeeting**—NetMeeting is voice/video conferencing software that enables you to have a live conversation with anyone else on the Internet who also uses this software.

- ☐ **FrontPage Express**—As a web page editing environment, FrontPage Express enables you to create and publish your own web pages, almost as easily as creating a document in a word processor.

- ☐ **Chat**—Chat is a unique chat client that presents the chat session on your screen in comic-strip form, turning each participant into a different cartoon character and displaying each character's words in a comic-style "word balloon."

Figure 2.6.

Microsoft's Internet Explorer home page, seen through the Internet Explorer web browser.

Summary

Your viewing window frames and colors your world, affecting your entire perception of it. If you were to look at a yard through a big, clean window and then again through a small, dirty, distorted window, you would experience two very different yards.

First and foremost, a computer and its Internet software are a technical requirement—the keys to the door of the online world. But more importantly, they are your window to that world. A person who visits the Internet through a slow, tired PC and modem or through inferior software does not perceive the same world that someone else with a capable PC and snappy software. When you choose your computer and software, you are defining the character of your Internet experience to come.

Workshop

Q&A

Q I saw an ad for an Internet account you can get through one of those pizza-size satellite dishes. What the heck is that all about?

A The same kind of digital satellite dish used by DSS and DBS TV receivers—such as those from RCA and Sony—can also be used to receive high-speed Internet transmissions. Unfortunately, it can't *send* anything.

Some companies, such as DirecPC, are offering an unusual system that allows you to utilize the Internet, by *receiving* data from the dish (at very high speeds) and *sending* data through your phone line (at a normal modem speed). Because most of the delays on the net are caused by receiving information rather than sending it, the system can provide dramatically faster Internet access.

Q **You said two-way cable TV lines are rare and not really a workable option for Internet access now. Will they be an option soon?**

A Cable companies are experimenting in limited regions with two-way, high-speed cable services that will enable you not only to use the Internet at very high speeds— possibly as fast as 10Mbps, over 300 times as fast as 28.8Kbps—but also to receive other enhanced cable services, such as video-on-demand.

Before you can take advantage of that technology, your local cable company must upgrade all its hardware for two-way communication and set up its Internet service. Also, you'll need a special cable modem, which may cost more than $500.

Quiz

Take the following quiz to see how much you've learned.

Questions

1. Which type of modem offers the best balance of speed and affordability for Internet access today?

    a. Cable modem

    b. 28.8Kbps

    c. 57,000bps

    d. Internal

2. Older PCs and Macs usually make poor choices for web browsing because they are underpowered for handling

    a. Java programs in web pages

    b. Multimedia (graphics, sound, animation, video) in web pages

    c. New, Internet-ready operating systems

    d. All of the above

3. Which of the following can you do with a WebTV terminal?

    a. Browse the web.

    b. Steam vegetables.

    c. Make juice from overripe fruit.

    d. All of the above.

Answers

1. (b) A regular 28.8Kbps modem, or 28,800bps, makes the most sense today. A 36.6K modem is also a good option, but it wasn't listed as an answer choice.

2. (d) All this challenges—or defeats—older computers and operating systems.

3. (a) I know (a) is true. If you've successfully tried (b) or (c), I apologize for the error.

Activity

Start watching for any ads or free offers from Internet providers and online services (such as America Online), and save the ads if you can. In Hour 3, you'll choose from among those options and others.

Hour 3

Internet Service Provider, AOL, or Other: Who's Best for You?

If you have a mailing address, you probably know about Internet providers. They're the companies who beg you to join by cramming free signup CD-ROMs and disks in your mailbox (creasing your *National Geographic*). Heck, you don't even need an address—you get free signup disks today in magazines, cereal boxes, and bundled along with any new computer.

The provider you pull out of your cereal box may be a perfectly good choice, but it's not the *only* choice—not by a long shot. In this hour, you'll discover the full range of different ways to get signed up for the Internet, so you can choose the provider that best matches your needs and bank account.

At the end of the hour, you'll be able to answer the following questions:

- ☐ What's an Internet provider, and why do I need one?
- ☐ What's an Internet account, and what types of accounts are there?
- ☐ How are commercial online services, such as America Online, different from other Internet service providers?
- ☐ How can I find local and national providers from which to choose?
- ☐ What types of pricing plans are there, and how do I know if I'm getting a good deal?
- ☐ What do I need to know about the providers to choose one that's right for me?

Why Do I Need an Internet Provider?

The communications hardware and other requirements of a dedicated, full-time connection to the Internet cost tens of thousands of dollars, and the annual leases for the data communications lines cost many thousands more. The companies that offer Internet access all have their own costly, high-speed, 24-hour Internet connections. Those Internet connections have the capacity to support hundreds or thousands of individual Internet users.

Personal, day-to-day Internet users like you and I can't afford our own full-time Internet connections; we must rent someone else's connection. For whatever fee we pay our Internet provider, we must buy the right to use our modems to call up the Internet provider's computers and tap into that Internet connection.

What's an Internet Account?

When you sign up with (that is, subscribe to) an Internet service, you get an *Internet account*.

With an Internet account, you get the right to use the provider's Internet service, your own email address (so you can send and receive email), and all the other information you need to set up your computer for accessing the Internet through the service. From most providers, you may also get any communications or client software you need (see Hour 2, "What Hardware and Software Do You Need?").

The several types of Internet accounts available are all described in the next section.

Dial-Up Accounts

Most Internet accounts are called *dial-up* accounts because you use them by "dialing up" the Internet provider through your modem and telephone line. Dial-up accounts are sometimes called IP accounts because they require your computer to communicate through TCP/IP

3

(see Hour 1, "What Is the Internet and What Can You Do There?"). Dial-up IP accounts are the principal general-purpose accounts offered by most Internet providers.

Dial-up accounts come in two types: PPP and SLIP. (You don't need to know what PPP and SLIP stand for; everyone always uses the abbreviations.) Using the Internet through either a PPP or SLIP account is an identical experience, because both support the same client programs and any of the popular software you've heard about: Internet Explorer, Netscape Navigator, and so on. With a PPP or SLIP account, you have access to the full range of Internet activities and you can use any client programs you want to.

The only important difference between PPP and SLIP is setting up, which can be a little more difficult for SLIP. Most programs created to make setting up an Internet account easier are designed to set up PPP accounts, not SLIP accounts. For this and other reasons, SLIP accounts are rapidly disappearing.

JUST A MINUTE

An account with an online service like AOL is also a dial-up account, but it's not the same as a regular Internet PPP or SLIP account. An online service account requires a different kind of communications software (supplied by the service) for accessing the service and its non-Internet content.

When you access the Internet through an online service, the service may temporarily switch you over to a PPP account, or it may funnel you to the Internet using a different communications scenario.

This is why online services often limit you to one or two different web browsers and other clients, instead of letting you choose the one you want. Any client software used through the service must be specially configured for the service's unique communications system.

Special-Purpose Accounts

Dial-up IP accounts are the norm now, and most of this book focuses on how you can use the Internet through such an account. There are also other kinds of accounts that you may find valuable. *Shell* accounts and *email only* accounts are offered by most Internet providers (but not online services) as low-cost alternatives to their PPP or SLIP accounts.

With a shell account, your computer doesn't need to run TCP/IP. Although graphical web browsing is possible through a shell account, most shell account users run special software (supplied by the ISP) that enables them to browse all the text on the web (and use email and newsgroups). This software doesn't enable them to use any of the multimedia, Java programs, or other advanced web page stuff, however.

Those two concessions enable you to use the Internet with a far less powerful computer and much slower modem than an IP account requires—you could use the Internet effectively with a 286 PC or 10-year-old Mac, and a 2,400 baud modem. (I once used a shell account through an IBM PCjr with 256KB of memory, no hard disk, and a 300 baud modem, and lived to tell.) Shell accounts also are far cheaper than IP accounts, often available for $10 or less per month.

JUST A MINUTE

> Besides those using shell accounts, there are millions of web surfers who use computers that cannot display multimedia. For this reason, web authors used to be good about designing web pages in such a way that nothing crucial was lost when the page was viewed through a browser that displayed only text. The multimedia served as decoration, not essential content.
>
> Today, many web authors have decided that they only want to reach the folks who are using multimedia-capable computers (that is, people with apparent disposable income) and have stopped accommodating text-only browsers. More and more web sites have become virtually unusable to most shell account users.
>
> For this reason, I advocate a multimedia PC (see Hour 2) and an IP account as the only reasonable scenario for anyone who really wants to get the most out of the Internet.

With an email only account, you get full access to Internet email and nothing else—no web, no newsgroups, no chat, no shoes, no shirt, no service. You will have access to mailing lists, however (see Hour 14, "Joining a Mailing List"), which enables you to get much of what you'd see in newsgroups via email.

Email accounts can be run from the lowliest of computers and cost next to nothing. A few companies now offer you an email account free of charge, in exchange for the right to send you targeted advertisements.

What Are My Internet Provider Options?

You can get your Internet account from any of three main sources:

☐ A national Internet service provider (ISP)

☐ A local ISP that is headquartered in your city or town

☐ A commercial online service

Each of these three options is explained in the following sections.

3

No matter which one you choose, make sure the company offers a dial-up number for connecting to the Internet that is a local phone call from your PC's location. Otherwise, you'll end up paying long-distance fees to the phone company in addition to whatever your provider charges for Internet access.

In most cities, finding local access numbers is no problem—any local ISP, national ISP, or online service will have a local number you can use. In some suburbs and many rural areas, finding a local number gets more difficult. Your best bet in such circumstances is to find a local ISP (discussed later in this hour), or to find out if your local telephone company offers Internet access (many do).

Some services offer an 800 number that you may use to access the service when the ISP provides no local number. The 800 number is rarely a true toll-free, however, the ISP almost always charges a higher rate for using the service through the 800 number, kicking the toll back to you.

Commercial Online Services

You've no doubt heard of at least one of the major online services, such as America Online (AOL) or CompuServe (CSi). These services promote themselves as Internet providers, and they are—but with a difference.

In addition to Internet access, these services also offer unique activities and content not accessible to the rest of the Internet community. These services have their own chat rooms, newsgroup-like message boards (usually called *forums*), online stores, and reference sources that only subscribers to the service can use. Setting up for an online service is usually easy: You install the free software they provide, follow the onscreen instructions, and you're connected. Pow.

The main drawback to online services is the lack of flexibility. You often cannot choose and use any client software you want; you must use a single client environment supplied by the service or one program from among a limited set of options. When new, enhanced releases of client programs come out, ISP users can install and use them right away, while most online service users must wait until the online service publishes its customized version.

On the plus side, most online services do supply a customized version of either Navigator, Internet Explorer, or both for web browsing, making the look and feel of the web through an online service essentially identical to that of an ISP.

Another beef about online services concerns capacity. When America Online introduced more attractive pricing recently, it picked up far more subscribers than it was prepared to serve. The result was that subscribers often got busy signals when they tried to connect and could not get through to the overburdened system for hours. A few times, the system crashed altogether.

This is a legitimate complaint, as are the reports that the online services tend to supply slow, unreliable Internet access. To be completely fair, however, many ISPs also get overloaded and may be burdened by busy signals and poor performance.

You must be prepared for the possibility that you'll get fed up and switch to a different provider or service. You can't expect any provider to be perfect. The possibility of losing subscribers is the only incentive for providers to continually improve.

Online services used to be dramatically more expensive than ISPs. Lately, online services have adopted pricing policies that are generally competitive with the local and national ISPs, although you can still usually get a slightly better deal from a regular ISP than from any online service. For example, America Online offers a respectable $19.95 per month flat rate; if you shop around, you can get a flat rate from an ISP for as little as $15.

Also, in their advertising, the services often tout their ease-of-use. That claim refers exclusively to how easy it is to use the service's non-Internet content from its own client software, *not* to ease-of-use on the Internet. For all practical purposes, using the Internet is the same—no harder nor easier—no matter which online service or ISP you choose.

The following online service descriptions are intended to give you a general sense of each service, not to show exact prices or features. The services change their features and pricing policies rapidly, so the only way to get reliable prices and other information about each is to call the 800 number shown.

America Online (AOL)

Voice Number: 800-827-6364

America Online is the most popular of the online services, largely because of aggressive marketing and initial ease-of-use. The non-Internet content is indeed the easiest to use of all the services. However, the Internet access is notoriously slow, and busy signals continue to be a problem. AOL offers a wide range of pricing plans, including a flat rate, annual, and several pay-as-you-go plans (see "Plans and Rates," later in this chapter).

CompuServe (CSi)

Voice Number: 800-848-8199

CompuServe wasn't the first online service, but it's the oldest still in operation, and it was once the undisputed king. That legacy leaves CompuServe with an unbeatable range of local access numbers—thousands of them, all over the world.

Functionally, CompuServe is similar to America Online in most respects, and it still offers extensive non-Internet content. Its reputation for providing fast and reliable Internet service is somewhat better than America Online's. Its reputation for non-Internet ease-of-use is slightly worse. However, CompuServe can support almost any computer in the world, while AOL is essentially limited to popular personals: PCs and Macs.

Microsoft Network (MSN)

Voice Number: 800-FREE-MSN

Microsoft Network started out in 1995 as a service much like AOL. It has since evolved from the online service model, to the point where it is now more or less a regular national (actually international) ISP, although it still supplies some content accessible only to its subscribers. MSN offers true PPP access, so you can use any browser you want. Your choice of email and news clients may be limited, however, because of the way MSN limits access to its email and news servers. The service offers a variety of reasonable flat-rate and pay-as-you-go plans.

Signup software for MSN is built into every copy of Windows 95. If you use Windows 95 and choose to sign up for MSN, just double-click the MSN icon on your Windows desktop to start the signup process.

TIME SAVER

All the online services, and many ISPs (described in the following sections), provide software on a disk or CD that you can use to set up your computer for using the service. This software is required for the online services, but usually is optional for an ISP.

Even when it's optional, I strongly recommend getting any signup software your provider offers. The software leads you step-by-step through setting up your PC for the particular provider and makes setting up your computer properly a no-brainer. You'll learn more about using this software—and doing without it—in Hour 4, "Connecting to the Internet."

As soon as you've selected a provider, call the provider to request the software and instructions for your computer type.

Internet Service Providers (ISPs)

Unlike an online service, an Internet service provider (ISP) does not offer its subscribers special content that's not accessible to the rest of the net. You get Internet access, period.

ISPs offer greater flexibility than online services by providing dial-up IP (PPP or SLIP), shell, and email accounts. ISPs also enable you (through IP accounts) to use virtually any client software you want to, and to add or change that software whenever you like. Often, ISPs offer more attractive rates and better service than the online services, although that's not always the case.

TIME SAVER

Observe in Table 3.1 that the big long-distance phone companies—AT&T, MCI, and Sprint—all offer Internet access, as well. Usually, these companies offer a discount to Internet customers who are also long-distance customers.

There are many large, national ISPs that provide local access numbers all over the United States (and often across North America). Table 3.1 lists a few of the major national ISPs and their voice telephone numbers, so you can call to learn more about the service generally and about the availability of local access numbers specifically. Just in case you have access to the Internet through a computer at school, work, or cyber café, the table also shows the address of a web page where you can learn more about each service.

Table 3.1. A more-or-less random selection of national ISPs.

Company	Voice Number	Web Page Address
Earthlink	800-395-8425	www.earthlink.net
MindSpring	800-719-4664	www.mindspring.com
Netcom	800-638-2661	www.ix.netcom.com
GTE Internet	800-927-3000	www.gte.com
Sprint	800-747-9428	www.sprint.com
Global Internet	800-682-5550	www.gi.net
MCI Internet	800-550-0927	www.mci.com
Micro-Net	800-480-9925	www.micronet.com
AT&T WorldNet	800-967-5363	www.att.com/worldnet/wis/
PSINet	800-827-7482	www.psi.net
Voyager Online	800-864-0442	www.vol.com

JUST A MINUTE

If you choose Internet Explorer 4 for your web browser, while setting it up you'll be offered an option that connects you to a special service at Microsoft, through which you can choose an ISP.

However, Microsoft's service does not list all the ISPs that may be available to you. I recommend looking for an ISP on your own, and only relying on Microsoft's service as a last resort.

Finding a Local ISP

Besides the national ISPs, there are thousands of local ISPs in cities and towns all over the country. Typically, a local ISP cannot offer access numbers beyond a small, local service area of a few cities, towns, or counties. It can, however, provide reliable Internet access, personal service, and often the best rates you can get.

Unlike online services and national ISPs, local ISPs don't have the marketing muscle to advertise heavily or send out free disks. That's what makes them harder to find, but it's also why they're often cheaper. (Personally, I like to reward companies that don't pressure me; I have an inverse reaction to heavy advertising.) Finding a local ISP is getting easier all the time. Friends, coworkers, and local computer newsletters are all good sources for finding a local ISP. You can also check the Yellow Pages for ISPs: Look first under *Internet*, then try *Computers—Internet Services*. The folks at your nearest computer store or Radio Shack may also know of a good local ISP or two. (Just don't let the Radio Shack guys make you buy a cell phone in exchange for the information.)

TIME SAVER

If you have access to the Internet (through a friend's computer, your job, a local library, or a cyber café), you can search online for an ISP. A web site called the List (see Figure 3.1) at thelist.iworld.com is one of several that lists hundreds of ISPs in the United States and in many other countries.

Figure 3.1.

Using someone else's Internet account, you can visit the List to find a local ISP.

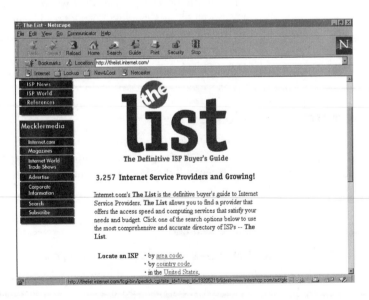

How Do I Choose?

Now that you know how to find the online services and ISPs, how do you pick one?

Beats me. If there were one reliable way to choose the best Internet provider, we'd all be using the same one. But different people have different priorities: For some it's price, for others it's range of access numbers, for others it's speed. You have to check out how each of your available ISP options addresses your own priorities.

Obviously, if you have friends who use the Internet, find out which services they use and ask whether they're happy. It's always a good idea to use a friend's Internet account to test the service the friend uses, and to explore your other options. Magazine reviews can help, but they rarely cover more than the online services and the largest national ISPs. To judge a local ISP, you need to listen to word of mouth information.

The next few pages describe various criteria you may want to consider when evaluating your options.

JUST A MINUTE

Stressed out over making a choice? Relax, and remember that unless you agree to a long-term deal, you can always quit and try another service if your first choice disappoints you.

The only caveat to switching services is that your email address changes any time you switch. But many services will forward your email to your new service for a few months after you quit, and you can always get in touch with all your email partners and let them know your new address.

Of course, switching services also provides an excellent opportunity to *not* tell some people your new email address, if they have been getting on your e-nerves.

Plans and Rates

Most providers offer a range of different pricing plans. (It's like choosing a long distance phone plan: Do you go with the plan that's a dime at night and a quarter during the day, or the one that's fifteen cents all the time, or the one that's 20 percent off after $20 and free on Tuesdays?)

The kinds of plans you'll see most often, however, are unlimited access, or flat rate, and pay as you go, both described next.

Unlimited Access or Flat Rate Plans

With a flat rate plan, for a monthly fee of between $15 and $25, you can use the Internet all you want. In the last few years, such accounts have become the norm, and are available from virtually all online services and ISPs.

3

Unless you expect to use the Internet only sparingly, flat rate plans make the most sense. While exploring the Internet, you don't want to keep one eye on the clock.

"Unlimited" does not mean you can stay online all day. To keep users from abusing their unlimited accounts, most providers automatically disconnect you from the service if you're "idle"—not actively using any Internet feature—for 10 or 15 minutes. This is not a big inconvenience; if you get disconnected while making a sandwich, you can just reconnect. But the practice does protect you from accidentally leaving your Internet connection open all day and hogging system resources that other, busy subscribers to the service may need.

Finally, some providers may attach strings to their best unlimited access rates. For example, a provider may offer unlimited access for $15 a month if you pay a full year up front, or $20 if you pay month to month. Always read the fine print.

CAUTION

> Some providers charge a startup fee—often as much as $30 to $50—that you pay on top of your first month's charges when you sign up. This trick is used most often by providers who advertise rates that look too good to be true; an $18 monthly rate plus a $30 one-time signup fee works out to $20.50 per month, for the first year.
>
> Better providers have long since done away with startup fees. When offered a deal that includes one, move on.

Pay-as-You-Go, or "Per Hour," Plans

These plans charge you according to the number of minutes per month you actually use the service. They typically start out with a monthly minimum charge (around $5 to $10) and a number of free hours you can use the service (usually from 5 to 20 hours).

In any month where you don't exceed the number of free hours, you pay only the monthly minimum. But in any month where you exceed the free hours, you pay the minimum plus an extra $1, $2, or more per hour for each hour over the limit.

To decide whether you should go with such a plan, you must guess the number of hours you expect to use the Internet each month, calculate the cost under pay-as-you-go, and compare that to the provider's flat rate plan.

Bear in mind that most newcomers to the Internet spend many more hours online than they think they will. There's also a tendency among newcomers to spend lots of time online for the first few months, then to spend less time as the novelty wears off and they learn to work more efficiently.

Because of these patterns, I generally recommend that new users first choose a flat rate plan with no long-term commitment, and to keep track of their monthly hours for six months or so. If you do that, you'll know whether you're getting your money's worth at the flat rate or should switch to a per-hour plan.

TIME SAVER

Throughout this book, you'll discover ways to cut your online time by applying smart tips for doing more of your Internet work offline. These tips are useful under any pricing plan, but obviously, they can save you big bucks if you choose a pay-as-you-go plan.

Billing Options

Most providers will bill your monthly charges automatically to any major credit card. Some local ISPs can bill you by mail, and some others can actually add your monthly Internet charges to your regular monthly telephone bill (itemized separately from your calls to Grandma, of course). All other things being equal, you may lean toward the provider who will bill you in the way that's most convenient for you.

Access Numbers

Obviously, you want a provider that offers a local access number in the area where your computer resides. But suppose you intend to use your account from both home and work, using two different computers or bringing a portable back and forth. Does the provider offer local access numbers that work from both locations?

What if you want to be able to use the Internet when you travel? Does the provider offer local access everywhere you and your computer might go? If you really want access from everywhere, you're probably going to wind up with one of the online services or larger national ISPs that offer the greatest number and range of local access numbers.

Supported Modem Speeds

Make sure the provider you select supports the maximum speed of your modem. If you use a 28.8Kbaud modem now, look for a provider that supports both 28.8Kbaud and 33.6Kbaud access now, so you can be sure to have a way to move up if you choose to.

Few providers support 56Kbaud modems now, although the list is likely to grow rapidly this year. If you want 56Kbaud access, be sure to find a provider that supports it and ask whether a higher price is charged for that access. Finally, keep in mind that 56Kbaud access demands a clean, clear phone connection. Even if your provider offers 56Kbaud access and you use a 56Kbaud modem, you'll probably notice that your Internet connection usually runs at a slower speed to compensate for line noise.

Also, there are two different kinds of 56Kbaud modems: One that works on a standard called *X2* and another, *Kflex*. Make sure the ISP you choose supports 56Kbaud access for the standard your modem uses, or for both standards.

If you'll need to use more than one access number, note that providers do not always offer their highest speed through all numbers. For example, you may find that the provider offers a 56K connection from your office, but only a 28.8K connection from your home. Look for a provider that gives you the speed you want on every access number you're likely to use.

Software Supplied

The online services require that you use a software package they supply for setting up your connection, using their non-Internet content, and often for using the Internet, too. That software may be included on the signup CD (the one you get in your cereal box or if you call the service to order it), or some of it might be transferred to your computer automatically from the service during signup.

Most ISPs can also supply you with any communications or client software you require, although using the ISP's software package is optional. If you need software to get started, you may want to consider what each ISP offers as a software bundle.

Web Server Space

If you think you might want to publish your own web pages (see Hour 23, "Creating Web Pages and Multimedia Messages"), you'll need space on a web server to do so. Some ISPs offer a small amount of web server space free to all customers; others charge an additional monthly fee.

Newsgroup Access

You'll learn all about newsgroups in Hour 15, "Reading and Posting to Newsgroups." For now, just be aware that there are roughly 14,000 newsgroups, and that not all providers give you access to all of them.

Some providers—including, to varying extents, the online services—take it upon themselves to censor newsgroups, preventing their subscribers from accessing any that might contain strong sexual or other controversial content. If that censorship appeals to you, keep in mind that the approach generally blocks access not only to genuinely racy groups, but also to many perfectly benign, G-rated groups that get lumped together with the racy ones.

Some other providers don't bother carrying all newsgroups. Instead, they carry only the newsgroups their subscribers have specifically requested. If you want to access a newsgroup that's not already carried by a provider like this, you must send in a request by email and wait a day or two to get access. That scenario prevents you from quickly finding information you need, which is what the net is all about.

If you want easy, universal access to all newsgroups, be sure to choose an ISP that supplies it.

Summary

In these first three hours, you've learned what the Internet is, what hardware and software you need to get on the Internet, and how to find and choose your Internet provider.

That's all the preparation you need—it's time to set up your computer and get on the net. You'll do that in Hour 4.

Workshop

Q&A

Q If I choose WebTV instead of a computer, which online service or ISP should I use?

A When WebTV (see Hour 2) debuted, buyers were required to use the WebTV Network as their ISP. Today, WebTV terminals can support a variety of ISPs (but not all), with one catch.

One of the main benefits of WebTV is the way it offers program directories and other services that enhance TV viewing. You can get these services only as a WebTV Network subscriber. If you use another ISP, you can still access WebTV Network services through your ISP, by paying WebTV Network a $9.95 per month fee in addition to what you already pay the ISP.

Q Should I be on the lookout for new online services?

A No. In fact, online services as we know them may be going away.

You see, when online services first came around, the Internet was difficult to use, so many people preferred to use the online services' non-Internet content. As interest in the Internet grew, the services recognized ISPs as competitors for subscribers and began offering Internet access as an option.

Today, web browsers and other client software have made the true Internet much easier to use, while the content on the Internet has expanded to cater to an infinite range of interests, tastes, and expertise levels. Few folks really need the online services' non-Internet content anymore. So slowly, the online services are either closing their doors or transforming themselves into regular ISPs.

Quiz

Take the following quiz to see how much you've learned.

Questions

1. Compared to an ISP, an online service
    a. Offers content only its subscribers may use, in addition to Internet access
    b. May limit your selection of client software
    c. May be more expensive, and may offer sluggish Internet performance
    d. All of the above

2. If you need to use the Internet from multiple locations (home, work, travel stops), look for an ISP or online service that offers
    a. Free snacks
    b. A local access number everywhere you may need one
    c. Internet access via TCP/IP, GE, IBM, AT&T, KFC, and FBI
    d. All of the above

3. True or false: The more popular an online service or ISP, the better it must be.

4. True or false: Online services make using the Internet easier.

Answers

1. (d) These are the essential pro (choice a) and cons (b and c) of online services.

2. (b) To avoid telephone toll charges, you need access numbers that are a local call from wherever you are. Snacks are optional. (Bonus: Can you identify each abbreviation in the meaningless, gratuitous list shown in choice c?)

3. False. As any cola drinker knows, popularity may be a measure of quality, or it may be a measure of successful advertising.

4. False. The Internet is the Internet. The main thing that determines ease-of-use is the client software you choose. The client software supported by the services is no easier to use than the client software you can choose to use with an ISP.

Activity

Take a quick flip through Hours 2 and 3, and take inventory. Have you selected your computer, operating system, client software source, and Internet provider? If so, you're ready to hit the Internet. If not, make your choices and proceed to Hour 4 when you're fully equipped.

Hour **4**

Connecting to the Internet

You've got your hardware and software, and you've selected a provider. It's time to get you and your computer onto the Internet.

To connect to the Internet, the communications software on your computer has to be supplied with certain information about your Internet provider. You can give it this information simply by running the signup program that you received from your Internet provider, or by configuring your communications software on your own. In this hour, you'll learn to do both.

At the end of the hour, you'll be able to answer the following questions:

- ☐ What are my Internet username and password, and why do I need them?
- ☐ What are the advantages of using a signup program?
- ☐ If my provider doesn't offer a signup program, how do I set up my computer by myself?
- ☐ How can installing Internet Explorer, Netscape Communicator, or Mac OS8 make setting up easier?
- ☐ After setting up, how do I get online?

Keys to Your Account: Username and Password

No matter how you set up your account and computer, you'll wind up with three pieces of information that are essential to getting online. The first piece of information is your local access number, the telephone number your modem dials to connect to your Internet provider.

The other essential pieces of information are your own Internet username and password:

☐ **Username**—To prevent just anybody from using its service, your Internet provider requires each subscriber to use a unique name, called a username (or sometimes user ID or userID), to connect.

☐ **Password**—To prevent an unauthorized user from using your username to sneak into the system, you must also have your own secret password.

Entering your username and password to go online is called *logging on* (or sometimes *logging in* or *signing in*) and the name used to describe that activity is logon (or login or sign-in). If you use a signup program to set up your Internet account and computer as described in the next section, you'll choose your username and password while running that program. If you set up your computer without a signup disk (as described later in this hour), you'll choose a username and password while on the phone with your provider to open your account.

Every user of a particular Internet provider must have a different username. If you choose a large provider, there's a good chance that your first choice of username is already taken by another subscriber. In such cases, your provider will instruct you to choose another username or to append a number to the name to make it unique. For example, if the provider already has a user named CarmenDiaz, you can be CarmenDiaz2.

JUST A MINUTE

Some rules have been set up regarding what you can and cannot use for your username and password. The rules vary by provider, but in general, your username and password must each be a single word (no spaces or punctuation) of five or more letters or numerals. Nonsense words, such as FunnyDad or MonkeyMary, are fine as usernames. For a password, avoid using easy-to-guess items such as your birthday or your kids' names. *Total nonsense*—such as xkah667a—makes the most effective password, as long as you can remember it.

Your username often doubles as the first part of your email address; if your username is Stinky, your email address might be something like Stinky@serveco.com. Before choosing a username, consider whether you also like it as an email address that will be seen and used by your friends and associates.

4

Some systems are *case sensitive*; that is, they pay attention to the pattern of uppercase and lowercase letters. On a case-sensitive system, if your username is SallyBu, you must type SallyBu to log on—sallybu, SALLYBU, or sallyBU won't work.

Using a Signup Program

A special signup program is required for each online service provider, and many ISPs also supply you with a signup program. I recommend using signup programs whenever they're available, even when they're optional.

You can get free signup disks by mail from the providers, just by calling them on the telephone (see Hour 3, "Internet Service Provider, AOL, or Other: Who's Best for You?"). Signup programs often come pre-installed on new computers, bundled in computer magazines, or sent directly to your door as junk mail.

Why Use a Signup Program?

The signup programs kill two birds at once: They sign you up with a provider *and* configure your computer to access that provider (see Figure 4.1). The program automatically takes care of all the communications configuration required in your computer, some of which can be tricky for inexperienced computer users.

JUST A MINUTE

Depending on the provider you select, the signup program may or may not set up all your client software.

After completing any signup program, you'll be able to connect to the Internet and to use your web browser to explore the web. In some cases, however, your email, news, and other clients may require a little further setup before you can use them. You'll learn about configuring each type of client software in the hour that covers it specifically.

Running a Typical Signup Program

Before running a signup program, make sure your modem is connected to a telephone line, because the signup software usually dials the provider at least once during the signup process. Also, make sure you have a major credit card handy; you'll need to enter its number and expiration date to set up payment.

Figure 4.1.

Programs like this one for AT&T's WorldNet service automatically configure your computer and lead you step-by-step through signing up.

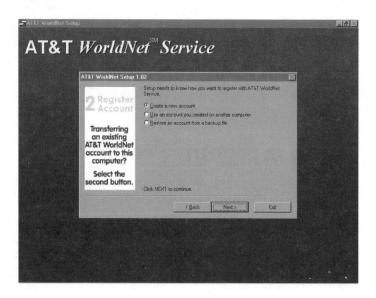

JUST A MINUTE

Signup programs are almost always designed to set up credit card payments for your Internet service. If you don't want to pay by credit card, you may not be able to use the signup program. (Actually, you may not even be able to use a particular provider; some accept payment solely by credit card.)

Call your selected provider to ask about payment terms. If the provider accepts other payment methods, but its signup program handles only credit cards, you can establish your account over the telephone, and then set up your computer without a signup disk, as described later in this hour.

You'll find instructions for starting the program on a page or card that accompanies it, or printed right on the CD or disk.

After you start the program, just follow its lead. The program will prompt you to type in your name, address, phone number, and credit card information. Then you'll be prompted to choose a logon username and password, email address, and email password. The program may also present you with a list of payment methods from which to choose (see Figure 4.2).

TIME SAVER

When you choose each of the following during signup, be sure to jot it down for later reference:

☐ Your logon username and password
☐ Your email address

4

☐ Your email password (different from your logon password; used to retrieve email others have sent to you)

☐ The telephone number of provider's customer service and/or technical support departments

Figure 4.2.

A typical signup program (such as this one for the Microsoft Network) prompts you to make all the choices required for setting up your account, such as choosing a payment method.

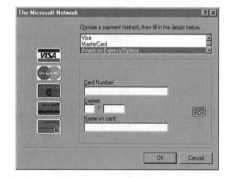

Once or twice during the signup process, the program uses your modem to contact the provider. It does this to verify your payment information, find the best local access number for you, check that your selected username is not already taken, and ultimately to send all the information it collected to the provider to open your account.

When the program closes, your computer and account are ready to go online and you are ready to explore.

Setting Up Without a Signup Program

Setting up your computer without a signup program is a little more difficult, but well within your capabilities. Besides, doing it yourself gives you that rich, satisfying feeling that comes only from braving a tricky task and succeeding—like replacing a toilet valve and then hearing that rewarding first flush.

JUST A MINUTE

The instructions in this section are for setting up dial-up IP accounts, the most popular type. If you intend to use another type of account, such as shell or email (see Hour 3), you must obtain specific instructions and software from your Internet provider for setup.

When you don't use a signup disk, you must set up your account with your selected Internet provider over the telephone first and then configure your computer. While setting up your account, your provider will tell you all the communications settings required for the service and will work with you to select your local access number, username, and password.

It's important that you make careful notes of everything your provider tells you because you'll use all that information when setting up. In addition to your access number, logon username, and password, you'll probably come out of the conversation with the following information:

- ☐ Whether the account is the PPP or SLIP type (see Hour 3).
- ☐ One or more IP addresses required for communicating with the provider (see the next section, "About IP Addresses").
- ☐ The addresses of the provider's email and news servers. (You'll need these addresses to configure your email client and newsreader; see Hour 13, "Sending and Receiving Email," and Hour 15, "Reading and Posting to Newsgroups.") Email server addresses may be described as SMTP or POP3 servers (you usually need one of each), and news servers may be described as NNTP servers.
- ☐ Your own email address that others can use to send email to you.
- ☐ Your email username and password that is required for retrieving email people have sent to you. (These may be different from your logon username and password.)
- ☐ The telephone number and hours of the provider's customer service or technical support departments.
- ☐ Any other special communications steps or settings the particular provider requires.

No matter how you go about it, setting up your computer for the Internet is a simple matter of entering this information in your communications software. After that's done, you can go online.

TIME SAVER

> If you use Windows 3.1 and do not use a signup disk, you can manually configure your Internet account, just as you can for the Mac or Windows 95. You need some special software first. See Q&A in the Workshop at the end of this hour for more information.

About IP Addresses

Sigh. Once upon a time, understanding the Internet's IP addressing system was essential to getting online, a required topic in the Internet 101 curriculum. Today, you usually don't ever have to deal with, or even know about, IP addresses. They're an issue *only* when you set up your computer to use a particular provider; after you're set up, you can forget about them.

4

If you use a signup program as described earlier, the program takes care of the IP addresses—you won't see them, so you don't need to know about them.

If you set up your computer without a signup program, however, you'll need to configure your communications software with one or more IP addresses that enable your computer to communicate with your provider and with the Internet.

So here is the least you need to know about IP addresses, if you need to know at all: Every computer on the Internet has its own unique address; that's why one computer on the Internet can find and communicate with any other. This address can be expressed in either of two ways: as an IP address or as a domain name.

An IP address is a set of four numbers, separated by periods, that expresses the Internet address of a particular computer. For example:

`195.25.100.14`

To make getting around the Internet easier, most activities support *domain names* rather than IP addresses. A domain name is a word-based equivalent of an IP address. For example:

`news.netco.com`

When a domain name is used, a computer called a *domain name server* (DNS) automatically converts it to an IP address behind the scenes, to locate the computer to which the domain name refers. For most Internet activities—including the web and email—you will deal exclusively with domain addresses.

When setting up your account, your provider may supply you with any or all of the following addresses for configuring your computer:

☐ **Your own Internet IP address**—Some providers do not require this; their computers automatically assign an IP address to you at each logon.

☐ **The IP address of one or more DNS servers**—When your provider gives you more than one DNS server address, one address is called the primary DNS server, and any others are called backup or alternate DNS servers.

☐ **The IP address of a *gateway***—A gateway is a device some providers use to manage Internet traffic on their service.

☐ **The IP address of a *subnet mask* (or *netmask*)**—A subnet mask is an address that identifies your computer to the ISP's local network.

☐ **Email and news server addresses**—These may be expressed as IP addresses, but are more often expressed as domain names.

4

Setting Up Windows 95 for an ISP

Short of using a signup program, the next easiest way to set up an ISP account on a PC running Windows 95 is to install Internet Explorer or Netscape Communicator (see Hour 2, "What Hardware and Software Do You Need?").

Each of these client software suites includes an easy-to-use program for configuring your Windows 95 Internet connection. These programs lead you through each step of the process, prompting you for all the required settings. Using these programs is almost as easy as using a signup disk, except that they don't sign you up with your ISP—you must take care of that first—and they prompt you for your IP address and other setup information, which a signup program can supply for itself.

The great thing about the setup software built into Internet Explorer and Navigator is that you may use them even if you don't intend to use the rest of the software. In other words, there's no reason you can't use Internet Explorer's setup program to configure your Windows 95 Internet connection, and then use a browser or other client software that's not part of Internet Explorer—the Internet connection and your client software operate independently of one another.

If you have Internet Explorer version 3, it usually includes the setup program called Internet Setup Wizard that works much like the wizard in version 4. To use the wizard in version 3, after installing the Internet Explorer 3 software, choose Programs | Accessories | Internet Tools from your Windows 95 Start menu.

The following To Do section shows how to use the setup program bundled with Internet Explorer 4—called Connection Wizard—to configure a PPP connection in Windows 95. Using Netscape's program is similar.

To Do: Run Internet Explorer 4's Connection Wizard

Before running the Connection Wizard, first install the IE4 software. Doing so takes just a few minutes and requires choosing options on a short series of dialog boxes.

After you finish installing the software, the Connection Wizard may open automatically to set up your Internet connection. If it doesn't, start it by choosing Programs | Internet Explorer | Connection Wizard. From the Welcome dialog box that appears, follow these steps:

JUST A MINUTE

To move from each step in the Connection Wizard to the next, click the Next button that appears on every dialog box. If you change your mind about any choices you made in earlier steps, click the Back button to go back to any earlier step and change your choices.

4

1. On the Welcome dialog box, click Next. The Setup Options dialog box opens.
2. In the Setup Options dialog box, choose one of the following options and then click Next:

   ☐ If you want Microsoft's help choosing an ISP (see Hour 3), select the top option, I Want to Choose an Internet Provider. Choose a provider from Microsoft's service, and move on to step 2 when finished.

   ☐ If you have already established an ISP account, choose I Want to Set up a New Connection.

3. The Dial-Up Connection dialog box appears. Choose Create a New Dial-Up Connection and click Next.
4. The Phone Number dialog box appears. Complete the area code and phone number used to connect to your ISP. Click Next. (Your communications software won't dial the area code when connecting you; it just needs the area code to know that your ISP is a local call.)
5. In the User Name and Password dialog box (see Figure 4.3), enter your Internet username and password and click Next. (When you type the password, asterisks appear onscreen instead of the password; that's so no one can peer over your shoulder while you type to steal your password.)

Figure 4.3.

Entering your Internet username and password in IE4's Connection Wizard.

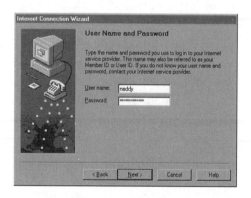

6. On the Advanced Settings dialog box, choose one of the following options and click Next:

   ☐ If your account is a PPP account in which your ISP automatically assigns you an IP address, click No and move on to step 7.

   ☐ If your ISP supplied you with an IP or DNS address, click Yes. You'll proceed through a short series of dialog boxes that prompt you for an IP address and other settings. When you arrive at the Dial-Up Connection Name dialog box, go to step 7.

7. (Optional). In the Dial-Up Connection Name dialog box, you can optionally type a name to identify your Internet account. If you don't type anything, the wizard names the connection "Connection to" plus the telephone number. Click <u>N</u>ext.

TIME SAVER

Steps 8 through 20 are required *only* if you want to use Internet Explorer's mail and news clients, and *only* if you want to configure them now.

If you want to use different clients, or want to wait and configure IE4's clients later, you can just click Next on every dialog box to click through the rest of the steps quickly. When a button labeled Finish appears, click it. Your Internet communications will be ready to go, but not email or newsgroups. To configure them later, simply start the Connection Wizard again.

You'll learn more about configuring email and news clients in Part IV, "Communicating with Email and Newsgroups."

8. Choose Yes in the Set Up Your Internet Mail Account dialog box.

9. Choose Create a New Internet Mail Account.

10. Type your full name in the Your Name dialog box.

11. In the Internet Email address account box, type your complete email address, as given to you by your ISP.

12. In the Internet Mail Logon dialog box, type your email username and password.

13. In the Friendly Name dialog box, give your email account a name to identify it. Use any name you like.

14. Choose Yes in the Set Up Your Internet News Account dialog box.

15. Choose Create a New Internet News Account.

16. In the Your Name dialog box, type your full name.

17. In the Internet News Email address dialog box, enter your complete email address (if it does not already appear in the box).

18. In the Internet News Server Name dialog box, type the news server address.

19. In the Friendly Name dialog box, give your news account a name to identify it. Use any name you like.

20. In the Set Up Your Internet Directory Service dialog box, choose whether to set up an Internet Directory Service (see Hour 12, "Finding People") now or leave it for another Connection Wizard session.

That's it! A dialog box appears, informing you that you've entered all the information Internet Explorer 4 requires. Click Finish to complete the setup.

4

To Do: Set Up a PPP Account in Windows 95 Through Control Panel

If you don't want Microsoft's or Netscape's help configuring Windows 95, you can fly solo. Setting up this way occurs in two basic steps:

1. Install and configure the Windows 95 TCP/IP program.
2. Create a Dial-Up Networking connection to dial your Internet provider.

CAUTION

Although the steps that follow should work for most ISPs, every ISP is a little different, and some require odd little extra configuration steps or other variations from the rule.

Always acquire any type of instruction sheet your ISP supplies, and favor the ISP's instructions over mine. My steps are probably better written, but they're generic; the ISP's instructions are specific to its own system.

First, you must install and configure TCP/IP:

1. Open Control Panel, and then double-click the Network icon.
2. In the Network dialog box, click the Add button.
3. In the list that appears, double-click Protocol. A dialog box appears listing Manufacturers on the left and Protocols on the right.
4. Select Microsoft from the list of manufacturers, and choose Microsoft TCP/IP from the list of Protocols.
5. Click OK to return to Control Panel.
6. Double-click the Network icon again.
7. Select TCP/IP from the list of Network components.
8. Click the Properties button. The TCP/IP Properties dialog box, like the one in Figure 4.4, appears.
9. Using the tabs of the TCP/IP Properties dialog box, enter all the IP, DNS, and other addresses and information your ISP gave you.

   For example, choose the IP Address tab to enter your IP address, and choose the DNS Configuration tab to enter your DNS server addresses. Do not change any setting or enter any information your ISP didn't mention.

TIME SAVER

If your ISP told you that the system automatically assigns you an IP address, choose the IP Address tab on the TCP/IP Properties dialog box and select the Obtain an IP Address Automatically check box.

Figure 4.4.

This dialog box is used to configure TCP/IP properties in Windows 95.

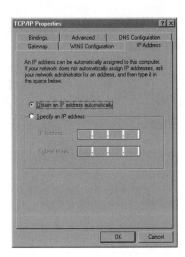

10. When finished entering TCP/IP information, click OK on the TCP/IP Properties dialog box, then click OK again to return to Control Panel.

11. Restart your PC.

Next, create your Internet Dial-Up Networking connection:

1. Open My Computer, and then double-click its Dial-Up Networking icon.

2. Double-click Make New Connection.

3. Type a name (Internet will do) for the connection, and then click Next.

4. Enter your local access number (area code and number), and then click Next.

5. Click Finish. A new icon, using the name you typed in step 3, appears in your Dial-Up Networking folder. This is your Internet connection—but it's not done yet.

6. Right-click the icon you created, and select Properties from the pop-up menu that appears.

7. On the Properties dialog box, click the Server Type button.

8. From the list at the top of the Server Types dialog box, choose PPP-Windows 95 | Windows NT | Internet.

9. If the check box next to Log On to Network is checked, click it to remove the check mark.

10. In the list of Allowed Network Protocols at the bottom of the dialog box, make sure only TCP/IP is checked.

11. Click OK to close the Server Types dialog box, and then click OK again to close the Properties dialog box.

4 ▲   Your new Dial-Up Networking connection is ready to connect you to the Internet.

Setting Up a Mac for an ISP

Just as in Windows 95, the easiest way to set up your Mac connection (short of an ISP signup program) is to install the Mac version of Internet Explorer or Netscape Communicator, and use the setup program each of these programs contains.

Also like Windows 95, a Mac running System 7 can be configured for the Internet with just a few minutes, a couple of dialog boxes, and a small dose of courage. The next To Do section shows you how.

TIME SAVER

The Mac's new operating system, OS8 (see Hour 2), includes signup software for America Online. If you use OS8 and have selected AOL as your Internet provider, double-click the AOL signup icon to sign up with AOL and configure your Mac for Internet/AOL access.

To Do: Set Up a PPP Account in System 7

Configuring System 7 to access an ISP requires two separate, simple procedures.

CAUTION

Although the steps that follow should work for most ISPs, every ISP is a little different, and some require odd little extra configuration steps or other variations from the rule.

Always acquire any type of instruction sheet your ISP supplies and favor the ISP's instructions over mine.

First, set up MacTCP:

1. From the Apple menu, choose Control Panels.
2. Open the MacTCP control panel.
3. Click the PPP icon.
4. Click the More button at the bottom of the MacTCP dialog box.
5. In the Obtain Address box (see Figure 4.5), choose how your ISP will handle your IP address:

   ☐ If your ISP automatically assigns you an IP address, choose the Server option button and move on to step 6.

   ☐ If your ISP has given you an IP address to enter, choose the Manually option button. In the IP address box, enter the letter corresponding to the first three digits in the IP address: for 001–126, enter A; for 127–191, enter B; for 192 and up, enter C.

Figure 4.5.
Use MacTCP to enter the connection settings your ISP gives you.

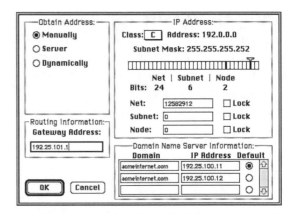

6. In the Domain Name Server box, enter the DNS server addresses supplied by your ISP. Click the Default option button to the right of the address for your primary DNS server.

7. If your ISP gave you a gateway address, enter it in the Routing Information box.

8. If your ISP gave you a subnet mask address, drag the triangular control on the scale under Subnet Mask until the address next to Subnet Mask is correct. (If you chose Manually in step 5, you must choose a subnet mask.)

9. Click OK to close the dialog box.

10. If you chose Manually in step 5, enter your IP address in the IP Address area on the MacTCP dialog box. If you chose Server, skip this step.

11. Close the MacTCP dialog box.

When you finish setting up MacTCP, configure your PPP connection:

1. From the Apple menu, choose Control Panels.

2. Open the Config PPP control panel.

3. Check the Hangup on Close check box.

4. Choose a modem from the PPP Server menu.

5. Click the Config button to open the Config dialog box.

6. Enter your local access number in Phone Num.

7. Click Done, and close the Config PPP control panel. Your Mac is ready to connect to the net.

TIME SAVER

On the Config dialog box, you can click the Connect Script button to open a dialog box on which you can type your Internet username and password, so your Mac can log in for you automatically.

Getting Online

After your account, connection, and client software are all set up on your computer, you can connect to the Internet at will by opening your connection program.

TIME SAVER

With an IP account, it generally doesn't matter in what order you connect to the Internet and your client software. You can either first connect to the Internet and then open your client software, or open your client software first and then connect to the Internet.

Exactly how you open your connection program differs depending upon your computer, the software you select, and whether you chose an ISP or an online service:

☐ Online services generally deposit an icon that looks like their logo right on your Windows or Mac desktop. To go online, you simply choose that icon. Often, the online services deposit a new menu item in your Programs or Apple menu, too.

☐ If you used an ISP signup program, you will probably also see a new icon or easily identifiable menu item for opening the connection.

☐ If you configured your connection on your own, you start it by opening the Dial-Up Networking icon you created in Windows 95 (you'll find it in My Computer's Dial-Up Networking folder) or the Config PPP icon in Mac System 7 (in the MacTCP control panel).

☐ Finally, if you used the Internet Explorer or the Navigator setup program, you may open your connection by opening the Internet Explorer or Netscape Navigator browser. Doing so automatically starts the connection software as well as the browser.

After the connection program opens, you're usually presented with a dialog box on which to type your Internet username and password (see Figure 4.6). To connect, simply type your username and password. (When you type your password, it usually appears onscreen as a series of asterisks, so no one can learn it by peering over your shoulder.) Then, click the button on the dialog box labeled OK, Connect, or Open.

TIME SAVER

Most connection dialog boxes, like the one in Figure 4.6, let you choose an option that enables the dialog box to "save" or "remember" your username and password, so you don't have to type them each time you go online.

This is a handy feature with two drawbacks you must consider. If you allow your connection software to remember your password:

☐ Anyone who has access to your computer—kids, coworkers, very smart dogs—can access the Internet using your account.

☐ Because you never type your password, and it does not appear on the dialog box (asterisks take its place), you may forget it. If you switch computers or install different connection software, you'll need to call your provider and request a new password.

Figure 4.6.

After opening your connection program, you supply your username and password to log on to the Internet.

The connection program instructs your modem to dial your Internet provider, and sends your username and password to log you on.

If all goes well, you'll see a dialog box or message indicating that you are connected. That dialog box is also usually used for disconnecting when you're finished using the Net. Choose Close or Disconnect on the dialog box, or just close the dialog box itself, to go offline.

JUST A MINUTE

From time to time, you won't be able to connect to your ISP. You may get a busy signal if your ISP is temporarily overcrowded, or temporary glitches in the ISP's system may prevent you from logging on successfully.

If your connection software can't get you online, it hangs up and tells you so. You can try again a few minutes later. (Some communications programs automatically retry for you every few minutes until they succeed.) You can have a cookie while you wait.

It's no big deal if your connection fails occasionally. If it fails often, you'll start running out of cookies, so you'd better shop for a more reliable Internet provider.

4

Summary

Now that you've seen what may be involved in setting up your computer without a signup program, I'm sure you'll agree with me that using a signup program from an online service or ISP is the easiest, most reliable way to set up your connection.

That said, I wouldn't choose a provider simply because the provider's signup program happened to be on my computer or in my Cheerios. If the provider that's best for you happens to be a little trickier to set up, so be it. You'll trade a little extra work today for far less frustration down the road.

Workshop

Q&A

Q How can I set up Windows 3.1 for the Internet?

A Some ISPs and online services still supply signup disks for Windows 3.1; as always, a signup program is your best option. In fact, if an online service doesn't supply a Windows 3.1 signup disk, you probably can't use that particular service.

To set up Windows 3.1 for an ISP that doesn't have a signup disk, you must ask the ISP for a copy of Trumpet Winsock, a Windows 3.1–based TCP/IP communications program that enables Windows 3.1 to use a PPP account. Better ISPs send out a copy of Trumpet Winsock that's preconfigured with an IP address, local access number, and all the other information you need to connect. Following instructions from the provider, all you need to do is install Trumpet Winsock, choose a few options, and you're ready to go.

Q Is configuring for the Internet getting any easier?

A Oh my, yes. Signup disks from ISPs are becoming far more common, and the slow death of SLIP and shell accounts has reduced the number of options, setting the stage for easy-to-use PPP setup programs. All new operating systems—such as the next version of Windows (to be released sometime in 1998) and Mac OS8—have easy Internet setup routines built into them. More and more ISPs are also supporting automatic IP address assignment and other techniques that make setting up on the user's end simpler.

Setup is simplifying itself so rapidly that, if you'd just waited another year or two, this hour of the book would have been only six minutes long. I could grant you a 54-minute nap and still stay on schedule.

Quiz

Take the following quiz to see how much you've learned.

Questions

1. An IP address is

    a. I used a signup disk, so I don't care. Leave me alone.

    b. The unique address of a computer on the Internet, expressed as four numbers separated by periods (for example, `255.101.56.92`).

    c. The street address of the place I usually P.

    d. The home of Iggy Pop, a rock idol of the 1970s.

2. Why shouldn't you use your Social Security Number as your Internet password?

    a. Immigration police will confuse you with the guy who uses the same number on his phony passport and deport you to Poland.

    b. You cannot use numerals in a password.

    c. You've used the number on credit applications and other documents, enabling a clever hacker to discover your password and commit general mayhem using your Internet account.

    d. It's hard to remember.

3. Your provider tells you the address of an email server so you can

    a. Configure your news server.

    b. Phone the server and request configuration information.

    c. Apply for an email license.

    d. Configure your email client.

Answers

1. (a) or (b) IP addresses are what makes the net work, but after you've got your computer set up, you don't have to worry about them.

2. (c) Any real word or number used as a password makes a hacker's job easy.

3. (d) You need an email server address (sometimes two) to configure your email client.

Activity

Now that your computer is all set up, scout around your folders and menus. Odds are that installing your client software and setting up your connection deposited some stuff on your computer you're not even aware of.

If you poke around, you may find clients you didn't know you had (installed by a signup program you used), document files containing instructions and reference information, and other goodies. You needn't deal with any of this stuff now, but it's important to know it's there, in case you need it later.

4

Part
II

Making the Web Work for You

Hour

Hour 5

Browsing the Web

Here it is, the $64,000 hour. The web is the main reason interest in the Internet has exploded in the last five years and the main thing that draws newcomers to it. In this hour, you'll pick up the basics of getting all around the web.

In fact, many web surfers never apply any skills beyond those you pick up in this hour. In Hours 6 through 12, you'll build upon what you learn here so you can not only travel the web, but also make the most of it.

At the end of the hour, you'll be able to answer the following questions:

- ☐ What's that web page that always appears as soon as I open my browser?
- ☐ What do all those web addresses mean, and how do I visit a web page address?
- ☐ How can I use links to jump from place to place on the web?
- ☐ How do toolbar buttons like Back and Home make navigating the web easier?
- ☐ What are frames, and how do they make getting around a web page different?
- ☐ How can I play online multimedia?

About Your Home Page

When you open your web browser and connect to the Internet, most web browsers are configured to go automatically to a particular web page. This page is generally referred to as the browser's *home page*.

NEW TERM A *home page* is a web page that a browser is configured to go to automatically when you open it, to provide a starting point for your web travels. It's also sometimes called the *startup page*. Remembering that the page is "home" is important, as you'll learn later in this hour.

Note that home page has two meanings in web parlance: It also describes a web page that serves as the main information resource for a particular person or organization. For example, www.toyota.com may be described as Toyota's home page.

For example, if you get Internet Explorer directly from Microsoft, it opens at a special "Start" page on Microsoft's web server. If you get Netscape Navigator directly from Netscape, it opens automatically to a similar startup page at Netscape. (Incidentally, these Microsoft and Netscape home pages were both shown in Hour 2, "What Hardware and Software Do You Need?" in Figures 2.5 and 2.6).

If you get your software from your Internet provider, however, your browser will probably have been reconfigured with a new home page, one that's set up by your provider as a starting point for its subscribers (see Figure 5.1). This home page also serves as a source of news and information about the provider and its services.

Figure 5.1.

Your browser goes automatically to its home page whenever you open it and connect to the Internet. The home page may be selected by the browser maker or (as shown here) by your Internet provider.

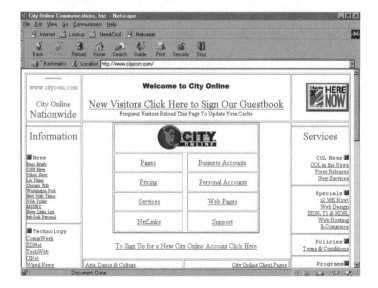

5

You don't have to do anything with your home page. You can ignore it and jump from it to anywhere on the web. Some home pages provide valuable resources, however, especially for newcomers. (Most home pages also contain a healthy dose of advertising. *C'est la web*.)

Often, you'll find a great selection of links on your home page to other fun or useful pages. If your home page happens to be one set up by your local ISP, the page may even contain local news, weather, and links to other pages with information about your community. Now and then, before striking out onto the web, be sure to give your home page a glance to check out what it has to offer.

NEW TERM A *link* is an object in a web page that you can click to jump to another page, or another part of the page you're on. Links can appear onscreen as blocks of text or as pictures. In most browsers, you go where the link leads simply by clicking it. See the section "Basic Jumping Around," later in this hour.

Don't like your home page, and wish you had a different one? In Hour 6, "Revisiting Places You Like," you'll learn how to change your home page.

Understanding Web Page Addresses

Using the web is easy and that's why it's so popular. But if there's one thing about web surfing that trips up newcomers, it's using web page addresses effectively. This hour will set you straight on web page addresses so you can leap online with confidence.

Although there are other types of addresses (you'll learn about them in Part V, "Beyond Browsing: Using Advanced Internet Tools"), for the most part, you'll deal with only two kinds of addresses for most Internet activities:

- ☐ **Email addresses**—They always contain an "at" symbol (@); for example, clinton@whitehouse.com. You'll learn all about email addresses in Hour 13, "Sending and Receiving Email."

- ☐ **Web page addresses**—They never contain an @ symbol. Web page addresses are expressed as a series of letters separated by periods (.) and sometimes forward slashes (/). An example is www.microsoft.com/index/contents.htm. (Web addresses often begin with www, but not always.) A web page address is generally referred to as a *URL*.

NEW TERM A *URL (Uniform Resource Locator)* is an address you can type in a web browser to access a particular resource. (You can pronounce it "U-R-L" or "earl.")

Although most URLs are web page addresses, other types of URLs may be used in a web browser for accessing newsgroups, local files on your computer, and other resources. You'll learn about web page URLs in this hour and learn about other types later in this book.

If you keep your eyes open, you'll see web page URLs everywhere these days. By typing a URL in your web browser (as you learn to do shortly), you can go straight to that page, the page the URL "points to." Just to give you a taste of the possibilities, and to get you accustomed to the look and feel of a URL, Table 5.1 shows the URLs of some fun and interesting web sites.

Table 5.1. A few of the millions of fun and interesting web sites.

URL	Description
www.cnn.com	Cable News Network (CNN)
www.doonesbury.com	The Doonesbury comic strip
www.epicurious.com	A trove of recipes
www.scifi.com	The SciFi Channel
www.uncf.org	The United Negro College Fund
www.rockhall.com	Cleveland's Rock & Roll Hall of Fame museum
www.un.org	The United Nations
www.nyse.com	The New York Stock Exchange
college-solutions.com	A guide to choosing a college
www.sleepnet.com	Help for insomniacs
www.nasa.gov	The space agency's site
www.adn.com	The Anchorage, Alaska *Daily News*
www.mommytimes.com	Parenting advice
us.imdb.com	The Internet Movie Database: everything about every film ever made
www.bookshop.co.uk	The Internet Bookshop
www.nhl.com	The National Hockey League

Anatomy of a URL

A URL is made up of several different parts. Each part is separated from those that follow it by a single, forward slash (/).

The first part of the URL—everything up to the first single slash—is the Internet address or the *domain name* (see Hour 4, "Connecting to the Internet") of a particular web server. Everything following that first slash is a directory path or filename of a particular page on the server. For example, consider the following fictitious URL:

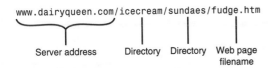

www.dairyqueen.com/icecream/sundaes/fudge.htm

Server address   Directory   Directory   Web page
                                                filename

The filename of the actual web page is `fudge.htm`. (Web page files generally use a filename extension of `.htm` or `.html`.) That file is stored in a directory or folder called `sundaes`, which is itself stored in the `icecream` directory. These directories are stored on a web server whose Internet address is `www.dairyqueen.com`.

Sometimes, a URL will show just a server address and no web page filename. That's okay—many web servers are set up to show a particular file to anyone who accesses the server (or a particular server directory) without specifying a web page filename.

For example, if you go to the URL of Microsoft's web server, `www.microsoft.com`, the server automatically shows you an all-purpose web page you can use for finding and jumping to other Microsoft pages. Such pages are often referred to as *top* or *index* pages, and often even use `index.htm` as their filename.

JUST A MINUTE

When a URL shows only a server address, it's generally described as the address of a web site rather than that of a web page, because the address is intended as a starting point on the server (site) for jumping to any of its pages.

TIME SAVER

Technically, every web page URL begins with `http://` or `https://`, but the latest releases of Navigator and Internet Explorer no longer require you to type that first part. For example, using either of those browsers, you can surf to the URL `http://www.mcp.com` just by typing

www.mcp.com

Because of this change, web page addresses often appear in advertising, books, and magazines with the `http://` part left off.

5

> If you use a browser other than the Big Two, or older versions of the Big
> Two, however, you probably have to include the `http://` part when
> typing URLs in your browser. For example, to go to www.pepsi.com, you
> must type
>
> `http://www.pepsi.com`

To Do: Find the URL of Your Home Page

1. Connect to the Internet and open your web browser. After a few moments, your
   home page should appear. (If no home page appears, your browser is not configured to use one. That's okay; skip to the next section, "Going Straight to Any Web
   Address.")

2. After your home page appears, examine your browser's toolbar area (above the area
   where the page appears) and status bar area (below the page, at the bottom of the
   browser window). If you see a URL in one of those places, it's the URL of your
   home page. (If you can't find the URL, peek ahead to the next section and Figure
   5.2 for help.)

3. Make a mental note of the spot where you saw the home page URL. In that same
   spot, you'll always see the URL of whatever page you're currently viewing. If you
   see the URL in a text box you could type in, that's also the place where you'll type
   URLs to navigate the web.

Going Straight to Any Web Address

Before you can jump to a page by entering its URL, you must find the place in your browser
provided for typing URLs. The term used to describe this area varies from browser to browser,
but to keep things simple, I'll just call it the *address box*. Figure 5.2 shows the toolbar area of
Internet Explorer, with the address box containing a URL.

Figure 5.2.

*In most graphical
browsers, you'll see an
address box in the toolbar
area where you type a
URL to go to a particular
web page or site.*

Address box with URL of current page

In both Internet Explorer and Navigator, you'll see the address box as a long text box somewhere in the toolbar area, showing the URL of the page you're currently viewing. If you don't see it, the toolbar that contains the address box might be switched off.

To switch on the toolbar that contains the address box:

☐ In Internet Explorer, choose View | Toolbars, and make sure a check mark appears next to Address Bar in the menu that appears. If not, click Address Bar. If you still don't see an address box, try dragging each toolbar to the bottom of the stack, so all toolbars are visible and none overlap.

☐ In Navigator, choose View | Show Location Toolbar. If it's collapsed, you still won't see it. Click at the far-left end of each line in the toolbar area, and it should appear.

If you use a different browser, you may see an address box in the toolbar area or at the bottom of the browser window. In some browsers, you may have to choose a menu item to display a dialog box that contains the address box. Look for a menu item with a name such as Enter URL or Jump to New Location.

Entering and Editing URLs

After you've found the address box, you can go to a particular address by typing the URL you want to visit in the box and pressing Enter. When the address box is in a toolbar, you usually must click in it first, then type the URL and press Enter.

TIME SAVER

Before you type a URL in the address box, the URL of the current page already appears there. In most Windows and Mac browsers, if you click once in the address box, the whole URL there is highlighted, meaning that whatever you type next will replace that URL.

If you click twice in the address box, the edit cursor appears there so you can edit the URL. That's a handy feature when you discover that you made a typo when first entering the URL.

When you type a URL to go somewhere, your starting point doesn't matter—you can be at your home page, on any other page, or in the middle of another activity (such as playing multimedia). From anywhere on the web, entering a URL takes you wherever that URL leads.

When typing the URL, be careful about the following:

☐ Spell and punctuate the URL exactly as shown, and do not use any spaces.

☐ Match the exact pattern of uppercase and lowercase letters you see in the URL. Some web servers are case sensitive, and will not show you the page if you don't get the capitalization in the URL just right.

☐ Some URLs that don't end in .htm or .html end in a final slash (/), and some don't. Servers can be quirky about slashes, and many print sources where you see URLs listed mistakenly omit a required final slash, or add one that doesn't belong. Always type a URL exactly as shown. If that doesn't work, and the URL appears not to end in a filename, try adding or removing the final slash.

☐ If you don't use a recent version of Internet Explorer or Navigator, you usually must include the http:// prefix at the beginning of the URL. For example, when you see a URL listed as www.discover.com, you must enter it in your address box as

http://www.discover.com

CAUTION

What happens if you type a URL wrong? Nothing bad—you just don't go where you want to. Usually, your browser displays an error message, reporting that the browser could not find the URL you requested. Check that you spelled, punctuated, and capitalized the URL correctly. If you discover a mistake, edit (or retype) the URL and press Enter to try again.

Note that web servers and their pages are not permanent. From time to time, a URL will fail because the page or server to which it points is no longer online, either temporarily (because of a system glitch) or permanently.

To Do: Go to the Macmillan Computer Publishing Web Site

Honest, I'm not shilling for Macmillan Computer Publishing (MCP) here, even though MCP published this book. It's just that web pages come and go. Most web site URLs for large organizations work fine for years, but addresses can change, and web pages and sites disappear from time to time.

To connect to the MCP web site:

1. Connect to the Internet and open your web browser.

2. Find your address box, and click in it once.

3. Type the URL:

   http://www.mcp.com

   (That URL will work in any browser, but if you use Internet Explorer version 3.02 or 4, or Navigator 4 (Communicator), you may optionally omit the http:// prefix.)

▼ 4. Press Enter. Macmillan's web site appears (see Figure 5.3).

5

Figure 5.3.

The MCP web site, a good place to go when practicing URLs because it has a really short one (www.mcp.com).

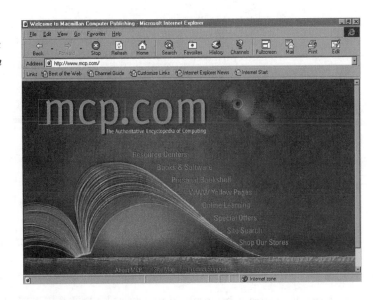

Basic Jumping Around

You've learned how to move about the web by entering a URL, but you can also jump from place to place without typing a URL. Most often, you'll just click a link or button.

Sorry to show the hard way before the easy way, but you're not always going to find a link that takes you exactly where you want to go. URLs are like cars—they take you directly to a particular place. Links are like buses—they often take you just to the right neighborhood.

JUST A MINUTE

Some web pages take a long time to appear, even if you have a fast modem and Internet connection. If some pages do seem terribly slow, don't worry that there's something wrong with your computer, modem, or connection. The problem is probably that the page you're accessing is complex.

You see, each time you display a particular web page, the whole page must travel through the Internet to your computer to appear on your screen. A page that's mostly text appears quickly, because text pages contain little data, and thus travel quickly through the net. Images, multimedia, and Java programs balloon the number and size of the files that make up the web page, and thus take much longer to appear. In most browsers, such pages tend to materialize on your screen incrementally: The text appears first, then the images, and so on.

5

Some browsers *cache* web pages—store them on your computer's hard disk. When you return to a web page your computer has previously cached, your browser first checks with the server to see what (if anything) on the page has changed. Anything on the page that hasn't changed is called up quickly from your hard disk instead of traveling through the Internet again. Because of caching, many pages show up much more slowly the first time you visit them than they do thereafter.

Finding and Using Links

Activating a link in most browsers is simple: Point to the link, click it, and your browser takes you wherever the link leads.

Most links lead to another web page or to another part of a long web page you're viewing. However, links can do much more. For example, some links may start the download of a software file (see Hour 11, "Finding Programs and Files") or play a multimedia file.

Using links is easy, but finding them in web pages that aren't designed well can be tricky. Links appear in a web page in any of three ways:

- **As text**—You'll notice text in web pages that appears to be formatted differently from the rest. The formatting differs depending upon your browser, but text that serves as a link is usually underlined (see Figure 5.4) and displayed in a different color than any other text in the page.

- **As images**—Any image you see in a web page may be a link. For example, a company logo may be a link leading to a page containing information about that company.

- **As image maps**—An image map is a single image that contains not just one link, but several (see Figure 5.5). Clicking on different parts of the image activates different links.

Figure 5.4.

In most browsers, when you point to a link, your pointer changes to indicate the link.

Text links are usually easy to spot because of their color and underlining. Image and image map links can be harder to spot at a glance. Most browsers provide a simple way to determine what is and is not a link. Whenever the mouse pointer is on a link, it changes from the regular

5

pointer to a special pointer (usually a hand with a pointing finger) that always indicates links (see Figures 5.4 and 5.5).

Figure 5.5.

Each part of this image map is a different link. You click different areas of the picture to do different things.

JUST A MINUTE

Users of nongraphical browsers can't use a mouse to activate links. Text-only browsers typically display a particular number or letter next to each link; the user activates the link by pressing its number.

Of course, such users also cannot use the links in images or image maps, because their browsers do not display images. That's why most well-designed web pages repeat all the links from images and image maps as text links somewhere else on the page, usually near the bottom.

5

Using Navigation Buttons: Back, Forward, Home, and Stop

In most browsers for Windows and the Mac, you'll see a whole raft of toolbar buttons, many of which you'll discover as this book progresses. By far, the most important are Back, Forward, Home, and Stop (see Figure 5.6). These buttons help you move easily back and forth among any pages you've already visited in the current online session and conveniently deal with the unexpected.

For example, when exploring a particular web site, you often begin at a sort of "top" page that branches out to others. After branching out a few steps from the top to explore particular pages, you'll often want to work your way back to the top again, to start off in a new direction. The Big Four buttons make that kind of web navigation simple and typing-free.

JUST A MINUTE

Nongraphical browsers lack the toolbars of graphical browsers, but usually support the same functions through keyboard commands and menu items. For example, in many such browsers, you use the Backspace key to do the same thing the Back button does in a graphical browser.

Figure 5.6.

The main toolbars in Navigator (shown here) and Internet Explorer prominently feature the invaluable Back, Forward, Stop, and Home buttons.

Back   Forward   Home   Stop

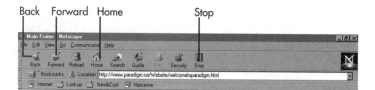

Here's how you can use each of the Big Four buttons:

- [ ] **Back**—Retraces your steps, taking you one step backward in your browsing each time you click it. For example, if you move from Page A to Page B, clicking the Back button takes you back to A. If you go from A to B to C, pressing Back twice returns you to A. When you reach the first page you visited in the current online session, the Back button is disabled; there's nowhere left to go back to.

- [ ] **Forward**—Reverses the action of Back. If you've used Back to go backward from Page B to A, Forward takes you forward to B. If you click Back three times—going from D to C to B to A—clicking Forward three times takes you all the way ahead to D. When you reach the page on which Back was first clicked, the Forward button is disabled because you can only move forward to pages you've already visited.

- [ ] **Home**—Takes you from anywhere on the web directly to the page configured in your browser as home, described at the start of this hour. Going Home is a great way to re-orient yourself if you lose your way and need to get back to a reliable starting point.

- [ ] **Stop**—Immediately stops whatever the browser is doing. If you click Stop while a page is materializing on your screen, the browser stops getting the page from the server, leaves the half-finished page on your screen, and awaits your next instruction.

5

TIME SAVER

Back, Forward, and Home don't care how you got where you are. In other words, no matter what techniques you've used to browse through a

> series of pages—entering URLs, clicking links, using buttons, or any combination—Back takes you back through them, Forward undoes Back, and Home takes you home.

Back and Stop are particularly useful for undoing mistakes. For example, if you click on a link that downloads a file, and while the file is downloading you decide you don't want it, you can click Stop to halt the download but stay on the current page, or click Back to halt the download and return to the preceding page.

To Do: Practice Using Links and Buttons

1. Go to the MCP web site at www.mcp.com.

2. Find any link on the MCP web page that looks interesting, and click it. A new page opens.

3. Click Back. You return to the top MCP web page.

4. Click another link. On the page that appears, find and click yet another link. (If you see no links, click Back to return to the top MCP page, and try another route.)

5. Click Back twice. You return to the top MCP page.

6. Click Forward twice. You go ahead to where you just came back from.

7. Try a new URL. Enter www.akc.org to go to the American Kennel Club site (see Figure 5.7).

8. From the AKC page, click Back once. You return to a page at MCP.

9. Click Home. Welcome home.

Figure 5.7.

The American Kennel Club page at www.akc.org. *Woof!*

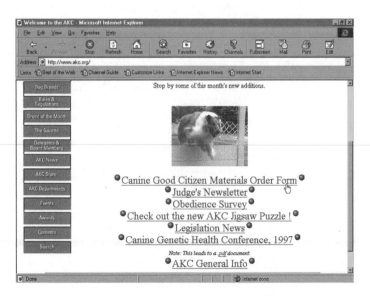

Fussing with Frames

Some pages you'll find are split up into *frames*, two or more separate panes (see Figure 5.8).

Each pane in a frames page contains its own separate web page. That enables each pane to operate independently of the others; for example, clicking a link in one pane can change the contents of another.

Figure 5.8.

Frames pages show two or more separate documents at once, each in its own pane.

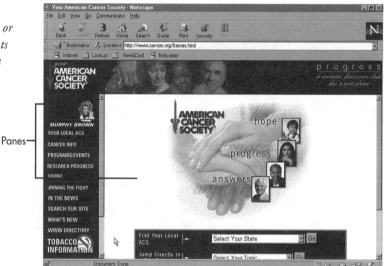

Some folks get all boxed up by frames, but using a frames-based page isn't really that tricky. Just remember the following tips:

☐ To use the links or other stuff in a particular pane, click anywhere within the pane to make that pane active. Then do what you want there. Anytime you move to another pane, click there before doing anything.

☐ Some panes have their own scrollbars. When you see scrollbars on a pane, use them to scroll more of the pane's contents into view.

☐ While you're on a frames page, the Back and Forward buttons take you back and forth among the panes you've used in the current frames page, *not* among pages. Sometimes, it can be tough to use Back to "back out" of a frames page to the page you saw before it; at such times, it's often easier to enter a new URL or click Home to break free of the frames, then go from there.

☐ Some pages use borderless frames, and so do not appear at first glance to be frames pages. After a little experience, however, you'll quickly learn to identify any frames page when it appears, even when the frames are implemented subtly.

TIME SAVER

Internet Explorer, Navigator, and a few other major browsers support frames, but many others do not. For this reason, many frames pages are preceded by a non-frames page that provides two links: One for displaying the frames page and another for displaying the same content in a no-frames version.

If your browser can't handle frames—or if your browser can handle them but you can't—just choose the no-frames version. Life's too short.

Playing Multimedia

Strictly speaking, *multimedia* describes everything on the web that's not text, including any images that appear in web pages. Images incorporated into the layout of a web page aren't really part of the whole multimedia issue, however, because there's no trick to seeing them. Any graphical browser can show the images in a web page.

When I say multimedia I'm talking about such advanced web capabilities as playing video clips, sound clips, and animation. I'm also talking about hearing and seeing live audio and video broadcasts through the web.

This multimedia comes in two basic types:

☐ **Inline**—Incorporated into the page so it plays or displays automatically when you go to the page. (Sometimes also known as *embedded* multimedia.)

☐ **External**—Stored in a separate file you open by clicking a link.

JUST A MINUTE

As you'll learn the hard way, external multimedia files may be large and may take a long time to travel to your computer before they play. A 30-second video clip may take a half hour or more to show up.

It's All in Your Browser's Power

So how do you learn to use multimedia? You don't—your browser does. For your part, playing multimedia on the web requires only skills you already possess—opening web pages and clicking links. The browser must know what to do with the multimedia files that you encounter while browsing.

Each type of online multimedia is a different kind of file, requiring a different program to play it. For example, there are at least a dozen different types of video and sound files, and each type requires a different program to play it.

5

A browser supports this multimedia in any of three ways:

☐ **Native support**—The capability to handle certain types of multimedia is built into the browser. Recent releases of Internet Explorer and Navigator include native support for the majority of popular multimedia file types. Older or less capable browsers usually contain native support for just a few file types or none.

☐ **Plug-in**—A plug-in is an optional add-in to a browser that endows it with new capabilities, such as support for a multimedia type the browser does not support natively. A plug-in creates the illusion of native support for the new features it adds to the browser.

☐ **Helper**—A helper application is a program separate from the browser that handles a particular file type. When encountering a file type for which it has no native support or plug-in, a browser may open another program on your computer to handle the file. For example, some lesser Windows 95 browsers lack native support for video files using the extension .AVI. However, Windows 95 has a built-in program, Media Player, that plays .AVI files. When such a browser hits an .AVI file, it automatically opens Media Player to play it.

You'll learn more about plug-ins and helpers in Hour 8, "Plug-ins, Helpers, and Other Ways to Do More Online." For now, what you must understand is that there is a long, complicated list of multimedia types online, and new ones are being invented all the time. Learning the names of all the multimedia file types won't really help you; only through trial and error can you truly learn what your browser can't handle:

☐ When you open a page containing inline multimedia your browser can't handle, a message appears telling you the name or type of the file your browser can't play. Usually, you can still browse the page with no problem—you simply won't see or hear some of its multimedia.

☐ When you click a link leading to a type of external multimedia file your browser can't handle, a message usually appears to tell you the browser doesn't know what to do with the file. Often, the message offers a choice between canceling the download of the file or continuing the download, in case you want to save the file and play it later in another program.

Whenever you learn the file type of a multimedia file your browser can't play, you need to install a plug-in or helper application to add support for that file type (if that file type matters to you). You'll learn how to do that in Hour 8. Until then, just browse around and see what happens. You may find that your browser already knows how to do nearly everything.

TIME SAVER

Internet Explorer and Navigator include native support for most common multimedia file types, but new ones are being introduced all the time.

5

When a web author introduces a new file type, he or she also supplies a new helper program or plug-in to enable existing browsers to play the new file type.

When you encounter a new file type, the web page may display a message telling you that a particular plug-in is required for playing the file. That message may contain a link you can click to download and install the plug-in right away. See Hour 8 for more information.

To Do: Play a Video Clip

Why not find out right now whether your browser is equipped for playing .AVI video clips? In the steps that follow, you'll download and play a movie trailer from the MovieLink site:

1. Go to MovieLink at web7.movielink.com. An image map of a theatre marquee appears.

2. In the marquee, click the word TRAILERS. A dialog box appears, prompting for more information about you. To supply that information, fill in an online form; you'll learn much more about forms in Hour 7, "Protecting Your Privacy (and Other Security Stuff)."

3. Click in the ZIP code portion of the form, type your ZIP code, and click on the button near the ZIP code labeled Submit. (You don't have to fill in any more of the form for this exercise.) A page like the one in Figure 5.9 appears, listing video-clip trailers and posters you can display for films in current release.

Figure 5.9.

MovieLink, which has links you may click to play video clips of Coming Attractions movie trailers.

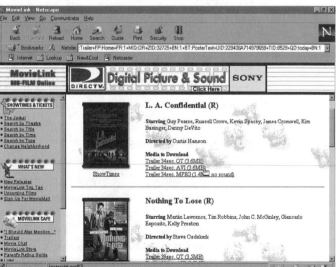

5

4. Find a trailer link that includes the extension `.AVI`. This indicates the file type of the clip. You'll see other types listed too, including MPEG.

5. Click the link. If your browser is equipped for playing `.AVI` video clips, the clip will be downloaded and will then play in a small window on top of the web page. (You may see a dialog box first, asking whether you want to Open (play) or Save the file to disk. Choose Open.)

Summary

That's all there is to basic browsing. Just by entering URLs, clicking links, and using buttons such as Back and Home, you can explore near and far. Little bumps such as frames and multimedia add complexity to the mix, but there shouldn't be anything you can't handle.

Workshop

Q&A

Q I've noticed that some server addresses end in `.com`, some in `.uk`, and others in `.org`. What's that all about? Should I care?

A The Internet's domain name rules include a set of suffixes that go at the end of server addresses to identify the type of organization that operates the server or to identify the server's geographic location. No, you really don't need to care about the suffixes; all you have to do is type the URLs correctly. But since you asked…

Most web server addresses you'll encounter end in `.com`, which is short for commercial and indicates a server used in a business. There are many different suffixes, but the most common include `.com`, `.edu` (educational, such as a server in a college or university), `.gov` (a government server), `.org` (an organization that doesn't fit in the other categories), and `.uk` (a server in the United Kingdom).

Q You said that the `http://` prefix indicates that a URL is a web page. If URLs are used only in web browsers, why would a URL need to point to anything *other* than a web page?

A Web browsers are the Swiss Army Knives of the Internet. Many web browsers are designed to serve as a client for several types of servers.

Of course, their main gig is showing web pages on web servers. But many web browsers can also show newsgroup messages on news servers, and interact with two other server types (FTP and Gopher) that you'll learn about in Hour 19, "Using Old-Fashioned Hacker's Tools: FTP, Gopher, and Telnet." Finally, a web browser can be used to view various types of files that are stored not on the Internet, but right on your local computer or network. (You'll learn more about that in Hour 24, "Moving Toward Web Integration.")

5

For each of the different types of resources a web browser can access, a different URL prefix is needed. For example, the URL for a resource on an FTP server begins with ftp://, not with http://. (Can you guess what the Gopher prefix might be?)

In upcoming hours, you'll learn more about accessing non-web stuff through a web browser. You'll also learn that it's often better to use a specific client for these activities, rather than your web browser. A real corkscrew or screwdriver usually works better than the one in your Swiss Army Knife.

Quiz

Take the following quiz to see how much you've learned.

Questions

1. To what web server does the URL www.nbc.com/today/Couric.htm point?

    a. Couric.com

    b. www.nbc.com

    c. today.show

    d. http://www.nbc.com/today/Couric.htm

2. In a magazine, you see the URL for the *Old Farmer's Almanac* shown as www.almanac.com. Which is the most reliable way to type this URL in a browser's address box?

    a. www.almanac.com

    b. http:/www.almanac.com

    c. http://www.alamanca.com

    d. http://www.almanac.com

3. You've just jumped from a page entitled John, to one called Paul, then to one called George, and finally to Ringo. From Ringo, how can you get back to John?

    a. Enter the URL for John in the address box.

    b. Click Back three times.

    c. Find a link on Ringo that happens to lead to John, and click it.

    d. All of the above.

Answers

1. (b) Just the first part of the URL—up to the first single slash—shows the Internet domain name of the web server. The rest of the URL shows the directory path and filename of a web page file on that server.

2. (d) Choice (a) could work, but only in browsers that permit you to omit the `http://` prefix. Choice (b) omits one of the slashes from the prefix, and choice (c) misspells the URL.

3. (d) Choices (a), (b), and (c) all work, although (b) would be easiest.

Activity

Okay, you and I both know that after you get the feel of the web, you're going to put this book down and explore awhile all by yourself. That's okay—I'd do the same myself. If you're not sure where to go first, take a look back at Table 5.1, and try some of the URLs you see there.

As long as you're cheating, try this: Anytime you arrive at a page you really like, jot down the URL so you can get back to it easily. I'll explain why in Hour 6.

5

Hour 6

Revisiting Places You Like

There are millions of web pages and only one of you. Yes, that's part of what makes you oh-so-special. But even though you're special, if you're at least a little bit like most people, your web surfing will eventually settle into a pattern wherein you revisit certain favorite pages often. If you revisit certain pages often, you need a more convenient way of getting there than having to type URLs all the time.

In this hour, you discover the various ways you can easily revisit places you've been, even when you don't remember the URL. You'll also learn about saving and printing what you see online, so you can revisit that information *offline*, any time.

At the end of the hour, you'll be able to answer the following questions:

☐ How can I change my home page so that I automatically visit my favorite page every time I go online?

☐ How can I create a way to go straight to a page I like without having to type its URL?

☐ How can I find and revisit a page I visited an hour, day, or week ago if I can't remember its URL?

☐ How can I save information I find on the web?

Changing Your Home Page

On your web travels, you'll discover many different pages you'll want to revisit. You may also discover one page you like or need so much that you want to visit it first, every time you go online.

If you find such a page, why not make it your browser's home page, so your browser automatically goes straight to it every time you go online and every time you click the Home button? Most browsers that use a home page—including Navigator and Internet Explorer—also enable you to choose that page.

To make any page your home page, just find your browser's dialog box where the web address of the home page is shown and replace that address with the address of the page you want to use as your new home page. You'll find that dialog box by doing the following:

☐ In Internet Explorer 4, choose View | Internet Options | General.

☐ In Navigator 4, choose Edit | Preferences, then choose Navigator from the list that appears in the left side of the Preferences dialog box (see Figure 6.1).

Figure 6.1.

To change your home page, find the dialog box used to customize your browser (Navigator's is shown here) and replace the URL of the current home page with your new home page URL.

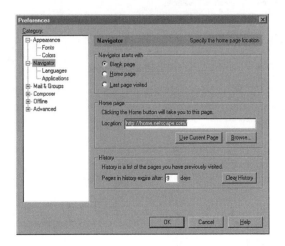

6

TIME SAVER

Both Internet Explorer and Navigator provide a way you can save yourself the trouble of typing the URL when configuring a new home page.

In either browser, begin by browsing to the page you want to use as your home page. Next, open the dialog box on which you change the home page. Then

☐ In Navigator 4, click the Use Current Page button.

☐ In Internet Explorer 4, click the Use Current button.

Creating Shortcuts to Pages You Like

Most browsers let you build and maintain a list of shortcuts to pages you plan to revisit often.

While viewing a page you know you'll want to revisit one day, you can create a shortcut to it so any time you want to visit that page, you needn't type (or even remember) its URL. You just choose the page's name from a menu, and your browser takes you there.

  The shortcuts you create for easily revisiting web pages are called *bookmarks* in Navigator and *favorites* in Internet Explorer.

Figure 6.2 shows a menu of these shortcuts, created in Internet Explorer. I can click on any item in this menu to go directly to the page it describes. Observe that some items in the list are folders. As the figure shows, clicking a folder opens a submenu from which you can select a shortcut or another folder.

Figure 6.2.

By creating bookmarks or favorites (like those shown in this Internet Explorer list), you give yourself an easy way to return to pages you like.

Adding a New Bookmark or Favorite

Before creating a new bookmark or favorite, go to the particular page you want to make a bookmark or favorite for. There you choose a quick button or menu item to create the shortcut.

To Do: Create a Bookmark in Navigator

To create a bookmark in Netscape Navigator, follow these steps:

1. Go to the page you want to create a bookmark for.

2. Click the Bookmarks button on the toolbar, or choose Communicator | Bookmarks from the menu bar.

3. In the menu, click Add Bookmark.

   The new bookmark is added to your list; its name is the title of the web page it points to. (If the page is untitled, its URL appears in the list.) If the title is not descriptive enough, edit the bookmark as described later in this hour to give it a new name.

To Do: Create a Favorite in Internet Explorer

To create a favorite in Internet Explorer, follow these steps:

1. Go to the page you want to create a favorite for.

2. From the menu bar, choose Favorites | Add to Favorites. A dialog box like the one in Figure 6.3 opens.

   Observe in Figure 6.3 that the name of the current page appears in a text box. That's the name that will appear in your favorites list. If the name shown is not descriptive enough to help you remember which page the favorite points to, you can optionally type a new name in the dialog box.

3. Make sure the top option button (next to No, just add the page to my favorites) is selected. Then click OK.

JUST A MINUTE

> The second and third option buttons on the dialog box, shown in Figure 6.3, are for *subscribing* to web pages and channels. Subscriptions automatically deliver selected web page content to your computer at regular intervals or whenever there's news. You learn about subscriptions in Hour 20, "Making the Web Deliver Pages to You: Channels and NetCasting."

Going Where a Bookmark or Favorite Leads

From the moment you create a new favorite or bookmark, it appears as an item in the bookmarks or favorites menu. To use bookmarks and favorites, you simply open the menu and choose an item from the list.

☐ To display Navigator's Bookmarks list, click the Bookmarks button on the toolbar, or choose Communicator | Bookmarks from the menu bar.

☐ To display Internet Explorer's favorites list, choose Favorites from the menu bar.

TIME SAVER

In Internet Explorer 4, as an alternative to clicking Favorites on the menu bar, you can click the Favorites button in the toolbar to display your favorites list in the Explorer Bar, a panel in the left side of the window that can display your favorites list, plus other kinds of lists. You'll learn more about the Explorer bar in Hour 9, "Getting Started with Searching."

Figure 6.3.

In Internet Explorer, choose Favorites | Add to Favorites to open this dialog box on which you can create a favorite for the current page or subscribe to a channel (see Hour 20).

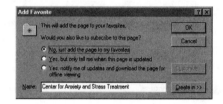

Managing Your List

Over time, your list of shortcuts can become too long and unwieldy. To make it more manageable, you can delete bookmarks and favorites you no longer use, or you can organize them into folders. You manage your shortcuts in a simple dialog box that lets you delete, move, or rename bookmarks and favorites much as you would do so with any group of file icons in a Windows or Mac folder.

To open the dialog box for managing shortcuts:

☐ In Internet Explorer 4, choose Favorites | Organize Favorites from the menu bar.

☐ In Navigator 4, click the Bookmarks button in the toolbar (or choose Communicator | Bookmarks), then choose Edit Bookmarks.

6

TIME SAVER

For favorites sites you want really fast access to, you can put a button right on a toolbar so clicking the button takes you straight to the site.

In Navigator 4, any bookmark you move into the Personal Toolbar folder appears as a button on Navigator's Personal toolbar. In Internet Explorer 4, any favorite you move into the Links folder appears as a button on the Links toolbar.

Reliving Your History

Bookmarks and favorites are the best way to go back where you've been. Suppose you want to revisit a page you didn't create a shortcut to, and you can't remember the URL. How can you find it?

Of course, getting back to any page you've visited in the current session is never a problem; you can use the Back button (see Hour 5, "Browsing the Web"). In addition to the Back button, most browsers can display a menu of sites you've visited in the current session. You'll find that list at the bottom of the Go menu in Navigator and on the File menu in Internet Explorer.

TIME SAVER

On the Back button in both Navigator 4 and Internet Explorer 4, you'll see a tiny, black, downward pointing arrow. If you carefully click on that tiny arrow, a list of pages you've visited in the current session drops down from the button. You can go straight to any page on the list by clicking it.

What about pages you visited yesterday or last week? To help you get back to those, browsers keep a record of where you've been: your history file (see Figure 6.4). To revisit any page you've visited lately, open your browser's history file, locate an entry describing the page, and choose that entry.

Figure 6.4.

From this history file in Navigator, you can return to any page you've visited recently by finding it in the list and double-clicking it.

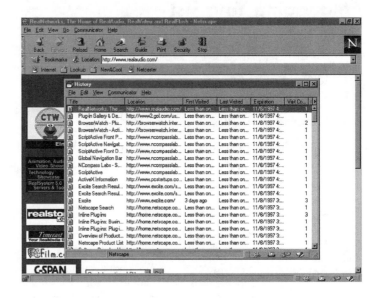

6

To find a particular page in the history file, it helps to understand that the file lists its entries from those you've visited most recently to those you visited longer ago. In other words, the farther you scroll down in the list, the older the entries are.

The history file keeps track of where you've been, no matter how you got there. Every time you go to a page—whether you get there by URL, link, bookmark, or favorite—the visit is recorded in your history file.

To open the history file:

☐ In Internet Explorer 4, click the History button, or choose View | Explorer Bar | History. The list opens in the Explorer Bar, a panel on the left side of the window.

☐ In Navigator 4, choose Communicator | History.

JUST A MINUTE

Browsers don't track your history forever; you'd wind up with a huge, unmanageable history file. Instead, browsers automatically delete all history file entries older than a set number of days.

By default, Navigator 4 deletes all history entries more than 9 days old; Internet Explorer deletes those older than 20 days. In either program, however, you can change the number of days the browser holds onto history entries. To do so

☐ In Internet Explorer 4, choose View | Internet Options | General.

☐ In Netscape Navigator 4, choose Edit | Preferences, then choose Navigator from the list that appears in the left side of the dialog box (refer to Figure 6.1).

Recalling URLs You've Typed

Your history file keeps every page you've visited, no matter how you got there. In addition to the history file, browsers keep a separate list of every URL you've typed in the address box. This list makes retrieving and reusing a URL you've typed much easier.

In either Navigator or Internet Explorer, you can take advantage of this list in either of two ways:

☐ **Drop-Down List**—At the far-right end of the address box, you'll see an arrow. Click the arrow, and a list of URLs you've typed drops down (see Figure 6.5). To visit any of the URLs listed, click it in the list.

☐ **AutoComplete**—Begin typing the URL in the address box. After you've typed enough of the URL for the browser to guess which URL you're typing, the browser fills in the rest of the URL in the address box. For example, if you've previously typed www.monkeys.com, and that URL is the only one in the list that begins www.mo, you need type only that much of the URL in the address box—the rest suddenly appears, and you can press Enter to go where it leads.

Figure 6.5.

The URLs you've typed are stored in a list that drops down from the address box, for easy recall.

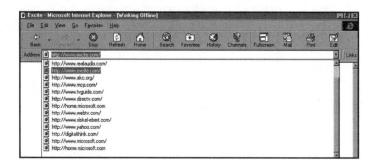

To Do: Recall a Typed URL

The following steps can be used in either Navigator 4 or Internet Explorer 4:

1. In your address box, enter the URL www.habitat.org, and learn about the good work Habitat for Humanity does.

2. Using URLs, links, or favorites, browse away from Habitat for Humanity.

3. Drop down your address box list and choose www.habitat.org. You return to Habitat.

4. Browse away from Habitat again.

5. In your address box, start typing www.habitat.org slowly. By the time you've typed as far as www.h or maybe www.hab, the rest of the URL should appear in the address box.

6. Press Enter to return to Habitat.

Printing and Saving Pages

You revisit a web page if you expect its content to have changed, because you want news. But for information that doesn't change, there's no reason to keep going back to the web page. Instead, save that information in a form you can consult offline, anytime.

The easiest way to do that is to print web pages. In most browsers, that's as easy as clicking a Print button on the toolbar, or choosing Print from a menu (usually a File menu). The browser prints all the page you're currently viewing, not just the screenful you see. If a page can be scrolled through multiple screenfuls of information, the whole thing is printed out, usually across multiple paper pages.

6

Alternatively, you can save web pages on your hard disk. On the File menu of most browsers, you'll find a Save As item. Choose that, and you can save the current web page as a file on your hard disk. You can then open and view the page in your browser anytime, offline. (You'll learn much more about working offline in Hour 20.)

JUST A MINUTE

When you save pages in some browsers, only the text of the page is saved, not its images. If the images are an important part of the information the page contains, print the page rather than saving it.

In Hour 23, "Creating Web Pages and Multimedia Messages," you'll learn special techniques for saving both the text and images in a web page.

In most browsers, the dialog box for opening saved web pages appears if you choose File | Open. If you simply open the folder in which you saved the page and then open the file icon for the web page, however, it will probably open in your browser automatically. When you install them, Windows and Mac browsers usually configure the operating system so any time you open a saved web page file icon, the browser opens automatically to display it.

Summary

You probably know that Magellan is famed for attempting to circumnavigate the globe. You may not know that he didn't make it—he kicked the bucket along the way.

The moral? Getting to new places, as you learned to do in Hour 5, is only half of navigating. The other half is getting *back* to places you've been. If poor Magellan had bookmarks (or favorites), a history file, or even a lowly Home button, he'd have made it full circle.

Don't even get me *started* on Columbus.

Workshop

Q&A

Q **Why does Netscape call them bookmarks and Internet Explorer call them favorites?**

A Navigator and its bookmarks were around before Internet Explorer, so Microsoft is to blame for the confusion. It's possible that Microsoft felt that using bookmarks might be some sort of infringement on Netscape—although that seems unlikely, because a) the two browsers already share many other terms, and b) Microsoft pretty much does whatever it wants (ask the U.S. Department of Justice). More likely, Microsoft just wanted to be different.

Q You said in Hour 5 that because web pages may go away or change their addresses, links and URLs can fall out of date and not work anymore. Will that happen to my bookmarks or favorites?

A Sure, eventually any bookmark or favorite can go bad, if the page to which it points moves or is deleted. One hedge against that is to point them to a site address or a "top" page from which you may then use a link or two to get to a particular page. Specific pages on a server come and go often, but that top page generally stays put.

Navigator 4 can check your bookmarks and optionally fix any that have fallen out of date. In the dialog box used for editing bookmarks (choose Communicator | Bookmarks | Edit Bookmarks), choose View | Update Bookmarks.

Quiz

Take the following quiz to see how much you've learned.

Questions

1. The difference between a bookmark and a favorite is
   a. One's a noun; the other's an adjective.
   b. A bookmark marks history, while a favorite indicates preference.
   c. A bookmark provides an easy way to return to a page in Navigator and a favorite does the same in Internet Explorer.
   d. A bookmark provides an easy way to return to a page in Internet Explorer and a favorite does the same in Navigator.

2. Your history file lists all pages you've visited
   a. Within the number of days for which your browser is set up to save history
   b. In your entire lifetime
   c. With conviction
   d. More than four times

3. Saved web pages always include all _____ that you see online, but may omit _____.
   a. Yin   Yang
   b. text   meaning
   c. images   color
   d. text   images

6

Answers

1. (c) Bookmarks are in Navigator; favorites are in Internet Explorer.

2. (a) Your browser is configured to save history entries for a number of days, which you usually can choose.

3. (d) Your saved web pages always include text but may omit images, depending on your browser.

Activity

By now, you probably already have a short list of web pages you like to revisit. Start building that bookmarks/favorites list. Also, use these shortcuts creatively. For example, I often hit a page that I know I want to explore, but I haven't the time right then. So I save a quick shortcut and return when I get a chance.

6

Hour 7

Protecting Your Privacy (and Other Security Stuff)

You may hear a lot on the news about what a dangerous place the Internet can be. Because you're reading this, you're brave enough to go online anyhow, even if you're a little concerned. (I like that about you.)

Although there are a few online pitfalls to watch out for, most of the stuff you hear about danger online is hype, and the few real risks are easily avoidable.

In this hour, you will learn the basics of keeping your computer out of trouble on the web. At the end of the hour, you'll be able to answer the following questions:

- ☐ How do I fill in online forms, and why must I be careful when doing so?
- ☐ What are certificates, and how do I use them?
- ☐ How does my browser protect my computer's security online, and how can I customize my security settings?
- ☐ What are cookies, and how can I control them?

JUST A MINUTE

In addition to the security tips you'll pick up in this hour, you'll learn other ways to protect yourself in hours to come:

☐ In Hour 11, "Finding Programs and Files," you'll learn about protecting yourself from computer viruses in files you download from the web.

☐ In Hour 18, "Chatting Live!," you'll learn about protecting your anonymity in a chat room.

☐ In Hour 21, "Finding Safe Family Fun and Learning," you'll learn how to self-censor the web to prevent the appearance of material you deem unsuitable for your kids or yourself.

Smart Surfing

There's one important browsing technique I haven't shared with you yet; it's filling in online *forms* (see Figure 7.1). I had a reason to stall: Forms are the one part of web browsing where you really need to be careful about your privacy.

  A *form* is an area in a web page where you can supply information that will be sent back to the web server.

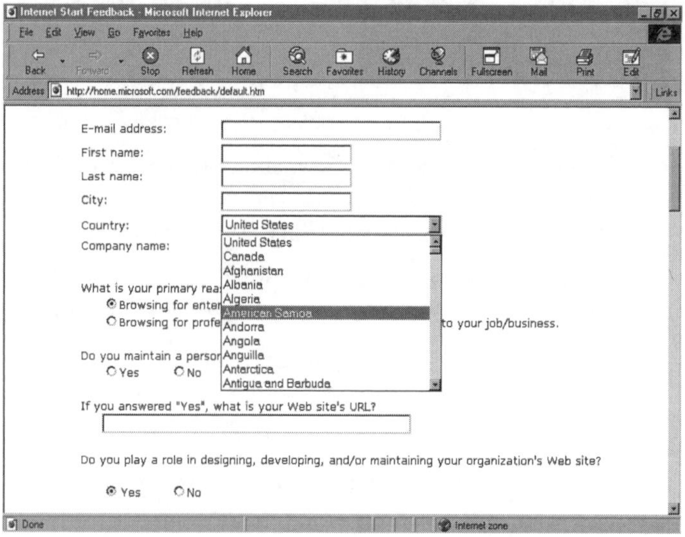

Figure 7.1.

An online form, including text boxes, lists, and radio buttons.

You'll practice filling in a form later in this section, after I've explained the security issues you must consider before using a form. But for now, I'll tell you that filling in an online form is pretty much like filling in any form in Windows or on a Mac. You'll see many of the same methods used for making selections or typing entries, such as

- [ ] **Text boxes**—This is an empty box where you can type something. You just click on the box and type.
- [ ] **Lists**—You may see a list of choices, in which you click an item to select it. Some lists work like Windows pull-down lists; you have to click an arrow on the list box to display the choices.
- [ ] **Check boxes**—A small, empty square in a form is a check box. Click it to put a check mark in it, which in turn selects or enables the item next to it. To remove the check mark, click the check box again.
- [ ] **Radio buttons**—A small, empty circle in a form is a radio button. Click it to fill it in (make it a black circle), which selects or enables the item next to it. To deselect a radio button, click it again.

JUST A MINUTE

Unlike filling in a Windows or Mac form, you often cannot use your Tab key to jump among the parts of the web form. You usually must point to and click each part of the form where you want to make an entry.

When you finish making all your entries and selections in a form, send it to the server. A button always appears near the form, usually labeled Submit, Send, or Done. (I'll just call it the submit button from here on, as long as you remember that it's not always labeled that way.) When you click the submit button, your form entries are sent to the server.

CAUTION

Nothing you do in a form goes to the server until you click the submit button. You can fill in all or part of a form, and as long as you don't click that button, you can jump to another page or go offline, and you will not have sent a word to the server.

Before you click the submit button, you also may go back and change any entries you made in the form.

Why Are Forms Risky Sometimes?

In general, when you visit a web site, you retrieve information from the server, but you don't *send* anything about yourself to the server. You can browse all you like, and you're basically anonymous.

7

When you fill in a form, however, you send the information you supplied in the form to the server. Most of the time, that's perfectly safe because the information you're sending isn't anything private. For example, as you learn in Part III, "Finding What You're Looking For," you perform most Internet searches by typing a *search term*, a word or two related to what you're looking for, in a simple form. A search term really doesn't reveal much about you.

However, some forms want more from you, including such potentially sensitive information as

- ☐ Your name
- ☐ Your email address
- ☐ Your mailing address or telephone number
- ☐ Your credit card number
- ☐ Your Social Security number

Most often, a form collects this information when you're making a purchase. (You'll learn much more about online shopping in Hour 22, "Buying and Selling on the Net.") If you join some sort of online organization or club, you may be prompted to supply detailed information about yourself. A growing number of sites prompt you to "join" the site in order to use it. To join, you must supply a little information about yourself, which the owner of the site typically uses for market research purposes.

To make the most of the web, you can't remain totally private; sooner or later, you're probably going to fill in a form with information about yourself. Before filling in any form, however, ask yourself three important questions:

- ☐ **Is the information requested by the form really necessary?** Some forms collect more information from you than is really required. Don't feel like you must fill in every blank. Include only as much information as you're comfortable sharing. If you find that the form requires you to fill in blanks you don't want to, consider whether the benefits of the form are worth the risks.

- ☐ **Do I trust the owners of this site with the information I'm providing?** Is the site operated by a known company (one you trust), or is it a company you've never heard of? Just as you would over the telephone, think twice about who you're dealing with before revealing anything about yourself. Of course, the more sensitive the information you're sending, the more you must trust the site. You can be much more casual about sharing your email address than about revealing your credit card number.

- ☐ **Is the site secure?** Sending information to a secure site does nothing to protect you if the site's owner is unscrupulous, but it does protect you against someone other than the site owner seeing the information you send.

7

New Term Some web sites that collect information through forms (especially sites that sell online) employ a security system in which information you send is scrambled when traveling between you and the server. The scrambling prevents anyone other than you and the server owner from seeing the information. These sites are called *secure sites*. Sites that do not use a security system are called *unsecure sites*.

Identifying Secure Sites

To use the security systems built into secure sites, your browser must be compatible with the security systems used. Both Internet Explorer and Navigator are compatible with the systems used by secure sites today.

When you send information to an unsecure site, it's possible (although difficult) for a criminal to harvest that information on its way. For example, if you send your name and credit card info, a crook could intercept that information en route between you and the server, and later use it to make a purchase or perpetrate some other kind of fraud.

Using a security-compatible browser to send information to a secure web site makes harvesting impossible; the information you send will be seen only by the owner of the site to which you send it. Of course, if the site owner is a crook, you still have a problem—that person can use your information, so you still need to be careful. Secure sites, on the other hand, do protect you from intrusion by a third party.

Most browsers show you whether a page you're viewing is on a secure site:

☐ Internet Explorer displays a locked padlock at the bottom of the window (near the center) when you're communicating with a secure site. The lock does not appear when you're on an unsecure site.

☐ In Navigator, a tiny padlock appears in the lower-left corner of the browser window (see Figure 7.2). When the padlock appears to be unlocked, as in the figure, you are not connected to a secure site. When the padlock is locked, the site is secure.

☐ In versions of Navigator before 4.0, a tiny gold key appears in the bottom of the browser window. When the key appears to be broken, you are not connected to a secure site. When the key appears intact, the site is secure.

Time Saver

In security dialogs and warnings in Navigator, secure sites are often described as *encrypted sites*. The meaning is the same.

7

Figure 7.2.

Navigator shows an unlocked padlock when the page you're viewing is not secure.

Padlock icon ———   Document: Done

In addition to little locks and keys, most browsers also have a fail-safe: They display a warning message (see Figure 7.3) to you before you send information to an unsecure site, so you have a chance to cancel (if you wish) before actually sending anything.

In fact, depending upon how they're configured, Internet Explorer and Navigator display such a warning before you send anything to any site, secure or unsecure. The dialog always informs you whether you're sending to a secure or unsecure site, and gives you a chance to cancel. You can click Yes to send the information or No to abort the transmission.

Figure 7.3.

Most browsers provide a warning before you send any information to an unsecure site, giving you a chance to cancel.

To Do: Fill in a Form

Now that you know what to watch out for, you can safely complete an online form. Try filling in this form to order a clothing catalog.

CAUTION

> You do not actually have to order the catalog—this is just for practice. In the steps that follow, I'll show you how to cancel the form after filling it in, so you don't order a thing.

1. Go to the Lands' End page at `www.landsend.com`.

2. Locate the link Catalog Request in the list of links at the upper left, and click it. A form like the one in Figure 7.4 appears.

3. Along the top of the page, a series of catalog cover photos appears, each with a check box above it. Choose one or more catalogs by clicking check boxes to put check marks there.

4. Scroll down to the lower half of the page, where a form for filling in your name, address, and other information appears.

5. Point to the text box next to First Name, and click.

6. Type your first name.

7. Point to the text box next to Last Name, and click.

8. Type your last name.

9. Fill in the rest of the form, skipping any boxes requesting information you don't care to share.

JUST A MINUTE

The Lands' End catalog request form includes text boxes for your telephone numbers. Phone numbers are generally required in forms for making purchases because they are needed for credit card verification.

However, in forms like this, they're usually optional and used solely for telemarketing. I recommend never entering your phone number in a form where it's not required, unless, of course, you really enjoy getting telemarketing calls.

10. Now, if you *don't actually want* the catalogs, click Back, or jump to any other page. You have not ordered anything, and Lands' End knows nothing about you that it didn't already know before you arrived at its web page.

If you *do* want the catalogs, click the submit button (yes, this time it's actually labeled Submit) in the form. Then go wait by the mailbox.

JUST A MINUTE

If you click the Submit button, your browser may warn you that you're sending over an unsecure site. The forms at Lands' End that collect credit card numbers for purchases are secure, but the forms for simple catalog ordering are not. That's pretty much the rule among online shops.

7

Figure 7.4.

Filling in a form.

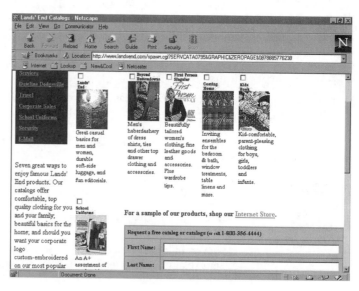

Knowing Who You're Dealing With: Certificates

If you use Navigator or Internet Explorer, now and then you'll come across a *certificate* on the web (see Figure 7.5). When you first see one, it seems like a big deal, but it's not. You won't see certificates often, and when you do, you can deal with them in just a click or two.

NEW TERM   A *certificate* is a dialog that appears when you enter some web sites to certify the identity of the site and its owner. It provides assurance that you're actually communicating with the company you think you're communicating with.

Figure 7.5.

A certificate identifies the site you're connected to.

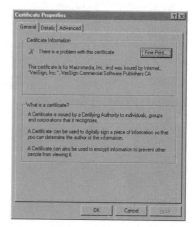

Because a certificate positively identifies the company you're communicating with, you can better decide whether to accept program code, send your credit card or other info, or do anything else that might expose you to risk.

When a certificate appears, your browser usually presents you with a few options for dealing with it: You can accept the certificate (and interact with the site) or reject it. The exact options differ depending on the certificate.

Sometimes, when dealing with the certificate, you'll be prompted to choose whether to accept Java or other *script* code from the site. If you don't trust the site, you are given the option to reject the certificate to prevent it from sending program code to your computer.

 A *script* is a program, such as a Java or JavaScript program, that a web site sends to your computer to be run by your browser. (You'll learn more about scripts in Hour 8, "Plug-ins, Helpers, and Other Ways to Do More Online.")

Protecting Yourself with Browser Security

Most browsers let you customize the way they handle security. You can often choose the circumstances under which a browser displays security warnings, choose which sites can run Java or other program code on your computer, and more.

CAUTION

I want to put you in the driver's seat, to give you as much Internet education as is possible in 400 pages, so that's why I'm describing here the ways you can customize your browser's security settings.

I *strongly* caution you, however, to leave your security settings alone until and unless you begin to feel that your browser is applying security that is too lenient or too strict for your particular needs.

The default security settings built into most browsers strike just the right balance between safety and convenience. So unless you have reason to think they're broken, don't fix them.

Customizing Security in Navigator 4

To open Navigator's security dialog (see Figure 7.6), click the Security button on the toolbar or choose Communicator | Security Info from the menu bar. When the dialog opens, it shows any security information pertinent to the site you're currently viewing, such as whether the site is secure and any certificates in force.

On the left side of the dialog, a list of items for which you can customize security appears. In the list, click Navigator.

7

Use the check boxes and lists in the Navigator security dialog to choose when warnings should appear. (For maximum security, make sure all check boxes on this dialog are checked.) To learn more about what each setting means, click the dialog's Help button.

Figure 7.6.

Customizing security settings in Navigator 4.

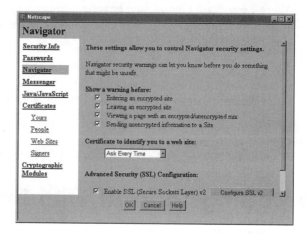

TIME SAVER

To control whether servers can run Java or JavaScript code on your computer, open Navigator's preferences dialog (by choosing Edit | Preferences) and click Advanced in the list on the left side of the dialog. A dialog opens in which you can check or uncheck check boxes to enable or disable Java and JavaScript.

Customizing Security in Internet Explorer 4

To open Internet Explorer's security settings dialog (see Figure 7.7), choose View | Internet Options to open the Internet Options dialog, then click the Security tab.

Figure 7.7.

The Internet Options dialog's Security tab, where you customize security in Internet Explorer.

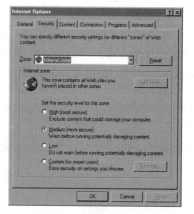

7

Internet Explorer's security system divides all sites into four different security zones:

☐ **Local intranet zone**—This includes all pages on your local intranet, if you have one.

NEW TERM An *intranet* is an internal, private network, usually a company network, that looks and acts like the Internet but isn't open to the outside world. If your computer is not part of a company network, you can ignore the local intranet zone.

☐ **Trusted sites zone**—This includes web sites you have selected as trusted sites (those for which you may want less strict security than others).

☐ **Internet zone**—This covers all Internet web sites that you have not included in your trusted sites zone or your restricted sites zone.

☐ **Restricted sites zone**—This includes sites you don't particularly trust, generally ones for which you'll want higher security than for other zones.

Using the Security tab, you can add sites to your trusted sites and restricted sites' zones, and choose security settings for each of the four zones.

To Do: Add a Site to a Zone

To add a site to a zone, complete these steps:

1. Open the Security tab (choose View | Internet Options | Security).
2. In the Zone list, select the zone to which you want to add sites.
3. Click the Add Sites button. A dialog opens, showing the URLs of sites already in the zone.
4. In the text box at the bottom of the dialog, type the URL of a site you want to add to the zone, then click Add to add it to the list.

Understanding Zone Security Settings

The security settings for a zone determine how aggressive the security system in Internet Explorer will be when communicating with web sites in that zone.

For example, you can always view pages on any site, regardless of security settings. (To completely block access to particular sites, use Internet Explorer's Content Advisor, as described in Hour 21) But within a zone for which high security is in effect, if a server attempts to send a script or other program code that could give your computer a virus or other problem, Internet Explorer prevents the code from reaching your computer.

The security levels you can assign to zones are

☐ **High**—All potentially damaging content (such as scripts) are automatically refused.

☐ **Medium**—Internet Explorer prompts you before accepting any potentially damaging content, giving you the opportunity to accept or reject it.

☐ **Low**—Open the gates. Internet Explorer will accept anything.

7

By default, each of the four zones has a reasonable security setting: high for restricted sites, medium for the intranet and Internet zones, and low for trusted sites.

However, if you tire of being prompted every time an Internet page sends some Java to your computer, you might want to change the security level for the Internet zone to low. Conversely, if you've experienced lots of problems with downloaded scripts, you might want to apply high security to the whole Internet zone. If you trust your coworkers, you might want to change your intranet zone to low security.

To Do: Choose Security Settings for Zones

To change the security level for a zone, complete these steps:

1. Open the Security tab (choose View | Internet Options | Security).
2. In the Zone list, select the zone for which you want to change security.
3. Select the security level you want.
4. Click OK.

I Want a Cookie! I *Don't* Want a Cookie!

Besides scripts, servers can put something else on your computer you may not know about: *cookies*.

NEW TERM A *cookie* is a small amount of information a server stores on your computer for later reference. Typically, a server stores an identifying code of some sort on your computer so that it can automatically identify you any time you visit.

Cookies are usually harmless and often useful. For example, an online store from which you've purchased once may put on your computer a cookie that identifies you. Any time you return to that site to shop, the server automatically knows who you are, and you needn't bother filling in a form to identify yourself.

But your computer is your domain, and you get to decide what someone else can put there. You can customize either of the big two browsers to accept or reject cookies.

Note that cookies, when accepted at all times, can begin to eat up tons of disk space. Even if cookies don't concern you, it's best to reject cookies you don't think you'll need.

To Do: Control Cookies in Navigator

To control cookies in Navigator, complete these steps:

1. Open Navigator's Preferences dialog by choosing Edit | Preferences.
2. In the list along the left side of the dialog, click Advanced. The Advanced dialog opens.
3. In the bottom of the dialog, choose how you want cookies handled:

    Choose Accept All Cookies to automatically accept any cookie.

7

Choose Accept Only Cookies That Get Sent Back to the Originating Server to accept most cookies, but to reject any that might be readable by servers other than the one who sent you the cookies. This prevents cookies on your computer from being read by any server other than the cookie's creators.

Choose Disable Cookies to reject all cookies.

Check the check box next to Warn Me Before Accepting a Cookie if you want Navigator to display a dialog before accepting a cookie, and to offer you buttons for optionally accepting or rejecting the cookie.

To Do: Control Cookies in Internet Explorer

To control cookies in Internet Explorer, complete these steps:

1. Open the Internet Options dialog (choose View | Internet Options).

2. Click the Advanced tab. The Advanced tab presents a long list of items you can enable or disable with check boxes and radio buttons.

3. Scroll down to the Security section of the list and find the Cookies choices at the bottom of the Security section.

   Choose Always Accept Cookies to automatically accept any cookie.

   Choose Prompt Before Accepting Cookies to instruct Internet Explorer to display a dialog before accepting a cookie, and to offer you buttons for optionally accepting or rejecting the cookie.

   Choose Disable All Cookie Use to reject all cookies.

CAUTION

Internet Explorer's Advanced tab is a valuable but tricky place. After you gain experience, you can use it to customize the browser to a high degree. But before you have experience, making random changes in the tab is likely to change your online life in ways you won't enjoy.

If you inadvertently change something in the Advanced tab and don't know how to fix it, click the tab's Restore Defaults button, which returns everything in the tab to its original setting.

Summary

Leading browsers have become very secure. By understanding what a server might do to your computer, and by deploying your browser's security force field intelligently, you'll protect yourself pretty well.

However, no browser can protect you from saying too much about yourself. You are responsible for preserving your privacy. Be careful what you say in a form and to whom you send that form. Avoid saying anything at all in a form that will be sent to an unsecure site.

Workshop

Q&A

Q Is it really safe to give my email address to anyone?

A Well, it's safer than some other kinds of information you can send, such as your real name. There are many good reasons to reveal your email address, such as signing up for a mailing list.

Still, if your email address falls into the wrong hands, you can be flooded with annoying junk email (called *spam*), or you might get weird or annoying messages from some online stranger. So the same watchwords apply: Never tell more about yourself than you have to, and be sure who you're dealing with.

You'll learn more about email privacy in Part IV, "Communicating with Email and Newsgroups."

Quiz

Take the following quiz to see how much you've learned.

Questions

1. After you've filled in a form, the information it contains is transmitted to the server
    a. Automatically
    b. As soon as you complete the last entry
    c. Within 24 hours
    d. Only after you click the submit button

2. True or false: It's a good idea to change your security settings at random, just to see what happens.

3. A secure site protects you from
    a. Sending information to an unscrupulous site
    b. Sending information that can be harvested from the Internet by a third party
    c. Buying junk you don't really want
    d. All of the above

7

Answers

1. (d) The server sees nothing you type in a form until you click the submit button, which might be labeled Submit, Send, or some other name that implies submission.

2. False. Leave your security settings alone unless you have a good reason to change them.

3. (b) Secure sites are a hedge against harvesting. You have to be careful about (a) and (c) yourself.

Activity

Open and explore your browser's dialogs for security and other forms of customization. Don't change anything on these dialogs; just examine what's there. In most browsers, you can control many aspects of your online experience, such as whether or not images in web pages display. (Switching off the display of images speeds up browsing, when time matters more than pictures.)

As you browse, think about the ways that customizing your browser might enhance or detract from your Internet experience.

7

Hour 8

Plug-ins, Helpers, and Other Ways to Do More Online

So much depends upon your browser. Your browser must know how to access web servers and display the web pages it finds there (which all browsers can do). To take advantage of all the web has to offer, your browser must be able to handle a wide variety of multimedia file types and run Java programs (which *not* all browsers can do).

Plus, your browser must be *extensible*; that is, it must have the capability to be refitted somehow to deal with file types and programs it was never designed for, all because petulant teenage geniuses keep inventing new file types and putting them online. That's where plug-ins and helper programs come in.

At the end of the hour, you'll be able to answer the following questions:

☐ How do web servers teach my browser new tricks?

☐ What are plug-ins and scripts, and how do I use them?

☐ How can I give my browser the power to play or display a new file type simply by giving my computer that power?

Understanding Plug-ins, ActiveX, and JavaScript

As part of being extensible, Navigator and Internet Explorer can, in effect, be reprogrammed through the web to acquire new capabilities. This happens chiefly through three types of program files:

- ☐ **Plug-ins**—Invented by Netscape for Navigator (but also supported by Internet Explorer), a plug-in is a program that implants itself in the browser to add a new capability. After you install a plug-in, that new capability usually appears to be a native, built-in part of the browser, as if it had always been there.

- ☐ **Scripts (Java, JavaScript)**—Both browsers support programs, called *scripts,* written in the Java and JavaScript languages (and sometimes other languages, such as VBScript). These scripts are used increasingly to enable advanced multimedia, forms, and other cool stuff on leading-edge web pages.

- ☐ **ActiveX files**—An ActiveX-enabled file includes program code that teaches the browser how to display it. For example, Internet Explorer doesn't know how to display a Microsoft Word file all by itself. In recent versions of Word, however, Microsoft has designed the Word file format as an ActiveX-enabled file type. When you open a Word file in Internet Explorer (see Figure 8.1), the ActiveX code built into the file teaches Internet Explorer how to display the file.

JUST A MINUTE

Internet Explorer has support for ActiveX built in. Navigator requires an ActiveX plug-in to handle ActiveX files. You can get the ActiveX plug-in for Navigator 4 from a company called NCompass Labs at

www.ncompasslabs.com

In general, you don't have to do anything special to take advantage of scripts or ActiveX; they're delivered to the browser automatically by web sites. Although plug-ins are occasionally delivered automatically, many times you have to download and install a particular plug-in to enjoy whatever it does.

Finding Plug-ins

When you come across a web site or a file that requires a particular plug-in, it's usually accompanied by a link for downloading the plug-in. In fact, when first entering the site, a message may appear on your screen informing you that a particular plug-in is required and giving you a link for downloading it.

Occasionally, the site doesn't help you get the right plug-in, and you have to go plug-in hunting.

8

Figure 8.1.

Because it's ActiveX-enabled, a Word file can be displayed in Internet Explorer.

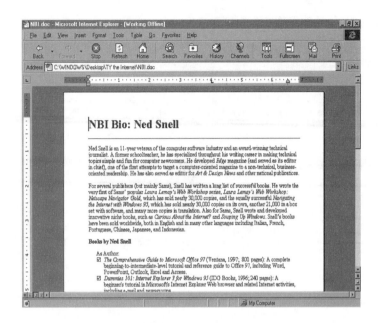

Several excellent indexes are devoted to plug-ins. The logical first stop is Netscape, where a full directory of plug-ins is maintained, along with links to the latest, coolest ones to come out (see Figure 8.2). You can reach Netscape's Plug-ins index at

```
http://home.netscape.com/comprod/products/navigator/version_2.0/plugins/
```

Figure 8.2.

Netscape offers a terrific directory of plug-ins.

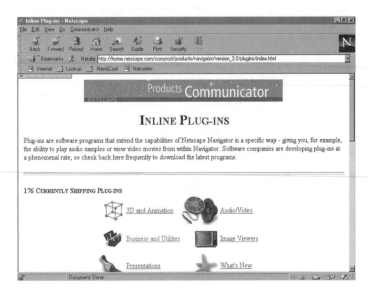

Another good source is the Plug-In Plaza (see Figure 8.3) at `http://browserwatch.internet.com/plug-in.html`. This page has an extensive list of all available plug-ins, as well as the companies creating the plug-ins.

From the site's top page, you can view the plug-ins by type (multimedia, graphics, sounds, and so on) or by platform (Windows, Macintosh, UNIX, and OS/2). Just select the listing type you want and scroll through the list and see what's available. You can download the plug-in directly from this page or visit the developer and read the latest news about the plug-in.

Figure 8.3.

The Plug-In Plaza offers lists of plug-ins of a particular type or for a particular platform.

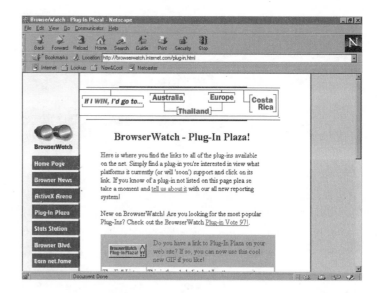

A third plug-in resource is the Plug-in Gallery & Demo Links page at `http://www2.gol.com/users/oyamada/`. Here, you can view the list of plug-ins for certain types of applications, such as video players and image viewers. If you're looking for a particular plug-in, just click on the list for that type, and select the name of the plug-in you're looking for (see Figure 8.4).

The list of plug-ins available from the Plug-in Gallery isn't nearly as complete as that in the Plug-In Plaza. You'll find the Plug-in Gallery useful, however, because it has tons of links to demo pages that rely on one or more particular plug-ins. Sometimes it's difficult to know whether you've successfully installed the plug-in; having a link to a site where you can test the plug-in is a great convenience.

8

Figure 8.4.

*The Plug-in Gallery &
Demo Links page offers
easy-to-manage lists of
plug-ins for specific types
of data.*

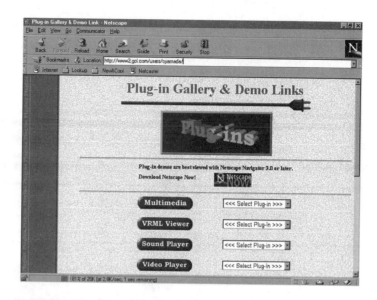

Installing and Using Plug-ins

Because plug-ins can come from any software publisher, no single method exists for installing them. Typically, you have to run some sort of installation program, and then specify the directory in which your web browser is installed. Some sophisticated plug-ins can even be installed into multiple web browsers, so you have access to the tool no matter which browser you use.

When you come across a link to a plug-in, carefully read any instructions you see, click the link, and follow any prompts that appear. You'll do fine.

Although there's no standard method of installing plug-ins, using them is pretty much the same across the board. Because they work with the browser, you never really see the plug-in. Sometimes, a plug-in adds a few new menu items or toolbar buttons to your browser that are useful when dealing with the type of file the plug-in handles.

Important Plug-ins to Have

In general, you should begin exploring with your browser just as it comes and install plug-ins only as they become necessary. You should consider getting two plug-ins right away, however, because they're so broadly exploited on the web.

The first is the RealAudio player, which you'll find at http://www.realaudio.com/ (see Figure 8.5), among other places. The RealAudio player enables your browser to play streaming audio feeds, from radio broadcasts to news updates to live music. The RealAudio home page also provides links to fun places where you can try out RealAudio.

Streaming audio and video are audio and video that begin to play on your computer before they have been completely downloaded. The main use of streaming audio and video is to present live web broadcasts of audio or video content, or to reduce your wait when playing a large audio or video file.

Figure 8.5.

Download RealAudio to play streaming audio through your browser.

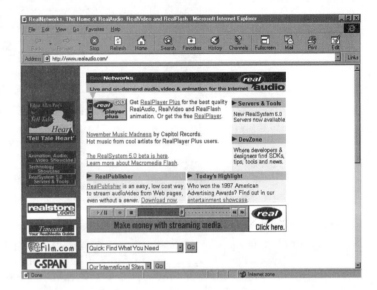

The other enhancement you'll soon need is Shockwave from Macromedia, at http://www.macromedia.com (see Figure 8.6). Shockwave is a set of plug-ins that install and work together, enabling your browser to play *shocked sites*, pages featuring highly interactive multimedia. The Macromedia site also features fun links to cool shocked sites.

TIME SAVER

The QuickTime player plug-in equips Navigator or Internet Explorer to play video clips stored in .MOV format, of which there are many online.

This free player is not quite as critical as the two I just mentioned because the Mac includes native support for QuickTime files, and most Windows systems already have a QuickTime player (it's installed automatically by many multimedia CD-ROM programs). If you have a Mac, or if your PC already has a player, Internet Explorer and Navigator will probably use the existing player as a helper application (see the next section, "Calling on Helper Programs") to play the file.

If you have trouble playing .MOV video files, however, get the plug-in at quicktime.apple.com.

8

Figure 8.6.

Download Shockwave to enjoy shocked web sites.

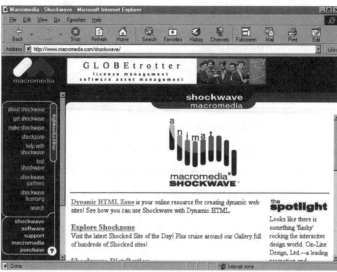

Calling on Helper Programs

Unlike plug-ins, helper programs do not work inside your browser. A helper program is simply any program on your computer that has been configured to handle a particular type of file or program that your browser can't handle itself. When the browser comes across such a file, it opens the helper program to get the job done.

For example, if you accessed a text file (.txt) on the web and your Windows browser could not display text files on its own, your browser might open the Windows Notepad program in a separate window to show you the file.

TIME SAVER

Need a helper program? In Hour 11, "Finding Programs and Files," you'll learn all about finding and downloading programs and other kinds of files from the web.

Adding Helpers to Older Browsers

Browsers other than the Big Two—and old versions of the Big Two, too—rely heavily on helpers because the browsers usually support few file types natively and almost never can be enhanced by plug-ins. In these browsers, you typically find a dialog box that lists the helper program assigned to each file type. You can add new helper programs by installing them on your computer and then adding them to the list in your browser's dialog box.

Adding Helpers to Internet Explorer and Navigator

The latest versions of the Big Two rarely rely on helpers because they feature native support for so many file types and can use plug-ins for so many more. When necessary, however, both have the capability to call on helpers.

When they do need a helper, Navigator and Internet Explorer don't need to be configured to use helper programs; they simply make use of the Windows or Mac file types registry. If Windows or the Mac system already has a program registered to automatically handle a given file type, that's the program the browser opens when you access that type of file. In particular, the file types registry keeps a tally of the program to use for each MIME file type. *MIME* (Multipurpose Internet Mail Extensions) is a standard that determines the file types for various objects that travel through the Internet, particularly such things as file attachments on email messages. Because the file types registry has entries in it for each common MIME file type, Internet Explorer and Navigator always knows what to do with any file you receive that falls under the MIME specification.

To install a new helper for Navigator or Internet Explorer, you usually just have to install the program on your computer. The installation routines for most programs automatically update the file types registry to make the program the default for the file type it handles.

If you install a helper program and still have trouble opening the file type it handles in your browser, you may have to open and edit your file types registry manually.

To Do: Examine Your Windows 95 File Types Registry

If you use Windows, you can open your file types registry to learn which programs are registered to handle which types of files. These are the programs Internet Explorer or Navigator will call upon to display files for which they have no native support or plug-in. To do so, follow these steps:

1. Open any folder and choose View | Options | File Types to view the File Types tab of the Folder Options dialog box (see Figure 8.7).
2. Scroll through the list to see which programs have been configured.
3. To see which extensions are associated with a particular program, click the program's name in the list.

To Do: Examine Navigator's Helper Applications Dialog Box

Navigator 4 features an easy-to-find dialog box for viewing and editing the file registry. Although the dialog box creates the impression that you're configuring helpers for Navigator alone, the dialog box is simply a new view on the Windows or Mac file registry; any changes you make affect not just Navigator, but your whole computer:

1. In Navigator, choose Edit | Preferences.
2. In the Preferences dialog box that appears, locate the word Navigator in the Category list.

8

Figure 8.7.

From any folder, choose View | Options | File Types to configure which helper applications work on which files.

3. Click the + sign next to Navigator to display the choices below it.
4. Click Applications. The file registry opens (see Figure 8.8).
5. To see which extensions are associated with a particular program, click the program's name in the list.

Figure 8.8.

In its Preferences, Navigator provides a dialog box for configuring helpers.

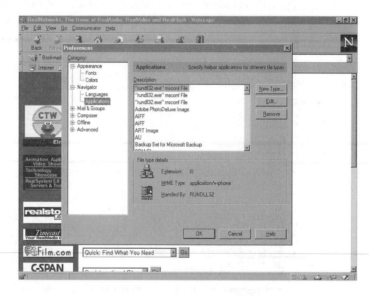

Summary

If you have the latest version of Navigator or Internet Explorer, your browser comes equipped to do so much that you'll rarely come across a situation in which it needs enhancement. Still, no matter how quickly developers enhance their browsers, the new file types and programs stay one step ahead. Knowing how to deal with scripts, plug-ins, and helper programs ensures that you won't get left behind when something new and wonderful hits the web.

Workshop

Q&A

Q You said earlier that I can prevent script code from reaching my computer if I think the code will hurt anything. How could code hurt anything?

A Realistically speaking, nothing terrible is likely to happen to your computer or browser if it picks up some script code that's badly written. The worst thing that's likely to happen is that the code fails to do whatever it was supposed to do, while you just browse ahead and forget about it.

Q Should I go out and get as many plug-ins as I can find, so I'm ready for anything?

A No. For the most part, plug-ins are rarely necessary. Smart web developers want to reach as many people as possible, and they know that forcing people to get a plug-in may scare some folks off (and eliminate those with browsers that don't support plug-ins). Also, plug-ins are known to slow your browser's performance; there's no sense bogging down your browser with plug-ins you may not use.

When you come across something you really want to see or do and it requires a plug-in, make your move. Otherwise, don't worry about it.

Quiz

Take the following quiz to see how much you've learned.

Questions

1. Which of the following is a type of program code that a web site might send to your computer?

    a. computer*jr* BASIC

    b. JavaScript

    c. DOS

    d. All of the above

2. The Windows or Mac file types registry

    a. Lists the file types your computer wants for its wedding

    b. Lists all the files installed on your computer

    c. Assigns a program to automatically handle each of many different file types

    d. Assigns your browser to handle all files

8

8

3. True or false: Plug-ins are installed automatically, whenever necessary.

4. To see the multimedia enhancements in a "shocked" web page, you need

    a. Nerves of steel

    b. Buns of steel

    c. The RealAudio plug-in

    d. The Shockwave plug-ins

Answers

1. (b) Of the choices, only JavaScript is a likely contender. Of course, anything's possible.

2. (c) The file types registry tells your computer (and maybe your browser) which program to open to handle each type of file.

3. False. Often, you must deliberately install a plug-in. Scripts, however, do their thing automatically.

4. (d) Only (d) gets the job done.

Activity

Are you using the very latest version of your browser? If you keep up with new releases, you'll always have the greatest range of native file support and access to the latest plug-ins.

PART

III

Finding What You're Looking For

Hour

Hour **9**

Getting Started with Searching

There's just too much on the web. It's like having a TV set with a billion channels; you could click the remote until your thumb fell off and still never find the *Law & Order* reruns.

Fortunately, a number of search tools on the web help you find exactly what you're looking for, anywhere on the web, and even *beyond* the web in other Internet arenas. In this hour, you'll discover what searching the web is all about and discover a simple but effective searching method: cruising categories. In the remaining three hours of Part III, "Finding What You're Looking For," you'll discover even more powerful targeted search methods.

At the end of this hour, you'll be able to answer the following questions:

- ☐ What are search tools, and where can I find them?
- ☐ How do I use features in my browser that can make searching more convenient?
- ☐ How can I conduct a simple search by clicking through a series of links?

What's a Search Tool?

Put simply, a *search tool* is a web page where you can conduct a search of the web. Such pages have been set up by a variety of companies, who offer you free web searching and support the service, at least in part, through the advertising you'll see prominently displayed on most search tool pages. Figure 9.1 shows a popular search tool, Excite.

JUST A MINUTE

> The term *search engine* is sometimes used to describe a search tool. This term, however, more accurately describes the program a search tool uses, behind the scenes, to perform searches. When you hear someone refer casually to a search engine, just remember that they probably mean a search tool.

Figure 9.1.

Excite, a popular search tool.

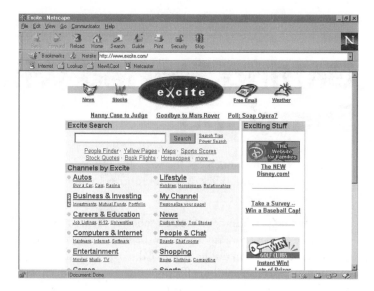

Although the various search tools are similar, each has its own unique search methods. But more importantly, each has its own unique set of files, called a *database*, upon which all searches are based.

You see, no search tool actually goes out and searches the entire web when you ask it to. A search tool searches its own database of information about the web. The more complete and accurate that database is, the more successful your searches are likely to be.

9

The database for a search tool is created in either (or both) of two ways:

☐ **Manually**—Folks who've created web pages, or who've discovered pages they want the world to know about, fill in a form on the search tool's web site to add new pages (and their descriptions) to the database.

☐ **Through a *crawler* (or spider, or worm)**—All of these creepy-crawly names describe programs that systematically contact web servers (at regular intervals), scan the contents of the server, and add information about the contents of the server to the database. (They crawl around the web like spiders—get it?) It takes the crawler a few weeks to complete each of its information-gathering tours of the web.

Where a search tool's database has been created by a crawler, the tool tends to deliver results that are more complete and up-to-date, whereas manually built databases tend to contain more meaningful categorization and more useful descriptive information. Also, most search tools with crawler-built databases do not offer you a way to search by browsing through categories—a valuable technique you'll pick up later in this hour. All search tools, however, support the main search method: entering a search term.

A *search term* is a word or phrase you type in a text box on a search tool's web page, to tell the search tool the type of information you're looking for. You learn all about search terms in Hour 10, "Searching for Information."

JUST A MINUTE

Because search tools search a database and not the actual web, they will sometimes deliver results that are outdated. You may click a link a search tool delivered to you, and find that the page to which it points no longer exists. That happens when a page has been removed since the last time the search tool's database was updated.

Despite differences in strengths and weaknesses among the available tools, the bottom line is this: Any of the major search tools may or may not locate a page or pages that meet your needs. If you can't find what you want through one tool, try another. Because each tool has its own database and each tool applies a different technical method for searching its database, no two search tools turn up exactly the same results for any given topic.

Where Are the Major Search Tools?

There are approximately a dozen general purpose search tools out there and many more specialized search tools (more about those in upcoming hours). Table 9.1 lists the major players. You can visit any search tool by entering its URL.

Table 9.1. The top search tools.

Tool	URL
Yahoo!	www.yahoo.com
Excite	www.excite.com
AltaVista	altavista.digital.com
Lycos	www.lycos.com
InfoSeek	www.infoseek.com
Magellan	www.mckinley.com
Open Text	www.opentext.com
HotBot	www.hotbot.com
WebCrawler	www.webcrawler.com

JUST A MINUTE

There's a confusion about search tools, created by some ISPs and browser sellers. In part to simplify their sales pitch for novices, these folks sometimes tout their products as "featuring all the best search tools," or words to that effect. That implies that a search tool is a feature in a browser, or a service provided by an ISP.

That claim is, oh, what's the word...hooey. A search tool is a web page, and anyone with a browser can use it. Browsers sometimes include features that can make accessing search tools easier, but no browser has a real built-in search engine, and no ISP can claim ownership of any of the important search tools.

To Do: Check Out the Search Engines

To Do

Before beginning to use search tools, take a peek at a few. While visiting these pages, watch for helpful links that point to

☐ Instructions for using the search tool

☐ A text box near the top of the page, which is where you would type a search term

☐ Links to categories you can browse

☐ Reviews and ratings of recommended pages

☐ "Cool Sites"—a regularly updated, random list of links to especially fun or useful pages you may want to visit just for kicks

▼   ☐ Other search engines

9

Let's take a tour; follow these steps:

1. Go to Yahoo! at www.yahoo.com. Observe that Yahoo! features a text box at the top for a search term (see Figure 9.2) and a table of categories below, for searching by category. Note also the graphical buttons at the top of the page, for displaying Cool Sites and such.

2. Jump to Magellan at www.mckinley.com. Observe that Magellan also features a search term box and category headings for a directory of sites for which Magellan has *reviews*, opinions about the sites' value.

3. Jump to AltaVista at altavista.digital.com. What familiar search tool features do you see?

Figure 9.2.
All search tools show a search term box, and a few (such as Yahoo!) also show categories you can explore.

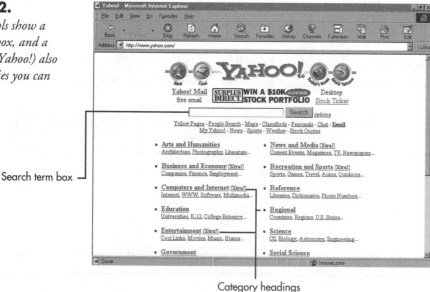

Search term box

Category headings

Using Your Browser's Search Button

Most major browsers have a search button on their toolbars or a search item somewhere within their menus. To use your browser's search features productively, you need to understand what they do.

In general, a Search button (or menu item) is preconfigured to take you to a particular search tool. The button doesn't really help you search; it just makes opening a search tool convenient.

> If your browser has a search button, that doesn't mean you're required to use it. You can enter a URL to go straight to any search tool, no matter which browser you use.

Some browser makers configure the Search buttons in their products to go to an "all-in-one" search page on the browser maker's web site (see Figure 9.3). An all-in-one search page lets you use several different search tools from the same page. The page is not really a search tool unto itself; rather, it accepts your searching instructions, passes them on to a search tool, retrieves the results from the tool, and displays them.

Besides the browser makers, some large ISPs also have set up all-in-one searches. If you got your browser from your ISP, it may be specially configured to go to an all-in-one search at the ISP's web site when you click Search.

Figure 9.3.

Clicking the Search button in Navigator opens this all-in-one search page.

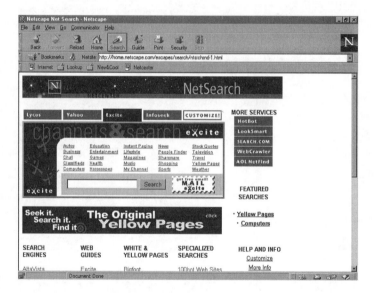

> The Search buttons in Internet Explorer 4 and Netscape Navigator 4 are configured to open all-in-one search pages, as described next, and cannot be reconfigured to go to a different search page.
>
> However, if you have an earlier version of these browsers, or any of a few other options, you can customize your search button so that it opens your favorite search tool. The dialog used for entering the URL of the page to which the Search button points is generally the same one you use for changing your home page (see Hour 6, "Revisiting Places You Like").

9

Using Navigator's Search Button

In Navigator 4, clicking the Search button opens Netscape's all-in-one NetSearch page (refer to Figure 9.3).

Atop the box labeled Channels & Search, notice the row of buttons, each naming a search tool (Lycos, Yahoo!, Excite, Infoseek). To use one of those tools, you click the button, which opens that tool's search term box and other tools in the box below the buttons.

Using Internet Explorer 4's Search Button and Explorer Bar

Clicking the Search button on Internet Explorer 4's toolbar opens the Explorer bar, a pane in the left side of the browser window (see Figure 9.4). The Explorer bar is also used in Internet Explorer for displaying your Favorites and History list (see Hour 6, "Revisiting Places You Like") and Channels (see Hour 20, "Making the Web Deliver Pages to You: Channels and NetCasting").

In the Explorer bar, the Provider-of-the-day (one of the major search tools picked daily at random) appears automatically. You can use that tool or drop down the list at the top of the Explorer bar to choose from among a few other tools, such as Excite or Yahoo!.

Figure 9.4.

Internet Explorer 4's Search button opens search tools in the Explorer bar.

Explorer bar

Whichever tool you choose, anything you do with that tool—whether you are clicking through categories or using a search term—happens in the Explorer bar. When you finally open a page from your search, that page appears in the main window, to the right of the Explorer bar. You can continue searching in the Explorer bar, or click the × button in the Explorer bar's upper-right corner to close it.

The Explorer bar can be a handy feature, but it also can be a pretty cramped place to work with a search tool. Always remember that you're not required to use the Search button; you can always enter a search tool's URL in Internet Explorer to work in that tool, full-screen.

Simple Searching by Clicking Categories

These days, all the major search tools accept search terms. A few, however, also supply a directory of categories (an index of sorts) that you can browse to locate links to pages related to a particular topic. Tools that feature such directories include Yahoo!, Excite, and Infoseek (refer to Table 9.1 for the URLs of these tools).

TIME SAVER

> Directory browsing is something of a sideline for other search tools, but it's the bread and butter of Yahoo!. When you want to search in this way, Yahoo! is almost always your best starting point.

Why Use Categories Instead of a Search Term?

When you're first becoming familiar with the web, foregoing the search engines and clicking through a directory's categories is not only an effective way to find stuff but also a great way to become more familiar with what's available on the web. As you browse through categories, you inevitably discover detours to interesting topics and pages that you didn't set out to find. Exploring directories is an important part of learning how the web works and what's on it.

Also, the more broad your topic of interest, the more useful categories are. When you use a search term to find information related to a broad topic (such as cars, dogs, music, plants), the search tool typically delivers a bewildering list containing hundreds or thousands of pages to you. Some of these pages will meet your needs, but many will be pages that merely mention the topic rather than being *about* the topic.

Some links a search term delivers will match the term, but not your intentions; a search on "plant" will likely turn up not only botany and houseplant pages, but others about power plants, folks named Plant, and maybe the Plantagenet family of European lore. Categories, on the other hand, help you limit the results of your search to the right ballpark.

Using a Directory

Everything in a directory is a link. To find something in a directory, you follow those links in an organized way.

You begin by clicking a broad category heading to display a list of related subcategories (see Figure 9.5). Click a subcategory heading, and you display its list of sub-subcategories.

9

You continue in this fashion, drilling down through the directory structure (usually through only two to five levels), until you eventually arrive at a targeted list of links to pages related to a particular topic. You may explore those page links one by one, and after finishing each, use your Back button to return to the search tool's list and try another link.

Figure 9.5.

A subcategory list in Yahoo!.

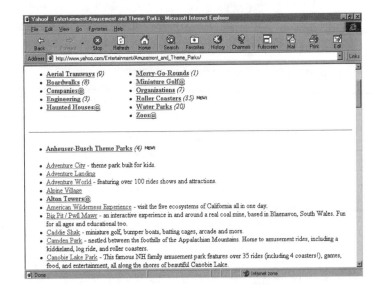

To Do: Explore Categories

Let's explore some categories. To do so, follow these steps:

1. Go to Yahoo! at www.yahoo.com.

2. In the list of categories on the top page, click Entertainment. A list of Entertainment subcategories appears.

3. Click Amusement and Theme Parks. A list of related subcategories appears.

4. Scroll down below the subcategories, and you'll find some links leading to pages about amusement parks. You can click one of the subcategories above to see more options or visit one of the pages below.

5. Click Back twice to return to the top Yahoo! page. Observe that you can try any path or page and then back out by as many levels as you want to so that you can try a different path.

6. Explore on your own, clicking down through the directory and then back up again with Back.

You'll learn tricks to finding what your looking for in the next hour.

Summary

A search tool is a web page. You can get to a search tool by entering its URL or by using your browser's Search button. Virtually all search tools support searching with search terms (see Hour 10), but some also enable you to find pages by browsing through a directory.

Workshop

Q&A

Q Why would I ever need more than one search tool? Can't I just pick my favorite and always use it?

A Every search tool has a different database and uses a different technical method for extracting results from that database. Although there will be overlap, you'll never see the same results from two different search tools.

Sure, if you have a search tool you're comfortable with, it makes sense to try it first. But to ensure the best hope of finding exactly what you're looking for, it's important that you know how to get to several different search tools, and how to operate each one.

Q I like exploring Yahoo!'s directory, but find it tiresome after exploring one branch to use Back to go back a few levels to try another route. Is there a shortcut?

A If you look carefully at any listing in Yahoo! (refer to Figure 9.5), you'll notice that a complete path appears in a large heading at the top, showing the full list, left to right, of the category and subcategories under which the list you're viewing appears. You can click on the name of any subcategory in that path to jump directly back to that subcategory's listing.

Quiz

Take the following quiz to see how much you've learned.

Questions

1. Which of the following is a way to get to a search tool?

   a. Enter the search tool's URL.

   b. Use a link to the tool, found on another tool's page.

   c. Click your browser's Search button.

   d. All of the above.

2. Which name describes a program through which a search tool builds its database automatically?

   a. Crawler

   b. Whiner

   c. Stinger

   d. Wiggler

3. Clicking through a directory's categories is an especially useful technique when you're

   a. Bored

   b. Looking for recipes

   c. Looking for pages related to pages related to pages related to themselves

   d. Looking for pages related to a broad, general topic

Answers

1. (d) Any of these will give you access to a search tool, either directly or through an all-in-one search.

2. (a) A search tool's database-builder is often called a crawler, spider, or worm.

3. (d) Directories are great for finding pages related to broad topics.

Activity

Explore Yahoo!'s or Excite's categories awhile, looking for topics that interest you. Try looking for something in Yahoo!, then looking for the same thing in Excite. How do the choices presented by each tool differ?

9

Hour 10

Searching for Information

Clicking categories, as you learned to do in Hour 9, "Getting Started with Searching," can be a productive way to search. But often, a more powerful method is called for, one that delivers to you a custom-made list of links related to any topic you can imagine.

That's what search terms do. In this hour, you'll learn how to use search terms and how to phrase them carefully to produce precisely the results you need.

At the end of the hour, you'll be able to answer the following questions:

- ☐ What's a search term?
- ☐ How do I use a simple search term to produce a list of *hits*, web pages related to the term?
- ☐ How do I phrase more complex search terms, for power-searching?
- ☐ How can I search for information just among the contents of a particular site?

Understanding Searches

Each of the search tools described in Hour 9, and just about any other you might encounter on the web, has a text box featured prominently near the top of its main page (see Figure 10.1). That text box is where you will type your search terms. Adjacent to the box, there's always a submit button, almost always labeled Search.

Typing a search term in a text box and then clicking the submit button to send the term to the search tool is known as *submitting a search term.* Such searches are sometimes described as *keyword* searches, because the search term serves as a key to finding matching pages.

Figure 10.1.

The text box you see near the top of any search tool page is where you may type a search term.

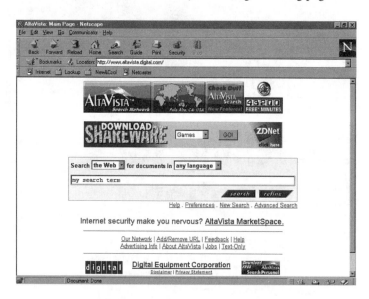

When you submit a search term, the search tool looks through its database of information about pages and locates any entries that contain the same combination of characters in your search term. Although the contents of the various search tool databases differ, the record for each page typically contains the page's URL, a title, a brief description, and a group of keywords intended to describe the page's contents. If your search term matches anything in that record, the search tool considers the page a match.

After searching the whole database (which takes only a moment or two), the search tool displays a list of links to all of the pages it determined were matches; this list is called a *hit list.*

NEW TERM   A *hit list* is a list of links, produced by a search engine in response to a search term you have entered. Each link is a *hit*, a page that contains a match for your search term.

10

Each hit in the list is a link (see Figure 10.2). You can scroll through the hit list, reading the page titles and descriptions, to determine which page might best serve your needs, then click the link to that page to go there. If the page turns out to be a near miss, you can use your Back button to return to the hit list and try a different page, or start over with a new search.

Some tools organize the hit list in smart ways, attempting to put the best matches at the top of the list so you see them first and weaker matches lower in the list.

Figure 10.2.

Excite organizes the hit list from best matches to worst and gives each a confidence rating.

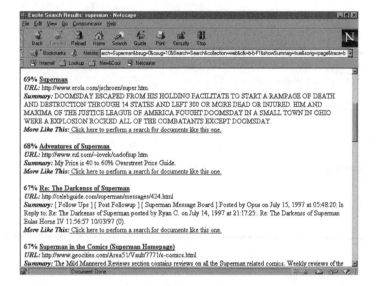

For example, suppose you use Godzilla as your search term. A particular search tool would tend to put at the top of the hit list all pages that use the word Godzilla in their titles or URLs, because those are the pages most likely to be all about Godzilla. Matches to keywords or the page's description come lower in the list, because these may be pages that simply mention Godzilla, but aren't really *about* Godzilla. Even lower in the list, a tool might show links to partial matches, pages to which only part of the search term, such as those containing the word God or the partial word zilla.

In addition to organizing the hit list this way, some search engines put a confidence rating of sorts next to each hit. The rating—usually expressed as a percentage (refer to Figure 10.2)—indicates how well the page matches your search term, with 100% being a perfect match.

TIME SAVER

In Internet Explorer 4, you can search straight from the address box.

Click in the address box, and instead of typing a URL there, type the word GO (or find, or ?), followed by a search term, and press Enter. The search term is automatically forwarded to a search tool (selected at random by Microsoft), and the hit list appears.

This isn't the greatest way to search: You don't pick the search tool, and you can't take advantage of directories or any special search options. But when you're in a *big* hurry...

Phrasing a Simple Search

You can get awfully artful and creative with search terms, but 9 times out of 10, you needn't get too fancy about searching. Go to the search tool, type a simple word or phrase in the text box, click the Submit button, and wait a few moments for the hit list to show up.

If the list shows links that look like they hold what you're after, try them. If not, try another search term.

TIME SAVER

You can use multiple words in a search term; an example of this might be someone's full name (such as Michael Moriarty) or another multiword term (such as two-term presidents). But when you use multiple words, some special considerations apply. See the "Phrasing a Serious Search" section later in this hour.

Here are a few basic tips for improving your search success:

☐ **Use the simplest form of a word**—The search term Terrier will match references to both Terrier and Terriers. However, the term Terriers may fail to match pages using only Terrier. Some search tools are smart enough to account for this, but some aren't. Try to use the simplest word form that's still specific to what you want.

☐ **Use common capitalization**—Some search tools don't care about capitalization, but some do. It's always a good habit to capitalize words as they would most often be printed, using initial capitals on names and other proper nouns, and all lower-case letters for other words. Be careful to observe goofy computer-era capitalizations, such as AppleTalk or FrontPage.

10

☐ **Be as specific as possible**—If it's the German Shepherd you want to know about, use that as your search term, not dog, which will produce too many hits, many unrelated to German Shepherds. If the most specific term doesn't get what you want, try less specific terms. For example, if German Shepherd fails, go ahead and try dog. You may find a generic page about dogs on which there's a link to information about German Shepherds.

☐ **Try partial words**—Always try full words first. But if they're not working out, you can use a partial word. If you want to match both puppies and puppy, you can try pup as a search term, which matches both.

To Do: Try a Simple Search

Let's try a simple search. Follow these steps:

1. Go to AltaVista at `altavista.digital.com`.

2. Locate the search term box in the middle of the page. (You can't miss it, but refer to Figure 10.1 if you need to.)

3. Click the search term box, and type `DaVinci` for a search term.

4. Locate the submit button, which is below the search term box and labeled Search. Click the button, and wait a few moments for the hit list to appear (see Figure 10.3).

10

Figure 10.3.

At the bottom of each page of a hit list, links or buttons appear for moving to other hit list pages.

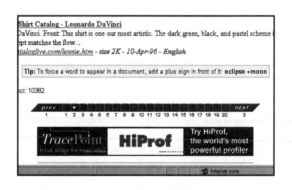

Shirt Catalog - Leonardo DaVinci
DaVinci. Front: This shirt is one our most artistic. The dark green, black, and pastel scheme
pt matches the flow...
taloglive.com/lennie.htm - size 2K - 10-Apr-96 - English

Tip: To force a word to appear in a document, add a plus sign in front of it: eclipse +moon

ci: 10382

prev   •   next
1   1 2 3 4 5 6 7 8 9 10 11 12 13 14 15 16 17 18 19 20   3

TracePoint   HiProf   Try HiProf, the world's most powerful profiler

Internet zone

TIME SAVER

A hit list may show no hits at all, or it may have hundreds. Zero hits is a problem, but hundreds really aren't. Remember, most search engines put the best hits at the top of the list, so even if your hit list has hundreds of links, the links you want may appear somewhere within the top 20 or so.

Regardless of the number of hits, if you don't see what you want somewhere in the first 30 to 50 links, you probably need to start over, with a new search term. If your first search turned up hundreds of hits, use a more specific term in your second try.

TIME SAVER

Observe that the search term box appears on every page of the hit list. You can start a new search at any time, from any page of the hit list, by entering a new search term.

Some search tools display the search term box only on the top page; to start a new search in those, just click Back until you return to the top.

5. Examine the hit list. What kinds of pages does a search on DaVinci turn up in AltaVista? Are they all about the artist/inventor, or are they about other stuff called DaVinci, as well?

6. Choose any hit in the list, and click it. The page to which it points appears.

7. Click your Back button to return to the hit list.

8. Scroll to the bottom of the page. Near the bottom, a row of buttons appears, with a button labeled Next at the right end. Click the Next button.

9. The next page of hits appears. Any time a search turns up more hits than can fit on one page, the hits are divided onto multiple pages.

   Each button in the row at the bottom of the page (refer to Figure 10.3) corresponds to a page in the list. You can click a button to go to a particular page in the list, or simply click the Next and Previous buttons at each end of the row to move among the hit list pages. All search tools use links or buttons similar to AltaVista's for moving among hit list pages.

10. Think of something you really want to know more about, and try a new search for what matters to *you*.

TIME SAVER

When you use a search term in Yahoo! (www.yahoo.com), the hit list typically shows not only pages, but Yahoo! categories related to the search term. You can try one of the pages, or start exploring related category headings from the head-start the search provides.

Phrasing a Serious Search

Sometimes, in order to phrase a specific search, you need multiple words. When you use multiple words, you may need to use *operators* to control the way a search tool works with those words.

10

In mathematics, an *operator* is a word or symbol used to specify the action in an equation, such as plus or minus. Operators are used in search terms to express a logical equation of sorts that tightly controls how a search engine handles the term.

Using Multiple Words in a Search Term

In a search term, you can use as many words as you need in order to make the term specific.

For example, suppose I want to learn about Boxer dogs. I could use the search term Boxer. While that term might turn up some hits about Boxer dogs, those hits may be buried among hundreds of other links about prizefighters, China's Boxer rebellion, Tony Danza (actor and ex-boxer), and people named Boxer. So to make my search more specific, I use two words: Boxer dog.

Now the search engine will look for pages that contain both Boxer and dog, which greatly increases the chances that hits will be about Boxer dogs, because most pages about all those other boxers I mentioned earlier will not also be about dogs. I still might see a link to a page about George Foreman's dog, if he has one, but the hit list will be a lot closer to what I want.

If my hit list is still cluttered with the wrong kind of pages, I might remember that a Boxer is a breed of dog, so a page about Boxer dogs probably also uses the term breed prominently. So I might try a third term to further narrow the hit list:

Boxer dog breed

Get the idea? Now, if you get *too* specific, you may accidentally omit a few pages you want; there may be Boxer dog pages that don't use breed anywhere that would show up in a search database. So it's best to start off with a happy medium (a term that's specific but not overly restrictive), see what you get, and then try subsequent searches using more or less specific terms, depending on what's in the hit list.

Time Saver

A few search engines support natural language queries. In a natural language query, you can phrase your search term as you might naturally phrase a question; for example, you might use the search phrase Who was the artist Leonardo DaVinci, and the search tool applies sophisticated technology to determine what you're asking.

Natural language queries are a good idea, and they're worth experimenting with. But in my experience, their results are usually not as good as you'd probably get with a really smartly phrased search term.

Using Operators to Control Searches

Whenever you use multiple words, you're using operators, even if you don't know it. Operators are words you use between the words in a multiword search term to further define exactly how the search tool will handle your term. Using operators in this way is sometimes described as *Boolean logic*.

There are three basic operators used in searching:

☐ **And**—When you use *and* between words in a search term, you tell the search engine to find only those pages that contain *both* of the words. Pages that contain only one or the other are not included in the hit list.

☐ **Or**—When you use *or* between words in a search term, you tell the search engine to find all pages that contain *either* of the words. Pages that contain either word alone, or both words, are included in the hit list.

☐ **Not**—When you use *not* between words in a search term, you tell the search engine to find all pages that contain the word before not, then to remove from the hit list any items that also contain the word following not.

Table 10.1 illustrates how *and*, *or*, and *not* affect a search tool's use of a term.

Table 10.1. How operators work in search terms.

Search Term	What a Search Tool Matches
Dodge and pickup	Only pages containing both Dodge and pickup
Dodge or pickup	All pages containing either Dodge or pickup, or both words
Dodge not pickup	All pages that contain Dodge but do not also contain pickup (gets all the Dodge pages, then eliminates any about pickups)
Dodge and pickup and models	Pages that contain all three words
Dodge or pickup or models	Pages that contain any of the three words
Dodge not Chrysler	Pages that contain Dodge but do not also contain Chrysler (gets all the Dodge pages, then eliminates any that also mention Chrysler)

Before using operators in search terms, check out the options or instructions area of the search tool you intend to use (see Figure 10.4). Most search tools support *and*, *or*, and *not*, but some have their own little quirks about how you must go about it. For example, Excite and AltaVista prefer that you insert a plus sign (+) at the beginning of a word rather than precede it with *and*.

10

TIME SAVER

Another powerful way to use multiple words is to do an *exact phrase match*, which most search tools support. In an exact phrase match, you surround the multiword term with quotes to instruct the search to match only pages that show the same words as the term, in the same order.

For example, suppose you want to know about the film *Roman Holiday*. A search on *Roman Holiday* will probably match any page that uses both of those words anywhere, in any order, together or separately. That'll still get you some good hits, but a lot of bad ones, too. A search on *"Roman Holiday"* (in quotes) matches only pages that use the exact phrase Roman Holiday, so the hit list will be much better targeted to what you want.

Figure 10.4.

Click the Options link near Yahoo!'s search term box to learn how Yahoo! supports operators and other advanced search techniques.

10

TIME SAVER

When you use multiple words and don't include operators, most search engines assume you mean to put an *and* between words. (See, you are using operators, even if you don't know it.)

For example, if you use the term *candy corn*, most search engines assume you mean candy and corn and match only pages that contain both words.

Some engines will apply *and* first, then use *or*. The *and* hits go at the top of the hit list, and the *or* hits go to the bottom, as low-confidence hits.

To Do: Try a Power Search

Try out multiword searches using the operators *and* and *or*:

1. Go to the search tool of your choice.
2. Enter the search term *star or trek,* and click the search button.
3. Examine the results. You should see many pages about *Star Trek*, but also others about other kinds of *stars* and other topics that include the word *trek.*
4. Return to the search term box. (If it does not appear on the hit list, press Back to redisplay the search tool's top page.)
5. Submit the search term *star and trek.*
6. Examine the results. Just about every hit should be about *Star Trek.*
7. Finally, try the exact phrase *"Star Trek"* (including the quotes). Does the hit list look different from the one you got in step 6?

TIME SAVER

In high school, they warned you that you'd need Algebra one day. If you ignored that warning (like I did), you've probably forgotten all of that stuff about grouping parts of equations in parentheses.

If you remember Algebra, note that you can apply those techniques for super searches. For example, suppose you wanted to find pages about pro boxers (the kind that hit each other). You'd need a hit list that matched all pages with *boxer* or *prizefighter*, but eliminated any that matched *dog* (to weed out the Boxer dog pages). You could do that with either of the following algebraic terms:

> *(boxer or prizefighter) not dog*
>
> *(boxer not dog) or prizefighter*

If you can apply these techniques, drop your old math teacher a note of thanks for a job well done.

About Site Searches

The major search tools mentioned in this hour and Hour 9 are for finding information that may reside anywhere on the web. Because they have that enormous job to do, they can't always find everything that's on a particular server.

However, large web sites often provide their own search engines, just for finding stuff on that site alone. For example, Microsoft's web site is huge, encompassing thousands of pages. So Microsoft supplies a search tool (you can open it from a Search link atop most pages) just for finding stuff at Microsoft. Even fairly small sites may have their own search tools; Figure 10.5 shows one for the Discovery Channel's web site.

10

You use a site's search tool just as you would any other, by entering a search term. Many such search tools even support multiword searches and operators. Always check the instructions accompanying the search tool to find out whether it supports fancy searches.

Figure 10.5.

The Discovery Channel supplies its own search tool just for finding stuff on its Discovery Online site
(www.discovery.com).

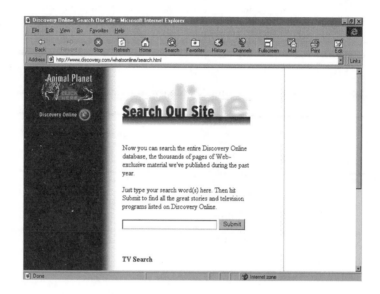

Summary

Most of the time, a search is a snap. Just type a likely sounding word in any search tool's text box, click the submit button, and wait for your hits. The more you know about narrowing your searches by choosing just the right word and using multiple words and operators, the better your odds of always finding exactly what you're looking for.

Workshop

Q&A

Q When searching for a name, such as Bill Clinton, should I use that old last-name-first gag and use *Clinton, Bill* as my search term?

A It doesn't matter. Search tools pretty much ignore commas, so whichever way you do it, the tool sees *Bill and Clinton* and comes up with the same hits. By the way, if you're searching for who I think you're searching for, note that he's not the only Bill Clinton in the world, and he sometimes goes by William, not Bill. The term *President Clinton* is a better choice.

Q **In some search tools, like AltaVista, I see options for searching Usenet. What's that all about?**

A Some search engines can search not only the web, but also the contents of newsgroups, which are sometimes collectively called Usenet. You'll learn about newsgroups, including searching them, in Hour 15, "Reading and Posting to Newsgroups."

Quiz

Take the following quiz to see how much you've learned.

Questions

1. You're searching for information about rabbits. Which is the best search term?

     a. Rabbits

     b. Rabbit

     c. Rabbit or bunny or hare

     d. Rabbit and bunny and hare

2. In the hit list, the search tool puts the hits it considers best

     a. In a special "premier" hit list

     b. At the top of the hit list

     c. At every fourth position in the hit list

     d. At the bottom of the hit list

3. Looking for information about the Puerto Rican city of Ponce, you used the search term *Ponce* and came up empty. Which is a good second try?

     a. Ponce, Puerto Rico

     b. ponce

     c. Ponce or Rico

     d. Puerto Rico and (city or cities)

Answers

1. (c) Only (c) gets you all pages that use any of the three terms for rabbit.

2. (b) The best hits go first.

3. (d) If *Ponce* turned up no good hits by itself, adding to that term (or using incorrect capitalization) won't help. You need to broaden your search, hoping to find a page about cities in Puerto Rico, one of which may include information about sunny Ponce.

10

Activity

While searching for information about your favorite subjects, you may produce a hit list that contains so many great hits you haven't time to visit them all right away (but you wish you could). While viewing the hit list, make it a Favorite (or a Bookmark), so you can reopen it anytime.

In most search engines, when you visit your new favorite hit list, the search will actually be repeated, so the list always shows the latest information, any time you display it.

10

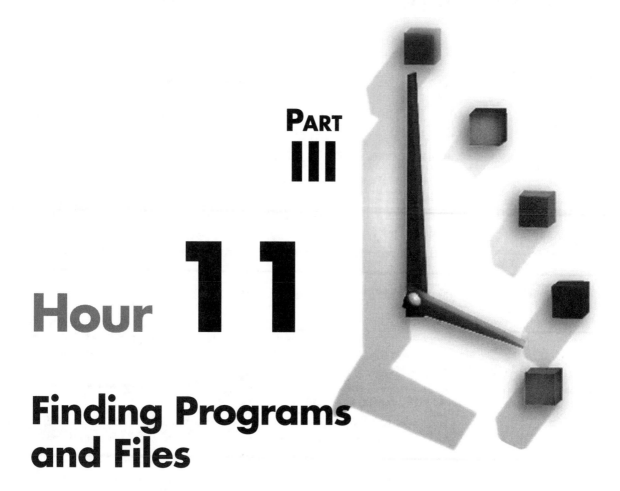

PART III

Hour 11

Finding Programs and Files

The huge, diverse group of people that use the Internet have only one thing in common: They all use a computer. So it's no surprise that computer programs and files are the most common "things" you can acquire through the Internet. You can find online all kinds of Internet software, other kinds of programs (such as games or word processors), documents (such as books or articles), and other useful files (such as utilities and plug-ins).

To find a particular file or program you want, you can apply the search techniques you've already picked up in Hour 9, "Getting Started with Searching," and Hour 10, "Searching for Information." In this hour, you'll learn how to use search techniques that are better focused and faster so you can find exactly the files you want. You'll also learn all about *downloading* the files you'll find, and about preparing those files for use on your computer.

At the end of the hour, you'll be able to answer the following questions:

- ☐ What is downloading?
- ☐ What kinds of files can I download and use on my computer?
- ☐ Where are the sites that can help me find and download files, and how do I use them?
- ☐ What's a compressed archive—or *ZIP* file—and what must I do with it before it will work on my computer?
- ☐ What's a computer virus, and how can I avoid catching one?

What Is Downloading?

Downloading is the act of copying a computer file from a server, through the net, to your computer so you can use it there, just as if you had installed it from a disk or CD-ROM. (Incidentally, you can also *upload*—send a file *to* a server—but you'll learn about that in Hour 23, "Creating Web Pages and Multimedia Messages.")

Click a Link, Get a File

Whether you've thought about it or not, when you're on the web, you're really downloading all the time. For example, every time you open a web page, the files that make up that page are temporarily copied from the server to your computer.

But here we're talking more deliberate downloading: You locate a link in a web page that points to a file or program you want (see Figure 11.1). To download that file, you click the link, then follow any prompts that appear. It's really that simple.

Figure 11.1.

You download files from the web simply by clicking links that lead to files, such as those shown here.

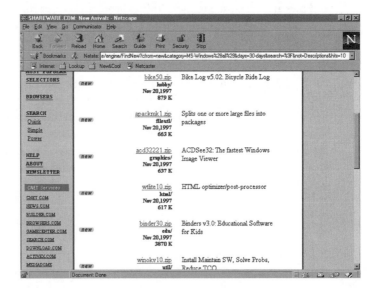

11

JUST A MINUTE

Observe that most of the file links in Figure 11.1 have the filename extension .zip. That extension indicates that these files are compressed archive files, also known as *ZIP* files. You'll learn more about ZIP files later in this hour.

JUST A MINUTE

The easiest and usually best way to find and download files from the Internet is by using a web link, as described in this hour. Another important way to download files is called *FTP* (File Transfer Protocol). FTP may be useful to you when the file you want is not available through a link in a regular web page.

You'll learn about FTP in Hour 19, "Using Old-Fashioned Hacker's Tools: FTP, Gopher, and Telnet."

How Long Does Downloading Take?

The larger the file, the longer it will take to download. That's why the size of the file is usually shown somewhere in or near the link for downloading it (refer to Figure 11.1). The size is expressed in kilobytes (K or KB) for smaller files or in megabytes (M or MB) for larger files. 1MB equals 1,024KB.

How long does it take to download a file of a given size? That depends on many factors, including the speed of your Internet connection and how busy the server is. But over a connection of 28.8Kbps or faster, a 1MB file typically downloads in around 10 minutes.

You'll find many items to download that are less than 1MB in size. However, many programs or multimedia files can be much, much larger. A download of the entire Internet Explorer 4 program from Microsoft's web site takes several hours, even through a fast 56K connection.

With experience, you'll develop a sense of how long downloading a file of a given size takes on your system. Always carefully consider the size of the file, and whether you want to wait that long for it, before starting the download.

To Do: Download a File

Just for practice, and to help you understand what to do after you locate a file you want, download the Adobe Acrobat reader—a program that enables you to display documents in the Adobe Acrobat (.pdf) file format, which are common online. If you already have an Adobe Acrobat reader, or just don't want one, you can cancel the download before it finishes.

1. Go to the page on Adobe's web site where you can download the reader: www.adobe.com/prodindex/acrobat/readstep.html.

2. From the list of systems, choose yours (see Figure 11.2).

Figure 11.2.

On many sites that offer file downloads, you first make some form choices or navigate through some links to select the product and system type.

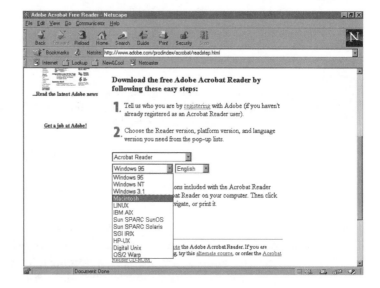

3. Near the bottom of the page, click the button labeled Download to submit the form. A page of instructions and links appears, containing information specific to the Adobe Acrobat Reader version for your system.

4. Scroll down to the list of Download Links (see Figure 11.3). Next to each link is a description of where the server to which the link points is located, geographically. You can use any link listed, but for best performance, choose the one that's closest to you.

Figure 11.3.

When you have multiple links for the same file, choose the one closest to you.

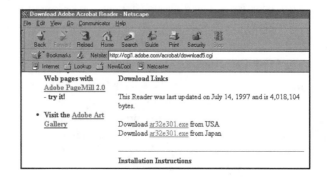

11

Popular files are usually available from multiple servers, spread across the continent or globe. Often, a downloading page will refer to the servers as *mirror sites*, because they all offer an identical copy of the file, a "mirror image."

5. After you click the link, one or more dialog boxes will appear, prompting you to make a few easy choices regarding the file you're downloading.

   The exact dialog boxes you'll see differ by browser and computer type, but typically, a dialog box opens to ask whether you want to just save the file to disk after downloading, or immediately open or run the file automatically.

When the link leads to a media file, such as a sound or video clip, your browser may open the file automatically after downloading to play it.

Another dialog box you may see prompts you to select the location (folder or desktop) and filename for the downloaded file (see Figure 11.4). You should choose a location so you can easily locate and use the file after downloading. Don't mess with the filename, because if you don't supply a new filename, the file will be stored on your computer under its original name, which is usually best.

Figure 11.4.

Most browsers let you choose the folder in which a file will be stored after downloading.

6. After you deal with any dialog boxes that appear, the download begins. A status message appears in a dialog box (see Figure 11.5) or in the status bar at the bottom of the browser window, informing you of the download's progress. The status message usually features a Cancel button, so you can quit the download before it finishes, if you want to.

   When the download is complete, the status message disappears. You may continue browsing, or use the file you just downloaded, which you can find in the folder you selected in the dialog box described in step 5.

Figure 11.5.

Throughout a download, a status message appears to track its progress.

TIME SAVER

In the download status message, some browsers also display an estimate of how much longer the download will take to finish. Although that estimate can be handy, it's just a guess, and should not be taken as an exact prediction of how long the download will take.

Choosing Files You Can Use

You can download any type of computer file; however, not every file or program you find online works on every type of computer.

You'd be surprised how often people forget this. Web browsing enables different kinds of computers to all look at the same online content, so after awhile people tend to forget that off the web, PCs, Macs, and other types of computers each use different kinds of files and programs.

When you search for files and programs, you must make sure that the ones you choose are compatible with your computer type, and often also with your operating system (Windows 3.1, Windows 95, DOS, Mac OS 7 or OS 8, UNIX flavor, and so on).

The Two File Types: Program and Data

Although dozens of different types of files exist, they all generally fall into one of these two groups:

☐ **Program files**—A program file contains a program such as a game, word processor, plug-in, utility, and so on. Program files are almost always designed to run on only one type of computer and operating system. For example, a program file designed for a Mac typically will not run in Windows. Many programs are available, however, in similar but separate versions, one for each system type.

☐ **Data files**—A data file contains information that can be displayed, or used in some other way by a program. For example, a word processing document is a data file, to be displayed by a word processing program. Like program files, some data files can be used only by a particular program running on a particular computer type. Most data file types can be used on a variety of systems.

11

Common Data File Types on the Net

When you encounter a link to a file, you'll usually have no trouble telling what system the file is made for.

Often, before arriving at the link, you will have navigated through a series of links or form selections in which you specified your system type, so when you finally see links to files, they all point to files that can run on your system. In other cases, the link itself—or text near the link—will tell you the system requirements for the file.

 System requirements are the computer type, operating system, and (for a data file) program required to use a particular file. Some files you'll encounter have special hardware requirements, as well, such as a particular amount of memory.

Even when the link doesn't fill you in, you can often tell a file's system requirements by its filename extension, the final part of the filename that follows the period. (For example, in the filename Monty.doc, the extension is doc.) Table 11.1 shows many of the most common file types found online.

Time Saver

> Data files can often be converted and used by programs other than those in which they were created. For example, nearly all full-featured word processing programs can convert Microsoft Word (.doc) files so you can read or edit them. Most spreadsheet programs can handle an Excel file.
>
> If you lack the required program for using a particular kind of data file, check out any similar program you already own to see whether it can convert a file of that type.

11

Table 11.1. File types you'll find online for downloading.

Extension	Type of File	Requirements
.exe, .com	Program file (a game, utility, application, and so on)	Runs on one (and only one) type of system. Always read any text near the link to be sure that a particular .exe or .com file will run on your computer.

continues

Table 11.1. continued

Extension	Type of File	Requirements
.doc	Word document	Can be opened and edited in either the Windows or Mac version of Word, or Windows 95's WordPad program, and also can be displayed by Internet Explorer 4, or by Navigator if it is equipped with the ActiveX plug-in (see Hour 8, "Plug-ins, Helpers, and Other Ways to Do More Online").
.pdf	Adobe Acrobat document	Can be opened in the Adobe Acrobat Reader program (available for a variety of systems) or in a browser equipped with an Adobe Acrobat plug-in. Can also be converted and displayed by some word processing programs.
.xls	Excel spreadsheet	Can be opened and edited in either the Windows or Mac version of Excel, and displayed by Internet Explorer 4, or by Navigator if it is equipped with the ActiveX plug-in.
.txt, .asc	Plain text file	Can be opened in any word processor or text editor on any system, and can be displayed by any browser.
.wri	Windows Write document	Can be displayed by Windows Write (in Windows 3.1) or WordPad (in Windows 95/NT).

11

Extension	Type of File	Requirements
.avi, .mov, .qt, .mpg, .au, .mid, .snd	Various types of media files	Can be run by various player programs, or by your browser if it is equipped for them (see Hour 8).
.zip	*Archive* containing one or more compressed files	Must be decompressed (*unzipped*) before the files it contains can be used; see "Working with ZIP Files" later in this hour.

Just a Minute

11

Few program files are designed to run on both Macs and PCs. If you use a PC, however, you should know that some programs work in multiple PC operating systems. For example, some programs are written to run in both Windows 3.1 and Windows 95, and sometimes also DOS, as well.

Programs written just for DOS or Windows 3.1 will usually also run in Windows 95 or Windows NT, although the reverse is never true. Any Windows 95 program will run in Windows NT, but some Windows NT programs won't run in Windows 95.

If you use a PowerPC-based Mac, you know that you can run some Windows programs on your Mac. You probably also know that those programs do not run as well there as native Mac programs.

A program always runs best on the system for which it was written, so favor choices that match what you have. For example, if you use Windows 95 and you're given a choice between Windows 3.1 and Windows 95 versions of a file, choose the Windows 95 version. Even if you have a PowerPC-based Mac, always favor true Mac files over PC versions.

Finding Sites that Help You Find Files

Where you begin looking for a file depends on the manner in which that file is offered on the web, or rather, in what way that file is licensed for use by those other than its creator. Most software falls into one of the following four groups:

☐ **Commercial**—The programs you can buy in a box at the software store. Many software companies have web sites, where you can learn about their products and often download them as well. Typically, you fill in an online form to pay for the software, then download it.

☐ **Demo**—Demo software is commercial software that has some features disabled or automatically stops working, or *expires,* after you use it for a set number of days. Demo software is distributed free on commercial and shareware sites, and provides a free preview of the real thing.

☐ **Shareware**—Shareware is software you're allowed to try out for free, but for which you are supposed to pay. After the trial period (usually 30 days), you either pay the programmer or stop using the program. Some shareware expires or has features disabled, like demo software, so you won't continue using it without paying.

☐ **Freeware**—Freeware is free software you may use all you want, as long as you want, at no cost.

All-Purpose Shareware Sites

Sites for downloading shareware appear all over the web. Many popular shareware programs have their own web sites, and links to shareware products may be found on thousands of pages, such as Yahoo!'s shareware directory at

www.yahoo.com/Computers_and_Internet/Software/Shareware/

But when you're looking for a shareware, freeware, or demo program to do a particular job, you'll have better luck if you visit a web site designed to provide access to a wide range of products, sites such as

☐ **Shareware.com**—Easy-to-remember URL is shareware.com (see Figure 11.6).

☐ **Download.com**—Again, its easy-to-remember URL is (you guessed it) download.com.

These sites are much like the search tools you used in Hours 9 and 10, providing search term boxes, directories, and other tools for finding files. The hits these sites produce are always either links to files that match your search, or links to other web pages from which those files may be downloaded.

11

Figure 11.6.

Shareware.com is a search engine for finding shareware, freeware, and demo software.

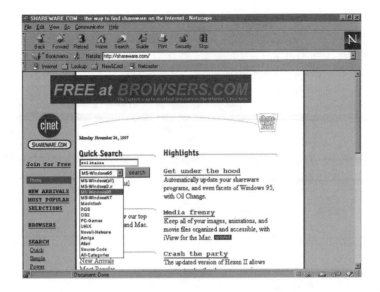

The key to using Shareware.com, Download.com, and similar file-finders is to make sure that your search specifies both of the following:

- ☐ The kind of file or program you seek: email, word processing, game, paint program, or whatever you want

- ☐ Your computer type and operating system: Windows 95, Mac OS8, and so on

If you include this information in your search, the hit list will show only files and programs of the kind you want, and only those that run on your particular system.

JUST A MINUTE

Note that sites like Shareware.com don't actually store the thousands of files to which they offer links on their own servers. Rather, they find and show you links that lead to files stored on other servers and mirror sites for those other servers.

To Do: Find a Program on Shareware.com

For practice, try finding a solitaire game for your system at Shareware.com:

1. Go to Shareware.com at shareware.com (refer to Figure 11.6).

2. In the box labeled Quick Search, type solitaire.

3. From the list below the Quick Search box, select your system type.

4. Click the button labeled search. After a few moments, a hit list of solitaire games for your system appears (see Figure 11.7). Each hit contains a link to the file, the file size and type, and a brief description of the file's contents.

Figure 11.7.

The hit list produced by a Shareware.com search includes links to the files, descriptions, file sizes, and system requirements.

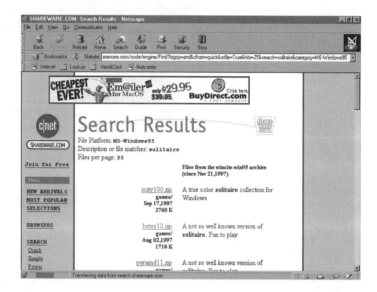

5. Choose a file link and click it. Depending on the file, the download may commence, or a new list of links appears, each pointing to the identical file stored on a different server. Click one to start the download.

TIME SAVER

If you use Windows 95, and a search for Windows 95 programs doesn't get you what you want, try another search for any Windows file of the type you want. For example, in Shareware.com, you'd choose MS-Windows (all) from the list of system types.

Such a search will turn up both Windows 95 and Windows 3.1 hits. You can substitute a Windows 3.1 program when no Windows 95 program is available.

Commercial Software Sites

As a web user, you have a lot to gain by frequenting the web sites of any commercial software companies whose products you use regularly. You can learn about new and enhanced versions of products you use and pick up tips, free enhancements, product support, and fixes for common problems.

11

In particular, it's important to know about the web site of the maker of the operating system you use on your computer: Microsoft's site (for Windows users) and Apple's (for Mac OS folks). On these sites, you can find all sorts of free updates and utilities for your operating system, fixes for problems, utilities, and news about upcoming new releases and enhancements.

Microsoft and Apple offer so many downloads that each provides its own search tools and directories for locating the file you need. The best place to start

- ☐ For Apple files, is at `support.info.apple.com/ftp/swhome.html` (see Figure 11.8).
- ☐ For Microsoft files, is at `www.microsoft.com/msdownload/`.

Figure 11.8.

Apple's support site offers a wealth of free files for Mac users.

Working with ZIP Files

The larger a file is, the longer it takes to download. Some files online are *compressed*—converted into smaller files—to cut the download time. After downloading, you must decompress a compressed file to restore it to its original size and be able to use it.

Most application programs are made up not just of one fat file, but of a collection of program and data files. A single compressed file can pack together many separate files, so they can all be downloaded together in one step. When you decompress a compressed file containing multiple files—which is sometimes called an *archive*—the files are separated.

Several forms of compression are used online, but by far the most popular form is called ZIP, a compressed file created by a program called PKZip. A ZIP file uses the extension .zip, and must be decompressed—*unzipped*—after downloading before you can use the file or files it contains.

You need a special program to unzip ZIP files. If you don't already have one, the most popular shareware unzippers are

☐ For Windows, WinZIP, which you can download from www.winzip.com.

☐ For Mac, ZipIt, which you can download from www.awa.com/softlock/zipit/ zipit.html.

After installing an unzipping program, you can decompress any ZIP file by opening the program, choosing the ZIP file you want to decompress, and then choosing Extract from a toolbar or menu.

TIME SAVER

One special type of .exe program file is called a *self-extracting archive*, which is a compressed file or files, just like a ZIP file.

Unlike a ZIP file, however, a self-extracting archive file does not require an unzipping program. Instead, it decompresses itself automatically when you open it (usually by double-clicking). Most large applications offered online, such as web browsers, download as self-extracting archives.

Viruses—Watch Out, but Relax

In the movie *Independence Day*, Jeff Goldblum stopped an intergalactic invasion by uploading a computer virus into the aliens' mothership and thereby scrambling the alien system.

 A *computer virus* is a program code secretly added to or attached to another file that makes mischief when the file is opened or run. Often, the virus is designed to reproduce and spread itself from the file it travels in—its host file—to other files.

Computer viruses are created by sorry, sick people who get a thrill out of cheap little tricks— viruses that display silly messages on your screen—or major attacks—viruses that crash whole computer systems.

If you saw *Independence Day*, you may wonder, "If Jeff Goldblum puts a virus on the Internet, and I happen to download a file containing that virus, what might happen to my computer? Would I still be able to conquer Earth? Can I get Jeff to come over and fix it?"

Viruses are like lightning: On one hand, your odds of getting struck are pretty slim, so there's no need to fret; on the other hand, there's no sense standing on a hill in a storm, holding a golf club skyward.

To play it safe, try to limit your downloading choices to commercial sites or reliable shareware sources (such as Shareware.com). Big suppliers regularly scan files for viruses, so you don't

11

have to. Also, don't worry when downloading any plain text (.txt or .asc) file; viruses typically cannot inhabit such files. (Note, however, that virtually any other type of file may contain a virus.)

If you venture beyond the reliable file suppliers (or if you just want to be extra careful), you may want to install and use a virus scanning program, such as Norton AntiVirus, which can find viruses in files and, in some cases, kill the virus while saving the file.

TIME SAVER

You can learn more about viruses, and find links to shareware and commercial virus scanners, from the AntiVirus Resources page at www.hitchhikers.net/av.shtml

Remember: A virus in a file does no harm until you open the file (or run the program, if the file is a program). So you can download anything safely, then scan it with the virus program before you ever open or run it. If the virus program detects a bug it cannot remove, just delete the file to delete the virus.

Summary

Finding the files you need begins with starting at the right site: a commercial software site, a shareware search site, and so on. When you start in the right place, and understand the simple steps required to select, download, and (sometimes) unzip files, getting any files you want is a snap.

Workshop

Q&A

Q **While a file is downloading, can I do other things on my computer, like browse other pages or run another program?**

A Some browsers built for Windows 95, or Mac 0S7 or 0S8, permit you to continue browsing during a download. When using one of these browsers—which include the Windows 95 versions of Internet Explorer and Navigator—you may explore another page, or even start another download, while one download is in progress.

I always recommend, however, that you leave your computer alone while downloading. Go get coffee, or play with the kids or something, until the download is complete. Using your computer for any other task—even an offline one—slows down both the download and whatever else you're doing, and raises the likelihood that the download might fail partway through, forcing you to start the download over again.

Quiz

Take the following quiz to see how much you've learned.

Questions

1. A file using the extension .exe may be

    a. A program file for Windows

    b. A self-extracting archive

    c. A program file for Macintosh

    d. Any of the above

2. Through a 28.8Kbps Internet connection, a 3MB file would most likely download in

    a. More than 2 hours

    b. Less than 1 hour

    c. 6 1/2 minutes

    d. 3MB (*minute-bytes*)

3. A ZIP file may contain

    a. A group of data files compressed together into one archive

    b. A single compressed file

    c. All the program and data files that together make up an application program

    d. Any of the above

Answers

1. (d) An .exe can be any one of the choices—but usually, *only* one.

2. (b) Download time is unpredictable, and if the server where the file resides is slow or busy, (a) is a possibility. But (b) is the most likely choice. (By the way, MB stands for megabytes, not minute bytes.)

3. (d) A ZIP can contain any of the choices described, plus one more—it can contain other ZIP files.

Activity

After Hour 12, "Finding People," you'll begin working with email. Do you have your email program yet? If not, now would be a good time to find and download one. Check out your browser-maker's web site or try searching for a program called Eudora.

11

Hour **12**

Finding People

Using mainly the search techniques you've picked up in the preceding three hours, you can find people on the Internet, or rather, the email addresses, mailing addresses, or telephone numbers through which particular people may be reached.

This people-finding power is among the Internet's most valuable and controversial capabilities. Applied properly, it can aid research, locate missing persons, track down deadbeats delinquent in their child support payments, reunite old friends, and even help adult orphans find their birth parents. Abused, this capability aids stalkers and overaggressive direct marketers. Unfortunately, as is always the case with freedom of information, no practical way exists to preserve the benefit of this capability without also enabling its abuse.

At the end of the hour, you'll be able to answer the following questions:

☐ Where on the web are search tools I can use to find the addresses, phone numbers, or email addresses of folks I want to contact?

☐ How do I use a people-finding search tool on the web?

☐ How can I also use a people-finding search tool from within my email program?

JUST A MINUTE

Throughout this book, I show screen images to illustrate an activity. In this hour, although I show you how to perform people searches, I never show the *results* of a people search. Showing those results would invade the privacy of whomever the search found.

Using People-Finding Sites

As with all types of search tools, every people finder on the web draws from a different database of names and contact information. For any particular name, a search using one tool may turn up no hits, although a search with a different tool may hit pay dirt. It's important to know where different search tools are, so if one tool fails, you can try another.

TIME SAVER

If there's a possibility the person you seek may have his or her own home page on the web, using a special people-finding tool may not be necessary. It's usually a good idea to first perform an ordinary search with a tool like AltaVista or Excite, using the person's name as your search term (see Hour 10, "Searching for Information").

Such a search will likely turn up that person's home page, if they have one (along with any references to other folks who have the same name, of course), and if you visit the home page, you'll find contact information on it.

You use these tools like any other search tool: Enter as much as you know about the person—name, city, and so on—and the tool finds matches in its database. That database contains only contact information, however, so your search won't turn up all sorts of references that have nothing to do with contacting someone.

Some of the better people finders are

☐ Yahoo!'s People Search, which can be found at www.yahoo.com/search/people/

☐ Excite's U.S. People Finder (for addresses and phone numbers), which can be found at www.excite.com/Reference/people.html

☐ Excite's E-mail Lookup (for email addresses), which can be found at www.excite.com/Reference/e-mail.html

☐ Bigfoot, which can be found at www.Bigfoot.com

☐ Four11, which can be found at www.Four11.com

12

Depending on the people finder you use and the options you choose, you may find a person's mailing address, phone number, or email address (or all three). Of course, you haven't learned how to use email yet, but that's okay—you'll learn all about it in the next hour.

For now, if a search turns up an email address of a person you want to contact, just jot it down. An hour from now, you'll know how to use it to send a message to that person.

To Do: Find Yourself in Yahoo!'s People Search

To Do

Because you're probably already familiar with Yahoo!, Yahoo!'s People Search is a great first place to try finding someone:

1. Go to Yahoo!'s People Search at www.yahoo.com/search/people. (You can also reach the People Search by going to Yahoo!'s home, www.yahoo.com, and clicking the link to People Search near the top of the page.) A page like the one in Figure 12.1 appears.

Figure 12.1.

Yahoo!'s People Search is an easy-to-use, reliable people finder.

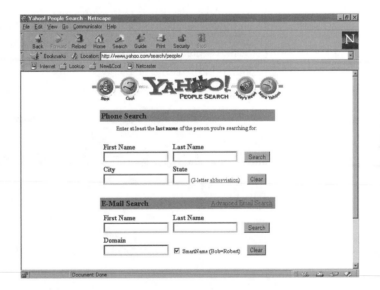

2. Complete the boxes in the Phone Search form with your own personal information: First Name, Last Name, City, and State.

3. Click the Search button to the right of the Phone Search form. After a few moments, any matches appear in a hit list.

4. Click Back to return to the People Search. This time, fill in the boxes under Email Search, and click the Search button to the right of the Email Search form. Did your email address appear?

5. Just for fun, try another Phone or Email Search, but this time, leave some boxes empty. For example, fill in your name, but not your city or state. The hit list will show others, all over the United States, who have the same name as you.

6. Finally, click the Advanced Email Search link. A new form appears (see Figure 12.2) on which you can supply more detailed information for performing an advanced search for someone's email address.

TIME SAVER

Observe that the screens shown in Figures 12.1 and 12.2 include a check box for SmartName. When this check box is checked, Yahoo! searches not only for the exact first name you supplied, but also for common variations of that name. If you entered Edward, the search might match records for Edward, Ed, Eddy, and maybe Ted. This increases the chances of finding the right person when you're not sure which name form the person uses.

In the Advanced Email search area (see Figure 12.2), a check box for enabling Flexible Search also appears. In a flexible search, you need to enter only the first part of a name you're not sure about, and Yahoo! will match all names that begin that way. Search for Jo, and matches include Joe, Joseph, John, and Jolene.

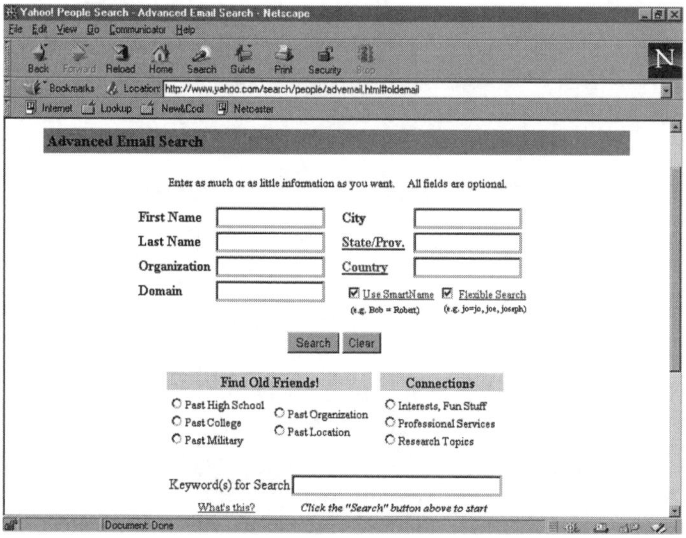

Figure 12.2.

Yahoo!'s Advanced Email Search lets you target your search more narrowly by providing more detailed information.

JUST A MINUTE

If you found yourself in your Yahoo! searches, you may be wondering, "How did my phone number, email address, or other information get on the web?"

Most of the information in the search tool databases—including names, addresses, and phone numbers—comes from public telephone records. By agreeing to have your name, address, and phone number listed in the phone book, you've agreed to make it public, so there's nothing to prevent it from winding up in a web database. Some databases may also obtain records from other online databases (such as your ISP's user directory), or even from online forms you've submitted from web pages.

Even if you have an unlisted telephone number (which phone companies call unpublished), a record about you may find its way into a database from another source. That's just one reason you must be careful about how and when you enter information about yourself in an online form. See Hour 7, "Protecting Your Privacy (and Other Security Stuff)."

Using People Finders Through Your Email Program

A family of people-finding directories, known collectively as LDAP directories, are specifically and solely made for finding email addresses, both in North America and worldwide.

 Lightweight Directory Access Protocol (LDAP) is a standard followed by some people finders that allows a single dialog box in an email program to be used to search any LDAP directory.

Some LDAP directories, such as Bigfoot (www.Bigfoot.com) and Four11 (www.Four11.com) are accessible through a web page. These and several other LDAPs may also be accessed from within some email programs. This enables you to search for an email address from within your email program—which is, after all, the place you need email addresses.

Now, I know we haven't covered email yet—that's in the next hour. However, because this hour is about finding people, it's a good place to quickly show how an email program can also be a people finder.

The two email programs included in the big two Internet Suites—Netscape Communicator's Messenger and Internet Explorer 4's Outlook Express—both support LDAP searches from within their *Address Book*, a utility that helps you keep track of email addresses.

Searching an LDAP directory from within your email program is just like using a people finder on the web: You fill in a name and other information in a form. The only difference

12

is getting to that form. Instead of opening a web page, you go online, open your email program and navigate to the LDAP search form as follows:

☐ In Messenger, choose Communicator|Address Book to open the Address Book, then click the Directory button in the Address Book's toolbar. A search dialog box opens (see Figure 12.3). Use the top list in the dialog box to choose the LDAP directory to search, fill in the other boxes in the dialog box, and click Search.

☐ In Outlook Express, click the Address Book button on the toolbar to open the Address Book, then click the Find button in the Address Book's toolbar. A search dialog box opens. Use the top list in the dialog box to choose the LDAP directory to search, fill in the other boxes in the dialog box, and click Find Now.

Figure 12.3.

Searching an LDAP directory from within Netscape Messenger's Address Book.

Other Folk-Finding Tips

The all-around easiest ways to find people online are those I've already described. If those don't pay off for you, however, try the methods described in the following sections.

Use a Company or School Directory

Do you know the name of the company the person works for, or a school he or she attends? Many companies, colleges, and universities have their own web sites, and those web sites often contain employee and student directories you can browse or search (see Figure 12.4). Just search for and go to the web site, then browse for a directory.

Try Name Variations

Might the person you're looking for sometimes use a different name than the one you've been using as a search term? Try alternate spellings (Sandy, Sandi) or nicknames. Try both the married name and birth name of people who may have married or divorced recently. You may even want to try a compound name made out of both the birth name and married name (such as Jacqueline Bouvier Kennedy); I know both men and women who use compound or hyphenated married names.

Use an Online Service Directory

If you use an online service and think the person you seek may use the same online service you do, try your online service's own directory of its users. You can access the directory from within the service's interface for non-Internet content.

12

Note that only the online service's customers can access its user directory.

Use Old Communications to Start the New Ones

Do you know either the mailing address or phone number of the person, and just want his or her email address? Don't be shy: Call or write, and just ask for the person's email address so you can conduct future communication online. Life's too short.

Summary

You know from earlier hours that you can find all sorts of information and files online. But until this hour, you may not have realized how easy it is to use the Internet to find an old friend or other contact you need. Most often, finding someone on the web is a simple matter of opening a people-finding search tool and typing a name.

If your search turns up an email address, you have a powerful way of getting in touch with that person; see Hour 13, "Sending and Receiving Email."

Workshop

Q&A

Q When my people searches turn up email addresses, those addresses appear to be links: They're underlined, and shown in the same color as other links. What are they links to?

A These links are called *email links* or *mailto links*, and they contain an email address. Some browsers are equipped to automatically open your email program when you click a mailto link in a web page (see Hour 13). If your browser is so equipped, you can click a mailto link and immediately begin composing a message addressed to that person.

Q I was looking for Carla Jones, and I found three people with that name. How do I figure out which Carla Jones is the one I want?

A Well, first you should try new searches, supplying as much information as you reliably know about the person. For example, include the state where the person lives; doing so may exclude the other choices. Try running your searches on different tools; another tool may display more detailed information, enabling you to choose the right Carla.

If you still have several choices, send a polite letter or email message (never phone) to all the Carlas, identifying yourself and the context in which you know Carla, and requesting that the right Carla reply. The wrong Carlas will ignore your message, and the right Carla will contact you (if she wants to).

12

In your note, say as little as possible, and be tactful. For example, if Carla is an old flame, consider the possible effect of your note on the boyfriends or husbands of the *wrong* Carlas when describing your relationship.

Quiz

Take the following quiz to see how much you've learned.

Questions

1. LDAP directories are accessible through

   a. The web site of the Long Distance Anthropology Project (LDAP)

   b. Any Chat client (see Hour 18, "Chatting Live!")

   c. `www.ldap.com`

   d. The Address Book of an LDAP-supporting email program

2. Your name and address probably got on the web from

   a. The secret devices Mulder and Scully found implanted in your spine

   b. Your local phone book

   c. Your prison record

   d. Your subscription to *Utne Reader*

3. True or false: Somewhere on the web, you can find a record about everyone in North America, Europe, and the Pacific Rim.

Answers

1. (d) Address Books in email programs are the window into LDAP directories. Some LDAP directories are also available through web pages—but I didn't give you that choice, did I?

2. (b) The most likely answer is (b), although I suppose (c) and (d) are remote possibilities. Only Mulder and Scully know if (a) is the Truth, or if the Truth is even out there.

3. False. There are billions of people in the world, and only a few measly million are in web people databases. Even among residents of high-tech places like North America, many, many people cannot be found by a web search.

Activity

When people first begin using the Internet, they often don't realize how many of their friends already use it. Search for your friends, and find out their email addresses. Sure, you can always just ask them. But sometimes it's fun to surprise someone with a friendly, unexpected email message. You learn how to send that message next.

12

PART IV

Communicating with Email and Newsgroups

Hour

Hour **13**

Sending and Receiving Email

Web browsing is the hottest Internet activity, but email is probably the most widely used and most productive one.

Using Internet email—which has become such an everyday fixture that many people now just call it *mail*—you can easily exchange messages with anyone else on the Internet. An email message typically reaches its addressee within minutes (or at most, an hour or so), even on the opposite side of the globe. It's faster than paper mail, easier than faxing, and sometimes just plain fun.

It's so easy, in fact, that I know people who haven't written a dozen paper letters in a decade but who write email daily. It's a great way to keep up with friends and communicate with business contacts. In fact, some businesspeople are so tied to their email that if you contact them in any way *other* than email, you probably won't get an answer.

At the end of this hour, you'll be able to answer the following questions:

☐ How do I recognize an email address?

☐ How do I set up my email program?

☐ How do I display a message so I can read it?

☐ How do I compose and send an email message?

☐ How do I receive messages others have sent to me?

☐ How can I reply to a message I've received, or forward that message to someone else?

☐ How can I keep track of all the email addresses I use?

Understanding Email Addresses

The only piece of information you need to send email to someone is that person's Internet email address. An email address is easy to spot: It always has that at symbol (@) in the middle of it. For example, you know at a glance that

```
sammy@fishbait.com
```

is an email address. In most email addresses, everything following the @ symbol is the domain address (see Hour 4, "Connecting to the Internet") of a company, ISP, or other organization. The part before the @ is the name (or user ID) of a particular employee or user. For example, the addresses

```
SallyP@genco.com
mikey@genco.com
Manager_of_Sales@genco.com
```

obviously belong to three different people, all of whom work for the same company or use the same ISP (whatever Genco is). Each online service has its own domain, too: For example, America Online's is aol.com, and Microsoft Network's is msn.com. So you can tell that the email address

```
neddyboy@aol.com
```

is that of an American Online user named neddyboy.

TIME SAVER

Online service users can omit the @ symbol and anything that follows it when sending to other users on the same service. For example, suppose you want to send email to

```
allieoop@aol.com
```

If you use a regular Internet ISP or any online service other than America Online (aol.com), you would use the address as shown. If you use America Online, however, you may address the message simply to

```
allieoop
```

13

Setting Up Your Email Program

Many different email programs are available. Internet suites such as Internet Explorer 4 and Netscape Communicator include an email client—but you must take care when installing these programs not to optionally omit the email component of the suite. Choosing the "full" installation option when setting up a suite ensures that you include all the suite's client programs.

In the suites, the programs are called

- ☐ **Messenger**—In Netscape Communicator, you can open Messenger from within the Navigator browser by choosing Communicator | Messenger.

- ☐ **Outlook Express**—In Internet Explorer 4, you can open Outlook Express from within the Internet Explorer browser by choosing Go | Mail.

If you don't already have an email client, you may apply the file-finding techniques from Hour 11, "Finding Programs and Files," to search for one, or browse a directory of email programs on Yahoo! at

```
www.yahoo.com/Business_and_Economy/Companies/Computers/Software/
Communications_and_Networking/Electronic_Mail/Titles/
```

Among the links you'll likely find in any search for email programs are links to various versions of a program called Eudora, one of the most popular email clients outside of the suites. If you simply want to go straight to learning about and downloading Eudora (which is available for both Mac and Windows in a freeware version called Eudora Light and a commercial version called Eudora Pro), visit the site of Eudora's maker at

```
www.eudora.com
```

JUST A MINUTE

If you use an online service, such as America Online or CompuServe, you may not be able to choose your own Internet email program; you may be required to use the online service interface—the tool you use for accessing the service's non-Internet content—to send and receive email.

Using an online service interface for email, however, is similar to using an Internet email program as described in this hour. From the online service interface, you can send email both to others on your service and to anyone on the Internet.

You need not configure email, as described next, for any online service. All email configuration is handled automatically when you sign up for the service and install its software.

13

Configuring Email

After installing an email program, you need to configure it before you can use it. All email programs have a configuration dialog box of some kind (or a series of dialog boxes) on which you can enter the information required for exchanging email (see Figure 13.1). You'll find the configuration dialog boxes:

☐ In Messenger, by choosing Edit | Preferences to open the Preferences dialog box. In the list of Categories, choose Mail & Groups. Complete the configuration settings in the Mail & Groups category's Identity and Mail Server subcategories.

☐ For Outlook Express, by completing the Mail dialog boxes of the Connection Wizard (see Hour 4). If you open Outlook Express without having configured it first, the Connection Wizard opens automatically.

TIME SAVER

The automated setup routines supplied with programs such as Netscape Communicator and Internet Explorer not only set up your browser and Internet connection, but can optionally collect the information required to configure their email components (Messenger and Outlook Express). See Hour 4 for more information.

If you open Messenger or Outlook Express without first having configured them, a dialog box opens automatically, prompting for the configuration information.

Figure 13.1.

In Netscape's Messenger, configure email settings in the Mail & Groups category of the Preferences dialog box.

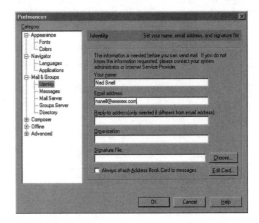

The configuration dialog boxes for most email programs require most or all of the following information, all of which your ISP will tell you:

13

☐ Your full name (Okay, so you don't need your ISP to tell you this one).

☐ Your full email address. (Some configuration dialog boxes make you indicate the two parts of your address separately: the *username*—the part of the email address preceding the @ symbol—and your *domain*—the part of the email address following the @ symbol.)

☐ The address of your ISP's *outgoing mail server*, sometimes called SMTP.

☐ The address of your ISP's *incoming mail server*, sometimes called POP3.

Also, to ensure that no one but you gets your email, most ISPs require you to choose and use an email password. Some email programs let you enter that password in the configuration dialog box so you needn't type a password each time you check your email.

Getting Around in Your Email Program

Before jumping right into sending and receiving messages, you should learn how to get around in your email program, move among its *folders* (lists of messages), and display messages you select from a folder.

TIME SAVER

When working with email, the only time you need to be connected to the Internet is at the moment when you actually send messages—transmit them to the Internet—or receive messages—copy them from the Internet to your computer. You can be online or offline while composing messages, reading messages you've received, or managing your messages.

Because of this, many email programs are integrated with the autoconnect capabilities built into systems such as Mac OS8 or Windows 95. When your system's autoconnect feature is enabled, the email program attempts to connect you automatically to the Internet when necessary. For example, if you've composed a message offline, when you attempt to send it, your Internet connection dialog box may open, prompting you to go online so the message can be sent. Some email programs try to connect you as soon as you open the program, so they can automatically check for any new email.

If your email program or system does not support autoconnect, it's no big deal. Just keep in mind that you must connect to the Internet before sending or receiving email, but when reading or writing email, you can stay offline.

13

Choosing a Folder

Messenger and Outlook Express divide their messaging activities into a family of folders. In each folder, you see a list of messages you can display or work with in other ways. The folders are

☐ **Inbox**—Lists messages you have received.

☐ **Outbox (called Unsent Messages in Messenger)**—Lists messages you have composed but saved to be sent later.

☐ **Sent**—Lists copies of all messages you've sent, for your reference.

☐ **Deleted (called Trash in Messenger)**—Lists messages you've deleted from any other folder.

JUST A MINUTE

> Outlook Express handles two different jobs: email and newsgroups. It, therefore, has folders not only for email, but also for newsgroups. Before performing an email activity in Outlook Express, always be sure that you're in an email-related folder, such as Inbox or Outbox, and not the News folder.
>
> You'll learn about using Outlook Express for newsgroups in Hour 15, "Reading and Posting to Newsgroups."

To switch among folders:

☐ In Messenger, drop down the folder list (which appears just below the toolbar), and choose a folder.

☐ In Outlook Express, click a folder name in the panel along the left side of the window (see Figure 13.2).

Displaying a Message

From the list displayed by each folder, you can display any message. You do this in either of two ways (the steps are the same in both Outlook Express and Messenger):

☐ Single-click the message in the list to display it in the preview pane in the bottom of the window (see Figure 13.3).

☐ Double-click the message in the list to display it in its own message window (see Figure 13.4).

In general, the preview pane is best when you're simply scanning messages and need to move quickly from one to the next. Use a full message window to read a long message, or to read a message you will reply to or forward (as described later in this hour).

13

Figure 13.2.

Choose a folder to select the messages you want to work with.

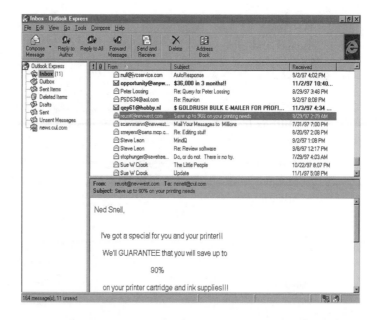

Figure 13.3.

Single-click a message in a folder to display the message in the preview pane.

Preview pane ——

13

Figure 13.4.

Double-click a message in a folder to display the message in a message window.

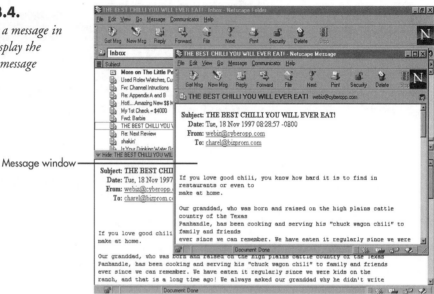

Message window ——

Composing and Sending a Message

If you have something to say, and the address of someone to whom you want to say it, you're ready to go.

Writing Your Message

In most email programs, you compose your message in a window that's very much like a word processing program, with a special form at the top for filling in the address and subject information—the message's *header*. Below the form for the header, you type your message text in the large space provided for the message *body*.

  The *body* of a message is the text, which you compose in the large pane of the message window. The address information you type—including your recipient's email address and the subject of the message—is called the *header* of the message.

To Do: Compose a New Message

The following steps show you how to compose a simple email message:

1. Open a new message window (see Figure 13.5), in which you can compose a message. You do this from any email-related folder, such as Inbox:

   In Messenger, click the New Msg button on the toolbar.

   In Outlook Express, click the Compose Message button on the toolbar.

13

Figure 13.5.

Compose and address email in the New Message box.

2. In the To line (near the top of the window), type the email address of the person to whom you want to send a message. To send the same message to multiple recipients, enter all the email addresses in the To line, putting a semicolon (;) after each message except the final one.

TIME SAVER

To cc (carbon copy) your email to recipients other than your primary addressee(s), just click the Cc: line under the To line and enter one or more email addresses there, separating multiple addresses with a semicolon (;).

3. Click in the Subject line, and type a concise, meaningful subject for your message. The subject line will appear in the message list of the recipient, to help explain the purpose of your message.

4. Click in the large panel of the new message window and type your message, just as you would in a word processor.

JUST A MINUTE

As a general rule, you cannot use text formatting (fonts, bold, italic, underlining, and so on) in an email message, so for now, stick to simple text. In Hour 23, "Creating Web Pages and Multimedia Messages," you learn how to do some fancy message formatting. You also learn that many email recipients cannot display such messages.

13

Sending a Message Now

After the header and body of the message are complete, you send your message on its way. In most programs, you do so simply by clicking a button labeled Send in the toolbar of the window in which you composed the message.

The message is immediately sent to your ISP's mail server, from which it will be routed to its destination. If you composed the message offline, and your email program supports your computer's autoconnect feature (see Hour 4), you'll be automatically connected to the net when you click Send.

JUST A MINUTE

> When you click Send in Outlook Express, the message is temporarily copied to your Outbox (see the next section, "Sending a Message Later") and then sent automatically as soon as Outlook Express determines that sending is possible.
>
> If you're online when you click Send, the message visits the Outbox for just a moment, and then is sent. If you're offline, the message stays in the Outbox until you connect.

Most email programs include a Sent folder, in which a copy of every message you send is saved. If you need to refer later to a message you've sent, find its copy in your Sent folder.

Sending a Message Later

When you're composing several messages offline, as you complete each one you need not connect and send, disconnect, connect and send, disconnect, and so on.

Instead, as you complete each message, you can save it in your Outbox or Unsent Messages folder instead of sending it right away. You can then send all the waiting messages at once, the next time you connect.

In either Messenger or Outlook Express, you save a message in your Unsent Messages or Outbox folder by choosing File | Send Later instead of clicking the Send button.

When you're ready to send all messages that are waiting:

☐ In Messenger, choose File | Send Unsent Messages.

☐ In Outlook Express, receive mail (as described in the next section). Whenever you attempt to receive mail with Outlook Express, all Outbox messages are sent automatically.

After the messages have been sent, copies appear in your Sent folder, as usual.

13

Receiving Messages

When others send messages to you, those messages go to your ISP's or online service's mail server, and wait there until you choose to receive messages. To receive messages:

☐ In Messenger, click the Get Msg button on the toolbar.

☐ In Outlook Express, open any email-related folder (Inbox is a good choice) and click the Send and Receive button on the toolbar.

JUST A MINUTE

As I mentioned earlier, your ISP provides you with a special password you use only when receiving email (you don't need it to send email). When you click the button to receive mail, a dialog box may appear to prompt for your password. Just type your password and press Enter to continue receiving email.

You can type your email password in the configuration dialog boxes of some email programs so that the email program will supply the password for you when you receive email, saving you a step. This feature is handy, but should only be used if your computer is located where no one else might try to retrieve and read your email if you strolled away from your desk while connected to the Internet.

Your mail program contacts your ISP, and checks for any new messages addressed to you. If there are none, the words No new messages on server appear in the status bar at the bottom of the window. If there are new messages, the messages are copied to your PC and stored in your Inbox folder, where you can read them any time, online or offline.

In the message lists displayed by most email programs, the messages you have not yet read appear in bold (refer to Figures 13.2 through 13.4).

Replying and Forwarding

Most email clients provide you with two easy ways to create new messages by using other messages you have received: *reply* and *forward*.

NEW TERM   *Replying* means sending a message back to someone from whom you have received a message, to respond to that message. *Forwarding* is passing a copy of a message you've received to a third party, either because you want to share the message's content with the third party or because you believe that, although the message was originally sent to you, the third party is a more appropriate recipient for it.

13

To reply or forward, you always begin by opening the original message. From the message window's toolbar, you then click a button or menu item with a label like one of the following:

☐ **Reply to Author (or Reply to Sender)**—Creates a reply to the person who sent you the message.

☐ **Reply to All (or Reply to Sender and All Recipients)**—Creates a reply to the person who sent you the message and to everyone else to whom the message was sent when it was sent to you.

TIME SAVER

> In Messenger, there's a single Reply button on the toolbar. Click it, and two choices drop down: Reply to Sender and Reply to Sender and All Recipients.

☐ **Forward Message**—Creates a new message containing the entire text of the original message, ready for you to forward.

Whichever button you click, a new message window opens. In the body of the message, a complete quote of the original message appears (see Figure 13.6).

NEW TERM   A *quote* is all or a portion of a message you've received, included in a reply to indicate what you're replying to, or included in a forward to carry the message you're forwarding.

You may edit the quote, cutting out any parts that aren't relevant and inserting your own comments above, below, or within the quote.

Figure 13.6.

A reply or a forward includes a quote of the original message.

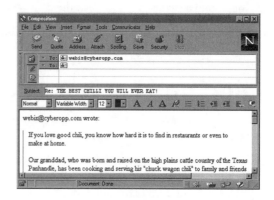

In the message window of a reply, the To line is automatically filled in for you, with the address of the person from whom you received the message (or multiple addresses, if you chose Reply to All). The Subject line is filled in with the original message's subject, preceded

13

by Re: (regarding, or reply to) to indicate that your message is a reply to a message using that subject. To complete the reply, just type your comments above, below, or within the quote, and then click Send.

In the message window of a forward, the To line is empty, so you can enter the address of the person to whom you want to forward the message. (As with any message, you may enter multiple To recipients and Cc recipients as well.) The Subject line is filled in with the subject of the original message, preceded by FW: (forward). To complete the forward, address the message, type your comments above, below, or within the quote, and then click Send.

Using an Address Book

Most folks find that there's a steady list of others to whom they email often. Keeping track of those all-important names and addresses, and using them, is easier when you use your email program's *Address Book*.

 An *Address Book* is a directory you create, containing the names, email addresses, and often other information (mailing address, phone, notes) about your contacts.

When an addressee's information is in your Address Book, you needn't type—or even remember—his or her email address. Instead, you can simply choose the person's name from the Address Book, and your email program fills in the address for you. Some Address Books also support *nicknames*—short, easy-to-remember names you type in the To line of a message instead of the full email address.

Adding to Your Address Book

In both Outlook Express and Messenger, the easiest way to add to your Address Book is to copy information from messages you've received. For example, if you've received a message from Sue, you can use that message to quickly create an address card you can use to send messages to Sue.

To create a new Address Book entry from a message, begin by displaying the message. Next:

- ☐ In Messenger, find the sender's email address, which appears as a link near the top of the body of the message (labeled "From"). Click that link, and a New Card dialog box opens (see Figure 13.7). Make sure the name and email address boxes on the Name tab have been filled in, and complete any of the other optional boxes you want. Click OK to save the new entry.

- ☐ In Outlook Express, choose Tools | Add to Address Book | Sender. Make sure the name and email address boxes on the Personal tab have been filled in, and complete any of the other optional boxes you want. Click OK to save the new entry.

13

Figure 13.7.

Fill in the name and email address boxes to create a new Address Book entry.

To create an Address Book entry from scratch (without beginning from a message you've received):

☐ In Outlook Express, choose Tools | Address Book | New Contact.

☐ In Messenger, choose Communicator | Address Book | New Card.

Addressing a Message from the Address Book

To use an Address Book entry to address a message (in Messenger or Outlook Express), begin by opening the new message window as usual. Then open the Address Book list:

☐ In Messenger, by clicking the Address button.

☐ In Outlook Express, by clicking the little Rolodex card icon in the To line.

In the list, click the name of an addressee, and click the To button to add the addressee to the To line, or Cc to add the addressee to the Cc line.

When done choosing recipients, click OK to close the address book, and complete the Subject and body of your message.

Summary

Wow! You learned a lot this hour. As you saw, the hardest part about email is getting yourself set up for it. Composing, sending, and receiving messages is a breeze, and techniques that can make you even more productive—such as using an Outbox or Address Book—are also pretty easy and always optional.

Workshop

Q&A

Q What's the Bcc line in the header about?

A The Bcc line works exactly like the Cc line, except that it sends a "blind" carbon copy.

Everyone who receives a message from you can see in the message header who else got the same message, either as a To or a Cc recipient. Bcc recipients don't show up in the header, however, so the only people who know that the message was copied to a Bcc recipient are the Bcc recipient and you. Use Bcc when your messaging relates to something you're doing that's especially private or sneaky.

Q Can I send a file, like a picture or a program, through email?

A Sure. A file sent through email is called an attachment because it's attached to a regular email message.

To attach a file, first address and compose the message as usual. Then click the Insert File button (the paperclip) in Outlook Express, or the Attach button in Messenger, to open a dialog box in which you can navigate to and select the file to attach. (Avoid attaching large files—they'll take a long time for you to send and also a long time for your recipient to receive.)

When you receive an attached file from someone else, you must separate it from the message to use it. The attachment typically appears in the message body as a file icon or paperclip icon; to save it as a separate file, drag the icon out of your email program into any Windows or Mac folder.

Quiz

Take the following quiz to see how much you've learned.

Questions

1. True or false: To compose or read email, you must first connect to the Internet.
2. Your Outbox or Unsent Messages folder holds messages that
    a. You've thrown out
    b. You've composed but not yet sent
    c. Contain *out*rageous statements
    d. Contain ideas that are not "in"

13

3. When a subject line in a message you've received begins with RE:, the message must be

    a. A *re*pulsive one

    b. A *re*cent one

    c. A *re*ply to a message you sent to someone

    d. A *re*publican one

Answers

1. False. You may use Outlook Express with Internet Explorer closed, and either online or offline.

2. (b) It's (b), of course.

3. (c) It must be (c), but of course any message might also be (a), (b), or (d), or all four (a repulsive, recent, republican message might indeed demand a REply, mightn't it?)

Activity

Have you been keeping notes of the email addresses of friends, family, and associates? Send all of them an email greeting today, so they will have your email address, the key to getting in touch with you. Check your email often for their replies.

13

Hour **14**

Joining a Mailing List

The Internet boasts two facilities commonly described as "discussion groups" that differ only in the medium on which the discussion takes place. In the first type of discussion group, *mailing lists*, you read the discussion in email messages you receive, and contribute to the discussion by sending email. In the second type of discussion group, *newsgroups*, you read messages on, and send messages to, a *news server* (more about newsgroups in Hour 15, "Reading and Posting to Newsgroups").

Regardless of the type you use, discussion groups are a great way to keep up with news about any imaginable topic, and to engage in conversation and debate with others online who share your interests.

The great thing about mailing lists is that you already know most of what you need to know to use them; you know how to send and receive email. All you need to learn is where and how to find the mailing lists that interest you, how to sign up, and how to quit a mailing list if you lose interest in it. At the end of this hour, you'll be able to answer the following questions:

☐ What are the two kinds of mailing lists, and the two different email addresses I need to use most mailing lists?

☐ How can I find the addresses for mailing lists covering topics that interest me?

□ How do I join a mailing list and contribute to it?

□ What rules of online courtesy—*netiquette*—must I observe when contributing to a mailing list?

The Two Types of Mailing Lists

For a mailing list to work, someone has to handle its management and administration: mostly signing up new members and removing members who have asked to be removed.

In a few mailing lists, that administration task is handled by a real person. Most mailing lists, however, are managed not by a person, but by a *listserv*. Sometimes, the mailing lists managed by people are called *manual* mailing lists, to distinguish them from the lists automated by listservs.

NEW TERM A *listserv* is a program that automatically manages a mailing list. Actually, several programs are available that manage mailing lists, including Listserv, Listproc, and Majordomo. But the term *listserv* is used generically to refer to all such programs, and often to the lists they manage, as well.

Finding a Mailing List

The first step in using mailing lists is finding one that interests you. When visiting web pages devoted to your favorite topics, you'll often see mention of related mailing lists, along with the email address required for signing up: the *subscription address*.

You may also visit any of several web pages that help folks find mailing lists related to a particular subject. A good first stop is FindMail (`www.findmail.com`), a search tool dedicated to helping you find and use mailing lists (see Figure 14.1).

You can browse through FindMail's categories to find a list, or use its search engine to find lists related to a search term you enter.

Besides FindMail, other good places to find mailing lists (and instructions for using them) include

□ The list of Publicly Accessible Mailing Lists at `www.neosoft.com/internet/paml`

□ Liszt, a searchable database of lists and instructions at `www.liszt.com`

□ Yahoo!'s directory at `www.yahoo.com/Computers_and_Internet/Internet/Mailing_Lists/`

14

Figure 14.1.

Use FindMail to browse for a mailing list or search for one.

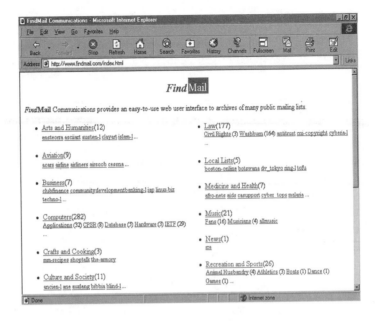

Subscribing to a Mailing List

To use any mailing list, you need to know two different email addresses:

☐ The address of the person, or listserv program, that manages the list. This address might be called the management or subscription address.

☐ The list address, an email address to which you send all your contributions to the list and the comments or questions you want all others in the list to see.

CAUTION

Sorry, sorry…Hate to break into an easy topic like mailing lists with a big fat Caution. But I really want to alert you to the one major mailing list mistake: Mixing up the list address with the management address, and vice versa.

If you accidentally send your list contributions to the management address, the others on the list won't see them. If you send management commands to the list address, those commands will not be carried out. Worse, the message containing those commands shows up in the mailing list of everyone in the list, which won't win you any friends.

Never forget: Contributions to the discussion go to the list address, commands for managing your subscription go to that other address (subscription, management, whatever), which is usually the same one you used to subscribe.

14

Composing the Subscription Message

When you're ready to sign up, you send a simple email message containing the command required to subscribe to the subscription address. Unfortunately, the command differs from list to list.

Most references to mailing lists—including those you'll turn up in the directories described earlier—include subscription instructions. Those instructions typically tell you the command you must send, and also *where* in the email message—in the Subject line or the message body—you must type that command.

Command instructions use a syntax diagram to tell you what to type. Even manually managed lists generally require a particular command syntax, although they're more forgiving of command mistakes than listservs are.

NEW TERM A *syntax diagram* shows what you must type to properly phrase a command to control a computer program, such as a listserv. In a syntax diagram, the exact words you must type are shown in normal type, and any parts of the command you must add are surrounded by brackets or shown in italics.

For example, to phrase the command indicated by the syntax diagram

```
subscribe lastname firstname
```

or

```
subscribe [lastname] [firstname]
```

I would type

```
subscribe Snell Ned
```

Notice that I replace any portions in italics or brackets with the information indicated, and that I do not type the brackets.

To subscribe to a list, read the instructions to find

☐ The syntax diagram for subscribing

☐ The part of the message in which to type the command (either the Subject line or body)

☐ The subscription address

Compose an email message containing only the command indicated by the instructions, and send it to the subscription address. Figure 14.2 shows a typical subscription message in which the command appears in the message body.

14

Figure 14.2.

You subscribe to a mailing list by phrasing a subscription command in an email message and sending it to the list's subscription address.

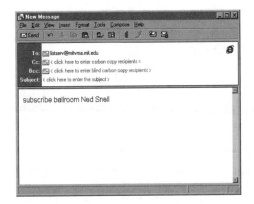

When composing your message, don't type anything the instructions don't ask for. If the instructions tell you to put the command in the Subject line, leave the message body blank. If the command belongs in the message body, leave the Subject line blank, and put nothing but the command in the body. (Many lists don't care whether you follow this rule, but because you can't predict which lists *do* care, it's best to always follow the rule.)

JUST A MINUTE

Because many listservs manage more than one list, the subscription command syntax often includes the name of the list, so the listserv knows which list you're subscribing to; for example:

```
subscribe listname firstname lastname
```

Reading the Welcome Message

Shortly after you send your subscription message, you'll receive a reply message from the list. A listserv may reply within a minute or two. After sending a subscription message to a listserv, stay online, wait a few minutes, and then check your email—the reply will probably be there. (Some listservs and manual lists may take a day or more to reply, so be patient, and don't resend the subscription message if you don't get an immediate reply.)

If you did not phrase your subscription message properly, the reply reiterates the subscription command syntax and usually includes instructions. You must compose and send another subscription message, carefully following any instructions in the reply.

After you subscribe successfully, you'll receive a Welcome message like the one shown in Figure 14.3.

14

Figure 14.3.

A Welcome message tells you that you've subscribed and also supplies general instructions.

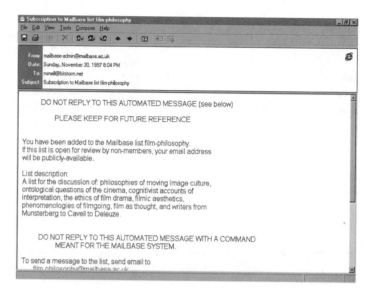

CAUTION

> Always, always, always read and save the Welcome message, if for no other reason than that it contains the instructions for *unsubscribing* to, or quitting, the mailing list if you choose to do so later.

The Welcome message contains a lot of valuable information, particularly

- ☐ A syntax diagram for phrasing the command to *un*subscribe. If and when you decide you no longer want to receive messages from the list, you'll need to send this command to the subscription address.

- ☐ The list address to which you must send all your contributions and the management address (which is usually the same as the subscription address, but not always).

- ☐ Syntax for other commands you may use to manage the way messages come to you. For example, many lists let you send a command to temporarily pause—stop sending you messages—if you go on vacation or want messages paused for any other reason.

- ☐ Any other rules or policies all members of the list are required to observe. These typically include the basic rules of netiquette (see "Observing Proper Netiquette" later in this hour).

14

JUST A MINUTE

Sometimes the Welcome message includes instructions to send a reply to the Welcome, to confirm your subscription. In such cases, you're not officially subscribed until you send a reply as instructed.

Always read and save the Welcome message, so you can refer to it when you need to know a command or policy or want to unsubscribe. If your email program lets you organize your messages in folders, create a special folder for Welcome messages, so they're easy to find and you don't accidentally delete them when cleaning up your Inbox. You may also want to print the Welcome message and file it.

Shortly after you receive the Welcome message (and reply to it, if so instructed), you'll begin receiving email messages from the list. How many and how often depends on the list, but it's not unusual to receive a dozen or more messages per day. Read anything that looks interesting; ignore (or delete) the rest.

JUST A MINUTE

Some mailing lists are purely informational. Mailing lists are designed not as a discussion forum, but to keep you abreast of news and developments in a particular company or other organization.

Usually, such lists don't have list addresses to which you can contribute. It's a one-way conversation; you just subscribe, and then read whatever shows up.

To Do: Subscribe to a List

To Do

Just for kicks, let's subscribe to a list. The following steps show you how to subscribe to the Ballroom list, which is devoted to ballroom and swing dancing, but if you've already found the address of another list you really want to subscribe to, feel free to substitute. (Also, if you go with the Ballroom list, I'll give you a chance to bail without subscribing, when the time comes.)

1. In your email program, start a new message.

2. In the To line, put the Ballroom list subscription address:

   `listserv@mitvma.mit.edu`

3. The instructions for the Ballroom list say that the command must be typed in the message body. So leave the Subject line blank, and skip to the body.

4. The syntax of the subscription command for this list is

   `subscribe ballroom your name`

14

Enter the command in the message body, replacing the words *your name* with your actual name. (Because the command does not say whether the name should be last-name-first or vice versa, it doesn't matter which you use.)

5. Send the message. After a few minutes, check your email. You will probably have received a Welcome message, prompting you to reply if you really want to subscribe.

6. To start receiving messages about ballroom dancing, reply to the message as instructed. To avoid subscribing, don't reply; the Welcome message expires in 48 hours.

Contributing to a Mailing List

You are not required to contribute to a mailing list. Many people simply read and enjoy the messages they receive, and never add their own comments or questions.

If you do feel inspired to contribute, just send a message to the list address. If the contribution is related to a previous message, use your email program's Reply feature to reply to the group, and include in the reply a quote of any portion of the original message that's relevant to your comment or question.

JUST A MINUTE

When using Reply to send a message to a mailing list, always double-check the To line in your message to be sure that it shows the correct list address.

Observing Proper Netiquette

How you communicate with private friends in email is between you and your friends. However, after you begin contributing to discussion groups—mailing lists and newsgroups—you're participating in a public forum, and have an obligation to follow a code of conduct that keeps the conversation pleasant and productive for all.

Netiquette—the unofficial code of online conduct—can be boiled down to the Golden Rule: Do unto others as you would have them do unto you. As you gain experience, you'll begin to notice things others do that bug you, such as quoting too much or writing sloppily. Obviously, those are the things you must remember not to do yourself.

The basics of being a good cyber-citizen, particularly in discussion groups, are given in the following list. Note that none of this stuff is law. If you skip a rule, the cyber-police will not show up at your door. Like all forms of courtesy, netiquette is not required, but highly recommended.

14

- [ ] **Don't shout**—SOME FOLKS LIKE TO TYPE ALL MESSAGES ONLY IN CAPITAL LETTERS, and some others overuse capital letters FOR EMPHASIS! Capitalize like a person, and use your word choices and phrasing for emphasis, saving the all-caps trick for rare, EXTREME EMPHASIS.

- [ ] **Stay on topic**—Nothing's more aggravating than subscribing to a list and then receiving all sorts of messages that veer off on tangents. If your message does not pertain directly to the discussion group's stated topic, don't send it.

- [ ] **Keep current**—Newcomers to a list or group, or folks who only drop in occasionally, tend to ask questions that have already been asked and answered a dozen times, which annoys the regulars. Keep up with the conversation, so you know what's going on. Read the FAQ, if one is available.

NEW TERM   *Frequently Asked Questions (FAQ)* is a file that contains a general list of common questions and answers pertaining to a particular list, newsgroup, web page, or other topic.

By reading FAQs (pronounced "faks"), you can quickly get up-to-speed on the background information shared by others in the group.

When a FAQ is available for a mailing list, you'll find instructions for obtaining the FAQ in the Welcome message.

- [ ] **Don't use sarcasm**—It's difficult to communicate sarcasm effectively in a written message. Often, exaggerated messages intended as sarcasm are taken literally by those who read them, and confusion or arguments ensue.

- [ ] **Keep personal discussions personal**—Before sending any message, ask yourself: Would this message interest the whole list, or is it really a personal message to just one member? If the message is really for one person, you can find that person's email address in the header information quoted in all list and newsgroup messages, and send your comment or question directly, in private.

JUST A MINUTE

> Avoid small, conversational contributions that add little information. For example, if someone posts a message with a great idea in it, don't send a reply to the group just to say "Great idea!" No one wants to go to the trouble of receiving and opening a message with so little to say.

- [ ] **Don't overquote**—When replying, cut quotes down to all that's necessary to show what you're replying to. When a series of replies builds up and nobody cuts the quotes, each message can be pages long even if it contains only one new sentence. Try to leave enough information so a newcomer to the conversation can tell what's being discussed, but cut everything else.

14

- ☐ **Write and spell well**—In the name of speed and efficiency, some folks boil their msg.s down to a grp. of abbrev.'s &/or shorthnd, or write toooo quikly and slopppilly. Do your readers the courtesy of writing whole words and complete sentences, and fix mistakes before you send.

- ☐ **Neither *flame* nor counterflame**—A *flame* is an angry tirade or attack in a message, the kind that flares when a debate grows into a spat. No matter how hot the argument gets, try to keep your cool. When flamed personally, don't rise to the bait: Flame wars only escalate, and no one ever wins.

  Some folks flame others for breaches of netiquette, but that's hypocritical. Take responsibility for your own online behavior, and let others worry about theirs.

- ☐ **Fit in**—Usually, I'm no fan of conformity. But every mailing list and newsgroup has its own, insular culture. After reading messages for awhile, you'll pick up a sense of the general technical level of the group, whether they're experts or novices (or both) on the topic at hand, the overall tone, catch phrases, vocabulary, and so on.

  By all means, be yourself—any group needs fresh ideas, new personalities. Try to be yourself within the style and culture of the group, to ensure that you can be understood by all.

Adding Personality with Smileys and Shorthand

Over the years, a system of symbols and shorthand has developed to enable folks to be more expressive in their messages: *smileys* and *shorthand*. You'll see both used online often, in discussion groups and in email.

JUST A MINUTE

Although I show you smileys and shorthand next, I'm doing so mainly to help you understand them in messages you receive. Except for the occasional, simple smiley face, I don't recommend using these in your contributions to discussion groups.

There are many newcomers online today who don't know smileys or shorthand, so if you use these, many of your readers won't understand you. Try to put all your meaning in your words, so everybody gets the message.

14

Smileys

Smileys are used to communicate the tone of a message, to add an emotional inflection. (In fact, smileys are sometimes called *emoticons*—emotional icons.) They're little pictures, usually of faces, that are built out of text characters.

To see the picture, you tilt your head to the left. For example, tilt your head to the left (or tilt this book to the right) while looking at the following smiley, which is made up of three characters: a colon, a dash, and a close parenthesis:

:-)

Looks like a little smiling face, doesn't it? Folks follow a statement with this smiley to indicate that the statement is a joke, or is made facetiously; for example:

Just for that, I'm leaving you everything in my will. :-)

Many different smileys exist, some so obscure that only the real net jocks use or understand them. You're likely only to see the basics, including the basic smile shown earlier, and also these:

:-(	Frown
;-)	Wink
:-0	Surprise
8-)	Smile with glasses or bug-eyed
:'-(	Crying
:-D	Laughing

JUST A MINUTE

> Some folks omit the nose from their smileys. For example:
>
> :)   ;)   :0

Shorthand

Shorthand abbreviations are used to carry a common phrase efficiently, to save space and typing. Some of these are commonly used offline, everyday, such as ASAP (As Soon As Possible). Another shorthand expression used commonly online is IMO (In My Opinion) and its cousin, IMHO (In My Humble Opinion). For example:

The Godfather is the greatest film of the '70s, IMHO.

Other popular shorthand expressions include

BTW	By The Way
B4	Before

14

FWIW	For What It's Worth
IBTD	I Beg To Differ
IOW	In Other Words
LOL	Laughing Out Loud (generally used to declare that a statement is laughable)
OTOH	On The Other Hand
ROTFL	Rolling On The Floor Laughing (generally used to declare that a statement is extremely laughable)

Summary

Mailing lists are easy. After you get straight on the difference between the list address and the management address, and learn how to phrase a subscription command, the rest is a cinch.

Mailing lists aren't for everyone, however. Personally, I don't use them much. I must manage so much work-related email traffic that the steady flow from a mailing list gets in my way. Fortunately, I can participate in the same kind of discussion in another way—*newsgroups*—that I find better suited to the way I work. You learn about newsgroups in the next hour.

Workshop

Q&A

Q I've seen forms in web pages that say I can fill them in to get on a mailing list related to the page's topic. How are those web-based mailing lists different from the regular ones?

A The lists you subscribe to through the web are not web-based. The web page merely supplies a convenient front-end to an otherwise normal mailing list.

You subscribe by filling in a web page form, but then the web page passes your form entries—name and email address—to a listserv, which emails you the usual Welcome message. From there, using the list is exactly like using any other mailing list.

Mailing lists you subscribe to through web forms are usually the informational type—designed to keep you posted about news and events in an organization—rather than the type intended for interactive discussion.

14

Quiz

Take the following quiz to see how much you've learned.

Questions

1. The command to subscribe to a mailing list

    a. Is always subscribe *listname firstname lastname*

    b. Is always subscribe [listname] [lastname] [firstname]

    c. Varies from list to list

    d. Must be expressed forcefully

2. True or false: It's a good idea to use smileys and shorthand expressions as much as possible, to give your messages character.

3. True or false: For a particular list, you usually send subscription commands and your questions and comments to the same address.

Answers

1. (c) The subscription command varies from list to list. Always read the subscription instructions.

2. False. Not everybody reads up on the net like you do. Many folks don't know what smileys and shorthand expressions mean, so it's best to avoid them except in email messages sent directly to people whom you know will understand them.

3. False. Lists generally have two separate addresses: One for management, one for list contributions. Don't mix them up.

Activity

Make a list of topics that interest you, then find a mailing list for each topic—but don't subscribe yet. In Hour 15, you'll learn how to find newsgroups. You can use your list of topics to find newsgroups related to each topic, then decide—for each topic—whether a newsgroup or mailing list would serve you best.

14

Hour 15

Reading and Posting to Newsgroups

Mailing lists (see Hour 14, "Joining a Mailing List") are a great way to keep up with a subject, but not always an efficient way. Some mailing lists can post 20 or more new messages a day, and many of those are trivial. Sure, you want to keep up with the subject, but you also don't want to be buried in email every day.

Newsgroups carry pretty much the same discussions that mailing lists do. In fact, many mailing lists and newsgroups covering the same topic carry the same conversation; they're hooked together so all messages sent to either the mailing list or the newsgroup show up in both. Unlike mailing lists, however, newsgroups don't come to you—you go to them. Whenever you want to catch up on the news, you access the newsgroup through your newsgroup client (newsreader), scroll through the list of current messages, and read just the ones that interest you.

At the end of this hour, you'll be able to answer the following questions:

☐ What are newsgroups?
☐ How do I set up my newsreader?

☐ How do I find and open a newsgroup?

☐ How do I navigate among the messages in a newsgroup and read them?

☐ How do I contribute to a newsgroup?

☐ How do I search for and display newsgroup messages through my browser?

Getting Started with Newsgroups

When you know how to use an email program, you know 90 percent of what you need to know to use newsgroups. Reading a message, composing a new message, and replying are all similar in an email program and a newsreader.

Where a newsreader differs, of course, is that it retrieves messages from, and posts messages to, Internet newsgroups, sometimes known as discussion groups or *Usenet*. The newsgroups and their messages are stored on a family of servers called *news servers* or *NNTP servers*.

 Sending a message to a newsgroup is known as *posting*, because you're publishing the message in a public forum, just as if you had posted a paper note on a bulletin board.

Your ISP or online service has a news server you are authorized to use for reading and contributing to newsgroups. Access to one news server is all you need; the messages sent to any news server on the Internet are automatically copied—at regular intervals—to all news servers.

On any news server, you can open any newsgroup and read any current message posted to that newsgroup, no matter which news server the message was originally posted to. That's why a newsgroup on an ISP's server in New York has messages on it from folks in Canada, California, and the United Kingdom.

Before you can open newsgroups and display their messages, you must configure your newsreader to contact your ISP's news server, and you must download the complete list of newsgroups from the server.

JUST A MINUTE

In general, all news servers carry the same newsgroups and current messages—but not exactly.

First, a few ISPs or online services do not carry all newsgroups, omitting those they deem potentially offensive to their customers, such as sex-oriented groups. A few ISPs carry only newsgroups specifically requested by their subscribers, instead of all 20,000+ groups. Some ISPs' servers carry special newsgroups of local interest that are not copied to other news servers.

15

15

> Beyond those differences, note that it takes a day or so for a message posted to one server to be copied to all the others. At any given time, a new message may be on some servers, but not yet on others.
>
> Finally, no news server keeps messages forever. After a set number of days, a newsgroup message is automatically deleted from the server. Each server has its own schedule for removing these old—*expired*—messages, so a message that's been deleted from one server may remain on others.

Configuring Your Newsreader

As with other types of clients, many different newsreaders are available. In the Big Internet suites, the programs are called

- ☐ **Collabra**—In Netscape Communicator. You can open Collabra from within the Navigator browser by choosing Communicator | Collabra Discussion Groups.

- ☐ **Outlook Express**—In Internet Explorer 4. Yep, it's the same program you use for email. You simply click your news server's name near the bottom of the folder list to shift Outlook Express into newsgroup mode. (Choosing the server changes the toolbar buttons and menu choices to those you need for newsgroups). You can open Outlook Express directly in newsgroup mode by choosing Go | News from within the browser.

If you don't already have a newsreader, you may apply the file-finding techniques from Hour 11, "Finding Programs and Files," to search for one, or browse a directory of newsreaders on Yahoo! at

www.yahoo.com/Computers_and_Internet/Software/Internet/Usenet/

JUST A MINUTE

> If you use an online service, such as America Online or CompuServe, you may not be able to choose your own newsreader; you may be required to use the online service interface—the tool you use for accessing the service's non-Internet content—to access newsgroups.

All newsreaders have a configuration dialog box on which you enter the information required for communicating with your ISP's news server. That dialog box always requires the address of your ISP's news server. If your newsreader is not part of a suite (and thus cannot copy configuration information from the email component), the configuration dialog box also requires your email address and full name.

You'll find the configuration dialog box

☐ For Collabra, by choosing Edit | Preferences to open the Preferences dialog box. In the list of Categories, choose Mail & Groups. Complete the configuration settings in the Mail & Groups category's Groups Server subcategory.

☐ For Outlook Express, by completing the News dialog boxes (see Figure 15.1) of the Connection Wizard (see Hour 4, "Connecting to the Internet"). If you choose your news server folder in Outlook Express without having configured first, the Connection Wizard opens automatically.

Figure 15.1.

Use the Connection Wizard to configure Outlook Express for newsgroups.

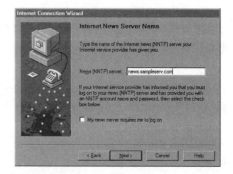

Downloading the Newsgroups List

After your newsreader knows how to contact the server, you must download the complete list of newsgroups, which usually takes just a few minutes. If you open some newsreaders (including Collabra and Outlook Express) without first having downloaded the list, a prompt appears, asking whether you want to download the list (see Figure 15.2).

Figure 15.2.

Before you can use newsgroups, you must download the complete newsgroups list.

If your newsreader does not prompt you, find a button or menu item for downloading the list:

☐ In Collabra, click the Subscribe button on the toolbar. On the dialog box that appears, click the Get Groups button.

☐ In Outlook Express, click the name of your news server, then choose Tools | Newsgroups. In the dialog box that appears, click Reset List.

15

15

TIME SAVER

The list of newsgroups changes periodically, adding new groups and removing others. Collabra, Outlook Express, and some other newsreaders detect automatically when the list changes and display a prompt, asking whether you want to update your list.

If your newsreader does not detect changes in the list, it's smart to download the full list again once a month or so, to keep current.

Finding and Subscribing to Newsgroups

After the list has been downloaded to your computer, you can find and subscribe to any newsgroups you want. While exploring web pages devoted to topics that interest you, you'll probably come across the names of related newsgroups. But newsgroups are easy to find, with or without a web page's help.

TIME SAVER

Unlike mailing lists, you are not required to subscribe to a newsgroup to use it. All subscribing really does is add the group to an easy-access list in your newsreader, to make visiting it convenient.

Most people have a small list of groups they visit often, so subscribing makes sense. In most newsreaders, however, you can pick a newsgroup out of the full list, or enter the group's name in a dialog box to open the list without subscribing.

Newsgroups are perhaps the one Internet activity where names are a reliable indicator of content. Newsgroups are organized under a system of names and categories. The leftmost portion of the name shows the top-level category in which the group sits; each portion further to the right more narrowly determines the subject of the group.

For example, the top-level category *rec* contains recreational newsgroups, those dedicated to a recreational—rather than professional—discussion of their topics. So the hypothetical newsgroup name

```
rec.sports.basketball.womens
```

indicates that the discussion focuses on a recreational interest in women's basketball. Thousands of rec groups exist, many `rec.sports` groups, several `rec.sports.basketball` groups, and just one `rec.sports.basketball.womens` newsgroup. See how it works?

Some of the other major top-level categories are

☐ **alt**—Alternative newsgroups, those in which the most free-wheeling conversations are accepted.

☐ **biz**—Business newsgroups and ads.

☐ **comp**—Computer-related newsgroups.

☐ **k12**—Education-related groups.

☐ **misc**—Miscellaneous.

☐ **sci**—Science-related groups.

To Do: Choose, Subscribe to, and Open Groups in Collabra

To subscribe to and open groups in Collabra, follow these steps:

1. Open Collabra, and display the newsgroup list (see Figure 15.3). It appears automatically right after you download the full list, but you can redisplay it at any time by clicking the Subscribe button.

Figure 15.3.

Choose groups from the full list to subscribe to them.

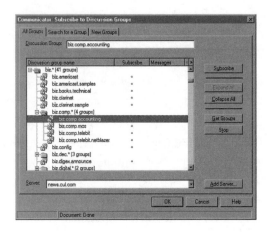

2. In the All Groups tab, display the group's name in the Discussion Group box. There are several ways to do this:

☐ If you know the exact name of the group you want to subscribe to, type the name in the box.

☐ Use the list to scroll to the group name, then click it. In the list, the groups are presented alphabetically and also organized by category; display a category's subcategories or groups by clicking the plus sign (+) that precedes it.

15

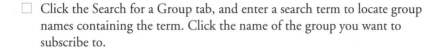

    ☐ Click the Search for a Group tab, and enter a search term to locate group names containing the term. Click the name of the group you want to subscribe to.

3. When the name of the group you want to subscribe to appears in the Discussion Group box, click the Subscribe button to subscribe to it. You can then select another group to subscribe to or click OK to close the dialog box.

4. In the Message Center (which appears whenever you open Collabra), your subscribed newsgroups are listed like subfolders under your news server name. If you don't see newsgroups listed under your server, click the plus sign (+) to the left of the server name to display them.

5. To open a newsgroup, double-click its name in the list.

To Do: Choose, Subscribe to, and Open Groups in Outlook Express

To subscribe to and open groups in Outlook Express, follow these steps:

1. Display the newsgroup list. It appears automatically right after you download the full list, but you can redisplay it at any time by choosing Tools | Newsgroups.

2. The list dialog box has three tabs: All, Subscribed, and New. Choose the All tab to display the full list.

3. To find a newsgroup, you can scroll down the alphabetical list. To locate a group about a particular topic, type a word related to that topic in the box at the top of the dialog box; Outlook Express narrows the list to groups whose names include that word.

4. When you see in the list the name of a group you want to subscribe to, click it to select it.

5. Click the Subscribe button to subscribe to the selected newsgroup. You can now select and subscribe to another group, or click OK to close the dialog box.

6. The name of your news server appears near the bottom of Outlook Express's folder list, along the left side of the window. Click it, and your subscribed newsgroups appear in the main pane. To open a newsgroup and display its current message list, click it.

Reading Newsgroup Messages

After you open and display a newsgroup's message list (peek ahead to Figure 15.4), reading messages is just like reading email messages in an email client. In Collabra or Outlook Express, you single-click an item in the list to display it in the preview pane or double-click it to display the message in its own window.

TIME SAVER

The message lists you see in an email program generally show messages that have been copied to your computer. But the messages in the list you see when you open a newsgroup are not on your computer; they're on the news server.

All that's been copied to your computer are the message headers, to make up the list. When you display any particular message, that message is then copied to your computer. Because the messages aren't copied until you request them, you must stay online while working with newsgroups.

Some newsreaders support *offline news reading*; you can configure them to automatically download messages from newsgroups so you can read them later, offline. In Outlook Express, you can download all messages from a newsgroup by choosing Tools | Download All.

The tricky part about reading news messages is organizing the list in a way that works for you. Most newsreaders let you arrange the messages in myriad ways: alphabetically by subject, by author, by date, and so on. (The options for sorting the message list in Collabra, Outlook Express, and most other Windows and Mac newsreaders appear on the View menu.) The most useful sorting, however, is by *thread*.

NEW TERM   In a newsgroup, a *thread* is one particular conversation—a message and all replies to that message (and replies to those replies, and so on).

In effect, threads group messages by subject. Two messages can have the same subject but not the same thread, if neither is a reply to the other (or a reply to a reply to the other). If you sort messages by thread, and then by subject, you'll get all threads on a given subject grouped together.

When you sort messages by thread (see Figure 15.4), you can follow the flow of the conversation by clicking your way, in order, through the messages to see how the discussion has progressed.

In most newsreaders, when messages are sorted by threads, the replies to a message do not appear automatically in the list; instead, a plus sign (+) appears next to the message's listing, to indicate that there are submessages—replies—to that message. To display the replies, click the plus sign.

15

Figure 15.4.

You can organize your newsgroup message list by thread, to better follow the flow of individual conversations.

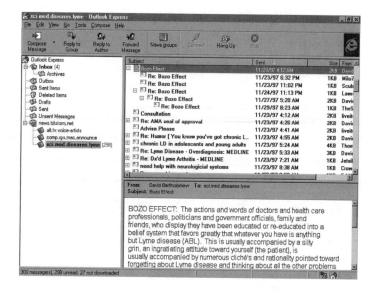

Composing and Replying to Messages

You compose and reply to messages in a newsreader exactly as you do in an email program. The only differences are in the message header, because instead of addressing a message to a person, you're addressing it to a newsgroup.

JUST A MINUTE

The only other important difference between sending email and newsgroup messages is the terminology you see applied on buttons and menu items:

- ☐ In email, you click Send to send a message; in a newsreader, it's either Send or Post.

- ☐ In email, you click Reply to reply to a message; in a newsreader, it's either Reply or Respond.

The easiest way to deal with that difference is to start in the right place. For example, when you want to compose a new message (not a reply) and post it on a newsgroup, begin by opening that newsgroup, then click your newsreader's button for composing a new message (it's New Msg in Collabra, Compose Message in Outlook Express). When the message window opens, you'll see that it's preaddressed to the currently open newsgroup.

When replying, open the message to which you want to reply; then click the Reply (or Respond) button on the message window in which that message appears. In the message window that opens (see Figure 15.5), the message is preaddressed to the appropriate newsgroup, the subject line is correctly phrased to add the reply to the same thread as the original message, and the original message is quoted in the message area. Just add your comments, and edit the quote as necessary.

Figure 15.5.

Start a new message or reply while viewing the message list of a newsgroup, and that message is preaddressed to the open newsgroup.

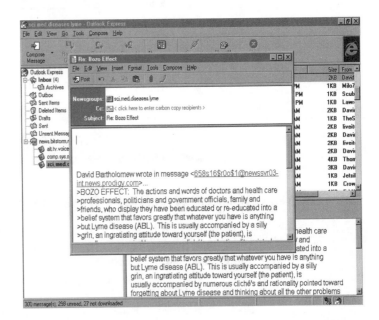

After completing a new message or reply, send the message by clicking the button or menu item labeled Send or Post.

TIME SAVER

When you choose to reply, most newsreaders provide the option of replying to the newsgroup or sending an email reply directly to the author of the message you're replying to. The email option is handy when your reply is really intended only for the author, not the whole group.

JUST A MINUTE

As in a mailing list (see Hour 14), always be mindful of your netiquette when posting to a newsgroup, and resist using smileys and shorthand.

15

Finding and Reading Newsgroup Messages Through Your Browser

15

Many web browsers can display newsgroup messages. Note, however, that you cannot use a web browser to contribute to a newsgroup, so you'll still need a newsreader to really get into newsgroups.

A web browser's display capability comes in handy when a search tool turns up a newsgroup message. Newsgroup messages show up in a search tool's hot list as links; if your browser can display newsgroup messages, clicking one of those links displays the message. (In some suites, the newsreader and the browser are linked so clicking a link that leads to a newsgroup message automatically opens the newsreader to display the message.)

AltaVista is among the search tools that can find newsgroup messages. In the following To Do, you'll use AltaVista to locate a message, then display that message in your browser.

To Do: Find and Display a Newsgroup Message in Your Browser

To find and display a newsgroup message in your browser, follow these steps:

1. Open your web browser, and go to AltaVista at `altavista.digital.com`.

2. Drop down the small list labeled Search, right above the search term box (see Figure 15.6).

Figure 15.6.

Choosing to search newsgroups (Usenet) in AltaVista.

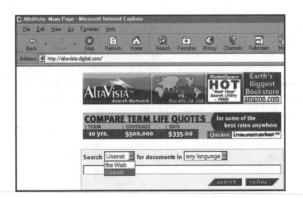

3. From the list, choose Usenet to instruct AltaVista to find newsgroup messages instead of web pages.

4. In the search term box, type a term for a topic you're interested in. (I typed Woodpecker, because there's one in my yard right now.)

5. Click Search. The hit list appears, showing links to newsgroup messages (see Figure 15.7). Observe that the link is also the subject of the message; to the right of the link appears the name of the group on which the message was posted.

Figure 15.7.

A hit list of newsgroup messages found by an AltaVista search.

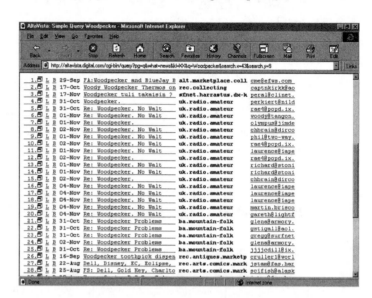

6. Click a link. The message appears in your browser (see Figure 15.8).

Figure 15.8.

Click a newsgroup link, and the message appears in your browser.

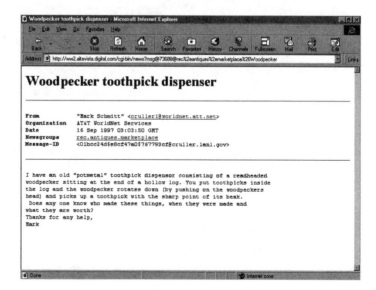

15

Summary

If the web is like a library, newsgroups are like a barber shop or beauty salon: The information you get from the former is generally more reliable and complete, but the information you get from the latter—although often pure opinion—is usually more personal, immediate, and fun.

Perhaps the best way to stay informed about any topic is to make sure you frequent both related web pages *and* related newsgroups, and use what you learn in each to balance the other.

Workshop

Q&A

Q When I search for newsgroup messages in my browser, lots of the links in the hit list seem to be dead ends. Am I doing something wrong?

A No, you're not doing anything wrong. Because of the inconsistencies among the contents of news servers, it's common to click a link to a message only to see a note appear that the message doesn't exist. The search engine has determined that the message exists on *some* news servers, but that's no guarantee that the message is on *your* news server. No big deal: Just keep trying the links in the hit list until you hit a good one, or try another search.

Quiz

Take the following quiz to see how much you've learned.

Questions

1. How many news servers do most folks access through their news readers?

    a. 1

    b. 8

    c. 74

    d. Roughly 1,024

2. *Threads* organize a list of newsgroup messages

    a. By author

    b. By importance, and within importance by date

    c. By grouping a message together with its anti-messages

    d. By grouping a message together with replies

3. The newsgroup `biz.manufacturers.jobs` is probably a

   a. Detergent-oriented newsgroup

   b. Showbiz-oriented newsgroup

   c. Business-oriented newsgroup

   d. A newsgroup dedicated to overworked, busy people

Answers

1. (a) Your ISP's one news server holds the same general collection of groups and current messages that all others do (give or take). In any event, 1 is probably all you've got.

2. (d) Threads follow a message with all replies to that message.

3. (c) Biz groups are about business.

Activity

Did you make a list of topics you're interested in, as I suggested at the end of Hour 14? Use that list now to find and explore related newsgroups, and begin selecting which information you want to have delivered to you via mailing lists, and which you want to get from newsgroups, as needed.

Hour 16

Putting a Stop to Junk Mail

Within a few weeks after you begin using the Internet, you'll make an unpleasant discovery: The same sort of take-no-prisoners direct marketing types who telemarket you at suppertime and stuff offers in your mailbox have found you online. Over time, you'll see an ever-increasing number of ads, offers, chain letters, pyramid schemes, and scams in your Inbox.

It's easy and cheap for an advertiser to automatically crank out an email ad to thousands—millions, even—of Internet users all at once. (Net veterans call these messages *spam* because they repeat and multiply the way the word spam does in a song from an old *Monty Python* skit.) These messages often have subject lines designed to entice you into reading the message (FREE $$$) or to trick you into doing so (MESSAGE FROM AN OLD FRIEND). As the Internet population has grown, so has the spam problem.

In this hour, you'll learn not only how to deal with spam and spammers, but also how to better manage and organize your incoming email. At the end of the hour, you'll be able to answer the following questions:

☐ How can I minimize my exposure to spam when surfing the net?

☐ Where can I get a utility to automatically delete or hide the spam I receive?

☐ How can I configure filters in my email program to deal with spam?

JUST A MINUTE

> I should say right up front that nothing today can prevent or eliminate spam altogether—the problem is too pervasive. By following the advice in this chapter, however, you can minimize spam to a tolerable amount. Until and unless it's outlawed, spam will remain as sure a fact of life as death and taxes.

Spam-Preventive Surfing

The more widely known your email address is, the more spam you'll get—it's that simple. So a logical first step in stopping spam is being careful about how and when you reveal your email address.

Unfortunately, you cannot fully enjoy the Internet while keeping your email address a secret. Many online activities, such as shopping or posting to newsgroups, create an online record of your email address. In fact, anytime you send email, an unscrupulous spammer may harvest your address by intercepting messages on their way across the net.

Still, you can effectively reduce the extent to which your address is known by making some smart surfing choices. In particular, be careful about

☐ **Forms**—Be careful how and when you fill out online forms or surveys. A growing number of web sites request that you complete a form to "register" to use the site; the form data is almost always used for marketing and often for spamming. On any site where you might complete a form, look for a link to a Privacy Policy; some web sites promise in that policy not to spam you or to sell your information to spammers.

☐ **Newsgroup postings**—When you post to a newsgroup, a spammer can easily learn two things about you: your email address and that you're interested in the newsgroup's topic.

That's valuable direct marketing information; if you post a message on a newsgroup about a particular kind of product, you can expect to receive spam trying to sell you such a product. If you post to a sex-related newsgroup, you will soon receive spam selling phone sex or other sex-related stuff. You can usually *read* newsgroup messages anonymously—but when you post, you reveal your address. So watch where you post.

16

JUST A MINUTE

Some people use their newsreader's configuration dialog box to enter a phony email address, to prevent spammers from learning their address from their postings. But this tactic has major drawbacks:

☐ First, a savvy spammer can still learn your address in other ways.

☐ Second, a phony address prevents others in the newsgroup from contacting you for legitimate purposes.

☐ Third, if your email program and newsreader are integrated (as they would be in a suite), this approach may prevent legitimate replies to your email messages from reaching you.

☐ Perhaps most important, hiding behind a phony identity is a trick the spammers use, and it's ethically iffy. You can't solve a problem by descending to the enemy's tactics.

16

☐ **Cookies**—Cookies are files on your computer stored there by a web site, such as an online store, to record information about you that the page can access next time you visit. Unfortunately, the cookies on your computer—which may contain your email address and other personal data—may be read not only by the servers that put them there, but by other servers you visit, who may use that information for spam. See Hour 7, "Protecting Your Privacy (and Other Security Stuff)," to learn how to control cookies.

☐ **Mailing lists**—When you subscribe to mailing lists, your name, email address, and your interest in the list's topic are recorded in a database that may be accessed and copied easily by a spammer, particularly if the list is managed by a listserv. (Some listservs let you keep your address private; read the list's Welcome message for information about a CONCEAL command.)

A newsgroup covering the same topic is a safer choice, as long as you don't post to it. If you will contribute to the discussion, the mailing list is still less spam-risky than the newsgroup.

JUST A MINUTE

Stopping spam is a little trickier for users of online services than for users of ISPs. The online services derive some of their revenue from advertisers, for providing access to you. So they're not too keen on letting you block those ads.

If you use America Online, you can reduce spam by signing up for the Preferred Mail function (keyword PREFERRED MAIL), which blocks messages from many spammers.

> Also, experts on AOL and spam advise users to avoid posting messages on AOL's forums, and to use Internet newsgroups instead. Despite the spam exposure risk in newsgroups, AOL forums are notoriously harvested by spammers.

Filtering Out Spam

If you can't stop the spam from coming, your next best bet is to avoid having to look at it. A variety of programs and techniques *filter* your incoming email to remove unwanted messages.

 You configure *filters* in email programs or utilities to selectively delete or file messages under specified circumstances.

For example, if there's a person whose messages you never want to read, you can configure a filter so all messages from that person's email address are deleted automatically upon receipt; you'll never see them.

Filters cannot completely remove spam. To set up filters to delete all spam messages, you'd have to know the address of every spammer. No master list of spammers exists (new folks start spamming every day, and slippery spammers change addresses often), but you can pick up lists of many of the worst offenders, and then import or manually copy the lists into your email program so you can create filters to block messages from them.

Use the URLs below to learn about and download lists of spammers for filtering:

- ☐ **The BadMail from Spam List**—www.webeasy.com/spam/
- ☐ **The Network Abuse Clearinghouse**—www.abuse.net/
- ☐ **Multimedia Marketing Group**—www.mmgco.com/nospam/
- ☐ **The Blacklist of Internet Advertisers**—www-math.uni-paderborn.de/%7Eaxel/BL/ #list

TIME SAVER

You can pick up utilities that combine a filtering system with a spammers database, for fast and easy configuration of anti-spam filters. Check out

SpamNet at www.spamnet.com

SpamKiller at novasoft.base.org

SpamBlaster (Mac) at www.gooware.com

eFilter at www.eflash.com

16

Finding Filters in Your Email Program

Most full-featured email programs have their own built-in filtering systems you can apply to manage incoming mail and, to a limited extent, control spam.

If you don't have a list of spammers, or if creating filters for a long list is too difficult, you can deal with spam by creating filters for your legitimate contacts.

It works like this: If you have a steady group of people you communicate with regularly, create a filter that automatically stores all messages from those people in a separate folder. When you receive email, all the important messages are automatically stored in the folder, while all the spam stays in your Inbox, where you can ignore it. (You'll still want to scan your Inbox from time to time to check for legitimate messages from folks you haven't added to your filters.)

You can find the filters dialog boxes:

- ☐ In Messenger, by choosing Edit | Mail Filters.
- ☐ In Outlook Express, by choosing Tools | Inbox Assistant.

To Do: Create Filters in Messenger

To give you an idea of how to set up filters, this To Do shows how to create filters in Messenger that will automatically move all messages you receive from your steady email partners into a new folder, leaving behind any other messages (including spam) in your Inbox:

1. Open your Inbox in Messenger.
2. Choose File | New Folder to open the New Folder dialog box.
3. Create the folder as a subfolder of the Inbox by typing a name (such as "Friends") and clicking OK.
4. Choose Edit | Mail Filters to open the Mail Filters dialog box.
5. Click the New button to open the Filter Rules dialog box (see Figure 16.1).

Figure 16.1.

To create a filter, you specify how a message matching certain criteria is to be handled.

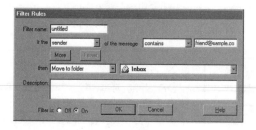

6. Create a new filter to move all mail from one of your email partners into the new folder as follows (refer to Figure 16.1 as necessary):
   - ☐ Following "If the," choose sender.
   - ☐ Following "of the message," choose contains.

- ☐ In the box to the right of contains, type the email address.
- ☐ Following "then," choose Move to folder.
- ☐ Next to Move to folder, choose the folder you created in step 3.
- ☐ Next to "Filter is" at the bottom of the dialog box, choose On.
- ☐ Click OK to save the filter and return to the Mail Filters dialog box.

7. Repeat steps 5 and 6 for each of your other legitimate email partners.

8. After receiving any email, you will find any messages from your steady partners in the folder you created in step 3, while spam and other messages remain in the Inbox.

TIME SAVER

Many spam messages leave the To or From line of the message header blank. Because any of your legitimate contacts will probably use the To and From lines, you can filter out some spam by creating a filter that automatically deletes, or moves into a separate folder, any messages with a blank To or From.

The Last Resort: Move

When all else fails, if you're still getting too much junk mail, there's one reliable (albeit temporary) solution: Change ISPs, or ask your current ISP to change your email address.

When you change your email address, spam directed to your old address can't reach you. (Be sure to inform all your legitimate email partners of your new address, and instruct your old ISP not to forward email to your new address.) If your address has found its way into lots of spam databases, you can get a clean start this way.

Eventually, spammers will find you. But if you start clean with a new address, and then diligently apply the steps you learned in this hour, you may be able to keep the spammers at bay.

CAUTION

Some folks try to stop spam by sending angry replies to spammers. This approach never works. Often, the "From" line in the spam is left empty, or filled with a dummy or "forged" email address, so a reply won't even reach the real spammer. When angry replies do reach spammers, they are generally ignored.

Many spam messages include "removal" instructions, telling you that if you reply to the message and include the words "REMOVE ME" or a similar phrase in the subject line, you'll receive no further messages. In some cases, doing so may work. But in many cases, the "REMOVE ME"

bit is actually a trick intended to make you verify your email address. In such cases, following the removal instructions won't remove you from the spammer's list, and may even *increase* the amount of spam you get.

The moral? Never do anything an unsolicited email tells you to do, even if the instruction claims to be for your benefit.

16

Summary

Spam can't be stopped, but it can be controlled. By watching where you surf and who gets your email address, and by deploying filters intelligently, you can prevent spam from intruding too severely into your day-to-day messaging activity.

Workshop

Q&A

Q At the start of the hour, you mentioned outlawing spam. Is that going to happen?

A Many efforts are underway to control or eliminate spam through legislation, but it's impossible today to say which, if any, of these efforts will succeed.

One of the most promising campaigns seeks not to enact new law against spam, but to extend an existing law—the prohibition of junk faxes—to also cover email. You can learn more about that campaign on the web page for CAUCE, the Coalition Against Unsolicited Commercial Email (www.cauce.org), which also provides links to many other anti-spam resources.

And if you really want to do something productive about spam, let your congressperson know how you feel. You can find your congressperson's email address from the web page at www.house.gov/writerep/.

Quiz

Take the following quiz to see how much you've learned.

Questions

1. True or false: A good way to stop spam is to send the spammer a nasty, scary message.

2. A spammer can get your email address:
   a. From your newsgroup postings
   b. From cookies on your computer
   c. From databases containing form entries you've made
   d. All of the above

Answers

1. False. That approach almost never works, and it makes *you* look like the problem.
2. (d) All are ways a spammer can get your address. They can also get your address from mailing lists you belong to.

Activity

Review your Inbox and estimate the number of spam messages you receive each day. After you implement any prevention measures, start keeping track of the number of spam messages you receive each week or month to determine the long-term effectiveness of your efforts.

16

PART
V

Beyond Browsing: Using Advanced Internet Tools

Hour

Hour 17

Voice and Video Conferencing

Both the Netscape Communicator and Internet Explorer 4 suites include a program for live, real-time conferencing through the Internet. In Communicator, it's called Conference, and in Internet Explorer, it's called NetMeeting, but no matter: The two programs are similar, and still more such programs are available from the web.

With one of these programs, you can have a live conversation—much like a telephone call—with anyone else on the Internet who uses the same conferencing program that you do. Depending on what you pay for Internet service and how far away your caller is, conducting such "Internet telephone" calls may be substantially cheaper than making a long-distance telephone call, because the call costs you nothing beyond what you already pay for your Internet account. You can, in effect, make a one-hour call to France for free (if your French friend has an Internet account and the same conferencing software you have).

These programs do more than just carry a conversation. You can have a text-based chat (like a chat client), draw and type messages on a collaborative whiteboard, and even add video to the conversation.

At the end of this hour, you'll be able to answer the following questions:

- ☐ What can I do with NetMeeting, Conference, and other Internet conferencing tools?
- ☐ What hardware do I need to have a voice or video conference?
- ☐ How do I set up and configure NetMeeting and Conference?
- ☐ How do I make a call?
- ☐ How do I accept a call from someone else?
- ☐ What advanced conference features can I use?

Understanding Conferencing and "Internet Phone Calls"

Conferencing is a different animal from the Internet activities you've explored so far. Before venturing into conferencing, it's useful to understand a little more about how it works.

How It Works—and Doesn't Work

Most Internet activities are *standardized*; that is, they're based on agreed-upon rules that enable all different programs and systems to interact. For example, because of standards, you can send a message with one email program, and your recipient can read it in another. The difference in programs doesn't matter, because all Internet email programs follow the same standards.

Conferencing has yet to be standardized (although standardization efforts are underway). For that reason, those with whom you share a conference must use the same conferencing program you do. Using NetMeeting, you can conference only with other NetMeeting users. Ditto Netscape's Conference.

JUST A MINUTE

The latest version of Netscape's Conference supports an emerging standard, called H.323, that enables different programs to join in a conference (as long as both programs support H.323).

This standard is supported by few other programs today, however, and even among supporting programs, compatibility is not reliable. For now, in general, you must conference only with others using the same program you use.

Obviously, this is a severe limitation; you cannot simply dial up any friend on the Internet and conference. Rather, you must first contact your conferencing partners by phone or email,

17

and agree upon what conferencing software you will use when you call one another. In effect, you must establish your own standard for your community of conferencing partners.

TIME SAVER

If your partners use a variety of programs, nothing prevents you from installing different conferencing programs and using different programs to talk to different folks.

Microsoft NetMeeting and Netscape Conference are included in their respective suites. You can also download them.

Get NetMeeting at

www.microsoft.com/netmeeting/

Get Conference at

home.netscape.com/comprod/products/communicator/conference.html

Other popular conferencing programs include

> Internet Phone at www.vocaltec.com

> PowWow at www.tribal.com/powwow

You can find other conferencing programs in Yahoo!'s Internet Telephone programs directory at

www.yahoo.com/Business_and_Economy/Companies/Computers/Software/
Internet/Internet_Phone/Titles/

Hardware You Need

The most popular form of conferencing through these products is *voice conferencing*, speaking and listening just as you would in a telephone call.

JUST A MINUTE

In addition to voice conferencing, some programs also support video conferencing, in which you see the person with whom you're speaking (and they see you), and text conferencing, which are conversations carried out through typed messages.

See "Advanced Conferencing Techniques" near the end of this hour.

To have a voice conference, you must have the following equipment installed and configured in your computer:

- ☐ A sound card
- ☐ A microphone, either attached to your sound card or built into your computer. In a voice conference, you speak into the mic.

☐ Speakers or headphones, attached to your sound card or built into your PC. You'll hear your partner's words through the speakers or headphones.

The sound quality of voice conferences is highly variable; an Internet voice conference never sounds as clear as a phone call, even on the best equipment. Still, it's important to know that the better your equipment, the more clear the call will sound.

In particular, more expensive, 32-bit sound cards enable a much clearer conversation than cheaper, 16-bit or 8-bit cards (although those work). An external microphone connected to your sound card is usually preferable to any built-in mic; built-in mics tend to be low-quality, and pick up too much background noise from the computer.

TIME SAVER

Most sound cards made recently support full-duplex communications; that is, when having a voice conference through them, you can talk and listen at the same time, just as you would in a phone call.

Older, cheaper cards support only half-duplex sound. When conferencing through a half-duplex sound card, you and your partner must take turns speaking and listening, as if you were using a speaker phone or walkie-talkies. ("How are you? Over!")

The speed of your Internet connection also plays a role. The faster your connection, the clearer the conversation. Connections of 28.8Kbps or faster provide acceptable sound; you'll hear heavy static and occasional interruptions.

Setting Up for Conferencing

Before you can use a conferencing program, you must supply it with a little information.

The first time you start Conference or NetMeeting, it launches a Setup Wizard to collect this information from you. Just work your way through the steps to configure your conferencing program.

The following To Do shows how to set up Microsoft NetMeeting. Note that setting up Conference is nearly identical.

To Do: Set Up NetMeeting

To set up NetMeeting, follow these steps:

1. Open NetMeeting. You can open NetMeeting from within Internet Explorer 4 by choosing Go | Internet Call. The wizard opens.

2. Read the introductory message, and then click the Next button to get started. The dialog box shown in Figure 17.1 appears.

The first thing you need to decide is whether you want to log on to a NetMeeting directory server when you start the application, and if so, which one. In most cases, this is a good idea because the directory server is where you will probably find the people you want to talk to. The server can also list your name in the directory so other people on the Internet know you're online and can call you.

I suggest leaving the Log On to a Directory Server When NetMeeting Starts check box checked, and leave the What Directory Server You Would Like to Use? list set to ils.microsoft.com for now. You can change both options later if you need to.

Figure 17.1.

The NetMeeting Setup Wizard helps you configure NetMeeting.

3. Choose your server options, and then click Next. The dialog box shown in Figure 17.2 appears.

   NetMeeting wants to know some things about you. This information will show up on the directory server that you chose in the preceding dialog box whenever you are logged on.

Figure 17.2.

Enter the information you want NetMeeting to use for you on the directory server.

4. Type the information you want to have listed, and click the Next button to continue.

CAUTION

Before the Setup Wizard will let you continue to step 5, you have to enter at least your first and last name and your email address in the dialog box shown in Figure 17.2.

As with Chat (see Hour 18, "Chatting Live!"), it pays to be discreet and cautious when using personal information in NetMeeting. Directory servers, like some chat servers, are cruised by some lonely, creepy people to whom you may not want to reveal too much about yourself. In the dialog box shown in Figure 17.2, consider using a phony name and email address, just to preserve your privacy.

5. On the next screen (see Figure 17.3), you decide which category in the directory to list yourself in: Personal Use, Business Use, or Adults-Only Use. Choose the option that is appropriate for how you intend to use NetMeeting, and then click the Next button to continue. A dialog box informing you that you're about to configure your sound card for NetMeeting opens.

Figure 17.3.

Choose the category that best describes how you will use NetMeeting.

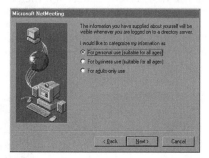

6. Click Next. A dialog box opens, listing your sound card as the *wave device* (sound card) that NetMeeting will use for recording (sending your voice to others) and playback (playing others' voices to you).

7. If the device listed is your sound card, click Next. Otherwise, use the drop-down lists to select the correct devices, and then click Next. The dialog box shown in Figure 17.4 opens. Here you tell NetMeeting what type of connection to the Internet you have.

17

8. Click the correct option, and then click Next. A dialog box appears in which you help NetMeeting set the microphone level so the people you talk to can hear you clearly.

Figure 17.4.

Choose the correct type of Internet connection.

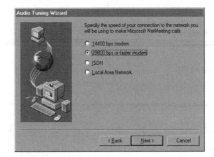

9. Click the Start Recording button, and then immediately begin reading the paragraph that begins "Microsoft NetMeeting enables you to...", speaking clearly and as loudly as you would speak during a voice call in NetMeeting. NetMeeting records your voice for about nine seconds, using your voice's strength to set a recording level for future NetMeeting sessions (see Figure 17.5).

10. When the Tuning Progress indicator reaches the end, NetMeeting stops recording. Don't worry if you haven't finished reading the paragraph; just click the Next button to continue.

Figure 17.5.

Set your microphone level so you can be heard clearly.

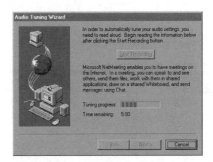

11. A final dialog box appears, reporting that you've configured NetMeeting. Click Finish to close the wizard.

NetMeeting starts and logs on to the directory server you chose. After you're logged on, you see a list of other users who are logged on to the same server. You can scroll through the list (which is sorted by email address) and find your name in there. Now anyone who wants to talk to you can find your name on the list and call you.

Getting Around in NetMeeting

NetMeeting has a simple interface that's easy to figure out. In the main screen (see Figure 17.6), the biggest section is the list of people logged on to the directory server that you chose. To its left are tabs that enable you to change what you see in the main view.

Above the directory listing are the Category and Server drop-down lists. Above those lists is the audio level adjustment toolbar. Finally, the toolbar and menus are at the top of the window, as with most Windows applications.

This section is a quick tour of each of these areas, one at a time.

Figure 17.6.

NetMeeting divides conferencing activities into a series of tabs.

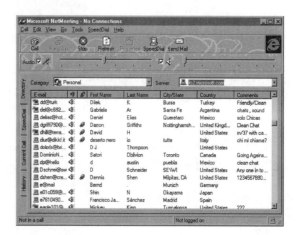

The Directory Listing

When you first start NetMeeting, you see a list of people. These are the people in the category you selected and on the server you selected when you ran the NetMeeting Setup Wizard. Because I chose ils.microsoft.com as my server and put myself in the For Personal Use category, I can see the list of everyone who made the same choices.

In this list, you see eight columns:

- ☐ **Email**—The person's email address.
- ☐ **Audio**—A small yellow speaker in this column means that this person can talk to you.
- ☐ **Video**—A small gray video camera in this column means that this person can send live video over the Internet.
- ☐ **First Name**—The person's first name.
- ☐ **Last Name**—The person's last name.

17

- [ ] **City/State**—The city and state that this person is currently in.
- [ ] **Country**—The country that this person is in.
- [ ] **Comments**—Comments, if any, that this person entered in the comments field.

CAUTION

> Keep in mind that all this information, other than that in the Audio and Video columns, is entered by the person using NetMeeting. Some people choose not to reveal their true identities or locations. You shouldn't accept the information listed here as 100 percent accurate.

By default, the listing is sorted by email address, but you can sort it by any information you like. To sort the entries by a different column, click the column header. For example, if you want the entries sorted by country, you can click the Country heading above the listings.

The Category and Server Lists

Above the directory listing are the Category and Server drop-down lists. These lists control who shows up in the directory listing. When you start NetMeeting, by default it logs you on to the server you chose in the NetMeeting Setup Wizard and displays the category you chose for your entry.

If you want to see the entries on a different server, just click the down arrow to the right of the Server drop-down list and choose the server that you want to use.

Similarly, to see the list of people in a different category than yourself, just choose the category you want to see from the Category drop-down list. Setting the Category field to, say, Business, will let you see the list of people who have designated that their information is For Business Use.

The Tabbed Call Windows

To the left of the directory listing are four tabs:

- [ ] Directory
- [ ] SpeedDial
- [ ] Current Call
- [ ] History

The Directory tab contains the Category and Server fields and the directory listing. The first time you start NetMeeting, the Directory tab is the one you see. Clicking the other tabs enables you to see different information pertaining to calls you can make, the current call, or calls you've received.

NEW TERM   *Current call* is how NetMeeting describes the conference in which you are currently
engaged.

You can use the SpeedDial tab the same way you would use a SpeedDial button on your
telephone. This tab keeps a short list of people you call regularly so you don't have to search
for their names in the main directory listing. You can also have people who frequent different
servers on the same SpeedDial list so you don't have to keep changing servers to find the
person you want to call.

After you've added someone to your SpeedDial list, NetMeeting starts on this screen instead
of the Directory screen, because you're more likely to want to call the person whose number
you've saved than someone you haven't talked to before.

The Current Call tab shows a list of the people in the current call. You will always find at least
two names in this list if you're in a call, or none if you're not. Also, if you or another person
is sending video, you'll see it in the video boxes on the right side of the screen on this tab. I'll
be talking about the Current Call tab in each of the other hours in this part of the book.

Finally, the History tab holds a list of all the calls you've received from other people. The
caller's name, the date and time of the call, and whether you accepted, rejected, or ignored
the call are all listed on this tab.

The Audio Level Controls

Using the audio level controls, you can change the level of your voice and the voice of the other
person on the call (see Figure 17.7).

Figure 17.7.

*The audio level controls
enable you to adjust the
volume of your voice and
the voice of the person
you're talking to.*

Just drag the slider for either the microphone (your voice) or the speaker (the other person's
voice) to the left to lower the level or to the right to increase the volume. In most cases, you
won't need to adjust the microphone level because that should have been set automatically
by the NetMeeting Setup Wizard. You can change the speaker volume to suit your taste for
each individual call, however. You can also use the check boxes on the audio level controls
to temporarily mute yourself or your conversation partner.

17

Answering a Call

To talk to someone on the Internet with NetMeeting, you have to call someone or someone has to call you. You'll learn how to answer a call in this section and how to make a call in the next section.

When someone calls you, the first thing that happens is you hear the phone ring. It's not really the phone ringing, however; the sound is coming out of the speakers of your computer. Next, you'll notice at the bottom right side of your screen a NetMeeting dialog box that says who is calling. It also has two buttons: Accept and Ignore. If you don't want to talk to the caller, click the Ignore button. To answer this call, click the Accept button.

After you accept a call, the NetMeeting window switches automatically to the Current Call tab. Here you'll see the name of the caller and your name, along with some information. To the right of each name are several columns:

☐ **Audio**—A little yellow speaker in this column means that this person can talk over the Internet.

☐ **Video**—A small gray video camera in this column means that you should also see live video in the Remote Video frame to the right (see "Advanced Conferencing Techniques," later in this hour).

☐ **Chat**—A small white and blue rectangle in this column means that the chat window is open (see "Advanced Conferencing Techniques").

It may take a few seconds for NetMeeting to complete the connection between your computer and the caller's computer. After it has finished you can start gabbing—your conference is underway.

When you finish talking to the caller, one of you has to hang up. In NetMeeting, this means clicking the Hang Up button on the toolbar. You can hang up at any time, just like you can on the telephone.

Placing a Call

Calling someone with NetMeeting is actually easier than using the white pages and a telephone. You don't need to remember or dial anyone's phone number; you just have to double-click a name in the directory list. After you've connected with someone, you can have NetMeeting automatically save the listing for you.

To Do: Make a Call

Let's make a call! To do so, complete these steps:

1. Prearrange the conference, via email or other means.
2. In NetMeeting, log on to the directory server where your partner is listed.
3. Find your partner's name in the listing (see Figure 17.8).
4. Double-click the name to make the call.

When your partner answers, NetMeeting switches over to the Current Call tab, and you may proceed with your conversation.

Figure 17.8.

Find the person you want to call in the directory listing.

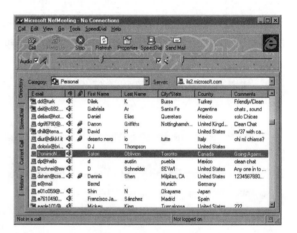

Advanced Conferencing Techniques

Most folks use their conferencing software for voice calls and nothing else. However, you may want to know about the three other forms of conferencing and collaboration enabled by Internet conferencing software: videoconferencing, text chatting, and whiteboard drawing.

Videoconferencing

Few conferencing programs today support videoconferencing, and for good reason: It doesn't work very well. Making live video look good requires moving and processing tons of data quickly, and even the fastest modems and computers are not up to the task. The video image you'll see of your conference partner (and the one they'll see of you) will be small, fuzzy, and jerky, like watching a bad station on a two-inch TV in a thunderstorm.

17

JUST A MINUTE

> Besides not always looking good, videoconferencing often degrades the audio quality in the call. You and your partner may find it preferable to shut off the video so you can hear each other more clearly.

That said, setting up and using video in NetMeeting—one of the few programs that supports it—is a breeze. All you really need to do is install a computer video camera on your PC or Mac. These cameras—usually designed to sit on your desk or mount on top of your monitor—come in color and black-and-white models, and can cost less than $100.

After a video camera has been installed and configured in a Windows or Mac OS, NetMeeting automatically senses and takes advantage of it. If your partner has a video camera installed, the image from that camera automatically appears in a small square on the right side of the Current Call tab; this is called the Remote Video Frame. If you have a camera installed, your partner also sees you.

Text Chatting

Text chatting is using your conferencing software to conduct a conversation through a series of typed messages, just like using Chat.

JUST A MINUTE

> It's important to remember that a text conference is not the same thing as IRC Chat, which you'll learn about in Hour 18. A text chat in a conference program is private, between users of a conferencing program, while bona fide IRC sessions take place on a public chat server among users of any IRC program.

Why would anybody have a text chat instead of a voice chat? Well, several reasons come to mind:

- ☐ One or more of the participants is speech- or hearing-impaired.
- ☐ One or more of the participants has insufficient hardware, or too slow a connection, to support a voice conference. Text conferences require no sound card, and work fine over slow connections.
- ☐ The conference requires the input of more than two participants. Voice and videoconferences are limited to parties of two; however, a text chat can include three, four, or more participants.

To hold a text chat in Conference or NetMeeting, you establish the call just as you would for a voice conference. All participants then switch to text chat mode by clicking the Chat button. Everyone types whatever they have to say, and all statements typed by all participants appear in a scrolling display in the conference program. Each statement is labeled with the name of the speaker, so everybody knows who said what.

Whiteboard

Ever been in a meeting where someone feels he needs to present his idea visually, so he jumps up and starts drawing on a blackboard, or the more modern office "whiteboard"?

In NetMeeting and Conference, you can do the same thing. Click the Whiteboard button while in a call, and a separate window opens—the *whiteboard*—a space in which you can draw and jot notes (see Figure 17.9). Whatever anyone in the call draws on the whiteboard appears to all participants, so partners can even add to one another's drawings.

Using a whiteboard is just like using any drawing program. You select a drawing tool from a panel of buttons, then use your mouse to draw lines or shapes in the drawing area. You can also click a colored square to choose the color the tool produces, and even click a text tool (the A button among the drawing tools) to type notes on the whiteboard.

Figure 17.9.

A whiteboard lets you present your ideas in a conference visually.

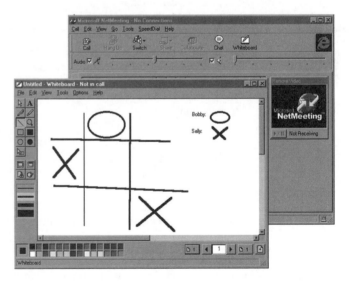

17

Summary

As you can see, using a conferencing program through the Internet is terrifically useful, as long as those with whom you like to converse or collaborate use the same program you do. This capability of the Internet has yet to grow up, but when it does, we'll all be using it in one way or another.

Workshop

Q&A

Q **I don't like using my mic and speakers to have a conference; I feel like a police dispatcher. Is there any way I can make voice conferencing more like a phone call?**

A Several companies have been working on that. You may see ads for devices that look just like telephones, but are really just a cleverly designed mic and speaker. You plug these "phones" into your sound card, so you can have a more phone-like experience.

Although these devices can be handy or fun, they still can't fix the fact that the sound of an Internet conference is not as clear as that of a regular telephone call. That problem has more to do with the Internet's limitations than with the device you speak into.

Quiz

Take the following quiz to see how much you've learned.

Questions

1. You store your name and email address on a directory server so that
    a. You can be billed a monthly NetMeeting usage fee
    b. You can receive great merchandise offers
    c. Other NetMeeting users can more easily find you and connect with you
    d. You can be mailed a monthly NetMeeting directory

2. The first time you open NetMeeting or Conference, a Setup Wizard opens automatically to
    a. Install the program
    b. Collect identification and server information
    c. Configure your sound card for use in voice conferences
    d. Both (b) and (c)

17

3. To have a voice conference, both participants must have

   a. A telephone

   b. At least four years of college

   c. The same conferencing software, a sound card, a microphone, and speakers (or headphones)

   d. A video camera

Answers

1. (c) Listing yourself on a directory server helps others find you.

2. (d) NetMeeting and Conference make you configure your sound card and enter information before you call.

3. (c) No sound card, no sound; no mic, no talk; no speakers, no hear. (No shoes, no shirt, no service.)

Activity

Email your friends, and ask whether they have the same conferencing program you do. When you can agree on a common program, arrange a time for a voice conference, and give conferencing a spin.

17

Hour 18

Chatting Live!

Feel the need to reach out and touch someone, "live" and (almost) in person? Chat puts you online in a live conversation with other Internet users, anywhere in the world.

Lots of chat clients are available, but the one Microsoft offers for free, Microsoft Chat, does everything most chat clients do. Microsoft Chat also displays the chat in a cool way, as you'll soon see. For that reason, you'll discover Internet chatting in this hour principally through Microsoft Chat, which is available either as part of the full installation of the Internet Explorer 4 suite or separately. (Note that Netscape Communicator does not include a chat client. If you use Communicator, you can download and use Microsoft Chat—or any other chat client—right alongside Communicator.)

At the end of this hour, you'll be able to answer the following questions:

- ☐ What is Internet chatting, also known as Internet Relay Chat (IRC)?
- ☐ How is Microsoft Chat different from a typical chat program?
- ☐ How do I join in an online chat session?
- ☐ How do I choose the identity by which I will be known in the chat?

☐ How do I enhance my contributions to the chat with expressions, gestures, and other touches?

☐ How do I exit one chat and enter another?

CAUTION

Be warned that a substantial amount of chat traffic on the Internet is dedicated to sex chats of various persuasions and fetishes. Many sex chat rooms exist, and sex-chat–oriented chatters often wander into non–sex-oriented rooms looking for new friends.

If you have an aversion to such stuff, tread carefully in Chat. If you have a *severe* aversion to it, it's best to stay out of Chat altogether.

Regardless of your own interests, I strongly advise against permitting children to use Chat, especially unsupervised. More about kids and Chat in Hour 21, "Finding Safe Family Fun and Learning."

Understanding Internet Chatting

When you're in an Internet chat, everything you type appears on the screens of everybody else participating in that particular chat. Thousands of different chats are underway at once, each in its own chat room. When you join a chat, you enter a room, and from then on you see only the conversation that's taking place in that room.

NEW TERM A *chat room* is a space where a single conversation is taking place. In Internet chat parlance, a chat room is sometimes known as a *channel*. But now the word *channel* has a new and completely different meaning on the Internet (see Hour 20, "Making the Web Deliver Pages to You: Channels and NetCasting"), so it's best to stick with the term *chat room*.

In most chat rooms, the conversation is focused around a given subject area. In a singles chat room, participants chat about stuff singles like to talk about. In a geology chat room, people generally talk about rocks and earthquakes.

When you're in a chat room, everything anyone else in the same room types appears on your screen, as shown in Figure 18.1. Each participant's statements are labeled with a nickname to identify who's talking. Those participating in a chat (known as *members*) choose their own nicknames and rarely share their real names. In a chat, you can be whoever you want to be, and so can everyone else.

NEW TERM Your *nickname*, which you choose yourself, is how you're known to others in a chat. Your nickname appears on every statement you make, so everyone knows who's talking.

18

Figure 18.1.

An Internet chat is conducted as an ongoing volley of typed statements between participants sharing a chat room.

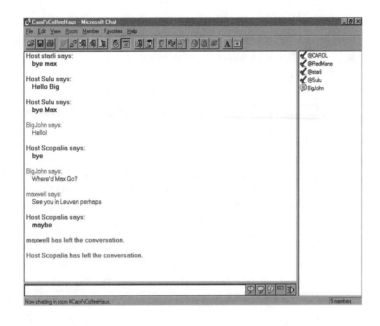

JUST A MINUTE

Other than IRC-type chatting, there's another type: web chatting. A web chat takes place within a web page, and is generally hosted as a discussion related to the web page's topic.

To join a web chat with your browser, you need the right plug-in for the type of web chat underway. Several types of plug-ins exist, but most web chats are supported by the ichat plug-in. You'll usually find a link for downloading ichat on any web page where a chat takes place. You can also get ichat right from the source at

`www.ichat.com`

About Microsoft Chat

To chat, you must have a program called a chat client. Internet Explorer 4's own chat client, included in the full installation (see Hour 1, "What Is the Internet and What Can You Do There?"), is called Microsoft Chat, and it's an unusual animal.

TIME SAVER

> If you don't have Microsoft Chat, but want it, download it from
>
> `www.microsoft.com/ie/chat`
>
> To learn about or download other chat clients, apply the file searching techniques from Hour 11, "Finding Programs and Files," or check out
>
> `www.yahoo.com/Computers_and_Internet/Internet/Chat/IRC/Software/`
> `Clients_and_Servers/`

Like any chat client, Microsoft Chat—henceforth to be known simply as Chat with a capital C—lets you communicate with chat servers. You can view the list of chat rooms, join a chat room, read what everyone says in the chat room, and make your own contributions to the discussion. What's different about Chat is the way it displays the conversation.

NEW TERM   A chat takes place on a *chat server*, more properly called an IRC server. (IRC stands for Internet Relay Chat, the full formal name for Chat.) Just as you need a web browser to communicate with a web server, you need a program called a *chat client* to communicate with a chat server.

Like the chat client shown earlier in Figure 18.1 (which is really just Chat in its text mode, which you'll learn more about later), most chat clients show the text of the conversation, a line at a time, and label each line with the speaker's nickname.

Chat, however, displays the conversation like a comic strip (see Figure 18.2), using little cartoon characters to represent members and showing the members' words in cartoon word balloons. Folks at Microsoft think this approach makes chatting feel more human, more fun. In its first versions, Chat was actually named "Microsoft Comic Chat."

NEW TERM   The *balloon* is the little bubble you see in comics in which the words and thoughts of characters appear.

It's important to understand that chat servers support any IRC client, so most folks you'll end up chatting with probably don't use Microsoft Chat. Many use ordinary text IRC clients; they see your statements labeled with your nickname but don't see your comic character.

On your display, Chat converts all statements in a chat—even those made by users of text-only clients—into comics. Other Chat users in the room with you appear as their chosen cartoon character. For users of other chat clients, Chat automatically assigns and shows an unused character.

18

Figure 18.2.

Microsoft Chat makes the chat look like a comic strip, with a different cartoon character for each participant.

Joining a Chat Room

Now that you understand what chatting is all about, it's time to hit a server and see it for real. On the way, you'll perform some automatic configuration that Chat needs to operate properly.

TIME SAVER

> Before opening Chat, you can be online or offline. If you're offline when you begin, Chat connects to the Internet automatically. Also, your browser need not be open for you to use Chat, although it won't hurt anything if it is open.

To Do: Start Chat and Display the Chat Rooms List

Let's begin by starting Chat and displaying the Chat rooms list:

1. Open Chat. (In Windows 95, you do so by choosing Programs | Microsoft Chat.) The Connect dialog box opens, as shown in Figure 18.3.

2. Select the Show All Available Chat Rooms option, and then click OK. After you're online, a list of all chat rooms available on the server appears. You are now connected to a chat server and ready to chat—except that, as a new user, you have not yet selected a nickname and a comic character, as described next.

Figure 18.3.

*The Connect
dialog box connects
you to a selected
chat server.*

Choosing an Identity

Before you can join in a chat, you must create a nickname. Because of Chat's unique presentation style, you must choose a comic character, too. In addition, you can select a background that appears behind the characters in each panel of the comic, as you see it on your screen.

After you choose a nickname, character, and background, Chat remembers them for future sessions. You do not need to choose them again, unless you want to change them.

To Do: Choose Your Chat Identity

To choose your Chat character and give yourself a nickname, follow these steps:

1. Choose View | Options. The Options dialog box appears.
2. Choose the Personal Info tab (see Figure 18.4), if it is not already open.

Figure 18.4.

*On the Personal Info tab,
you type a nickname.*

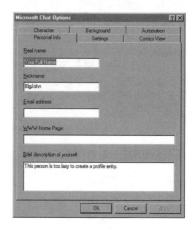

3. Click in the Nickname box and type a nickname for yourself. Your nickname should be one word, using no spaces or punctuation, and it should also be unusual to reduce the chances that another member has chosen the same nickname. If you

18

attempt to enter a room where someone is already using the same nickname as you, Chat prompts you to change your nickname before entering.

CAUTION

On the Personal Info tab, you can enter other information besides your nickname, such as your real name and email address. Think carefully before doing so, however. Whatever information you supply here can be seen by other members whose clients (like Chat) can display Member Profiles. If you want to keep your anonymity, enter your nickname and *nothing else*.

4. Click the Character tab. This is where you select your character.

5. Select the character you want to play by clicking a name in the Character column (see Figure 18.5). Note that someone else in the chat may use the same character as you. Chatters can share characters, but not nicknames.

The Preview column shows what the selected character looks like—what *you* will look like to other Chat users if you stick with that character.

TIME SAVER

When choosing a character in the Character tab, you can click the faces in the emotion wheel (beneath the character preview) to see what the character will look like when you apply to it a given emotion when making a statement. You learn about choosing emotions later in this hour.

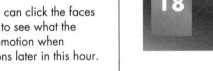

18

Figure 18.5.

Click a name in the Character column, and you see the character in the Preview column.

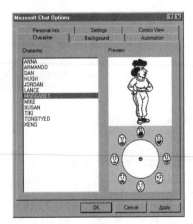

6. Click the Background tab. This tab enables you to select from several cartoon backgrounds to use when chatting.

7. Choose a background. When you select an entry in the Background column, the background appears in the Preview column.

8. Click OK.

Entering a Room

To enter a chat room, you select a room from the chat room list. Figure 18.6 shows the list of chats available on the server. Each server has its own list, and the lists change often.

TIME SAVER

The chat room list reappears after you finish selecting your identity. You can open the chat room list any time you're connected to the server by clicking the Chat Room List button on Chat's toolbar.

In the list, the name of each room begins with a pound sign (#). The name of the room is followed by the number of members currently in the room, and sometimes also by a description of the conversation that usually takes place there.

Figure 18.6.

To enter any room in the list, double-click its name.

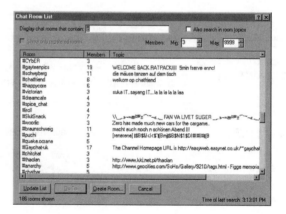

On most servers, there's a chat room specifically set up to practice chatting, called #Newbies. Give it a try.

To Do: Enter a Chat Room

1. Scroll down the chat room list (it's organized alphabetically) until you see the room #Newbies.

2. Double-click #Newbies. The Chat window opens, as shown in Figure 18.7, and you're in the chat.

18

Figure 18.7.
*Chats happen in
the Chat window.*

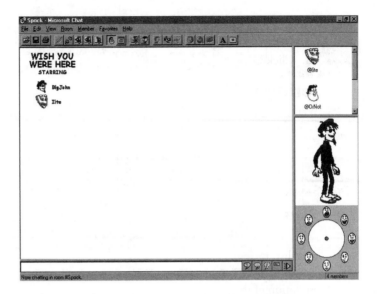

Observe that the Chat window is broken up into five sections, or *panes* (covered clockwise from upper left):

☐ The biggest pane is the viewing pane, where you see the chat session as it progresses.

☐ The small pane in the upper right is the member list pane, which lists all members in the current chat room.

☐ The pane showing your character is the self-view pane, which reminds you of who you are.

☐ The ring of faces is the emotion wheel, from which you can select your character's facial expression.

☐ The small text box at the bottom of the window is the compose pane, where you type your statements.

TIME SAVER

Instead of double-clicking the chat room name, you can click it once to select it, and then click the Go To button in the chat room list.

18

Just a Minute

When you first arrive in a room, you may not see any comic panels right away. The server shows you only what's been said *since* you entered the room. After you enter, statements begin appearing, one by one, as members make them.

Time Saver

You can switch Chat into a "text mode" (refer to Figure 18.1) so it skips the comic characters and displays the conversation as scrolling series of text messages, like any other IRC client. When the room is crowded (five or more members), you may prefer chatting in text mode.

To switch to text mode, choose View | Plain Text. To switch back from text mode to comics, choose View | Comic Strip. You can switch back and forth at any time, even in the middle of a conversation.

Contributing to the Conversation

Now that you're in a room, you can just *lurk* (listen in) to the conversation, or you can contribute to it by sending your statements for all others to see. Note that you are not obligated to add anything to the conversation. In fact, just lurking in a chat room is a great way to learn more about chats before diving in.

When you contribute, you can choose the style of the comic word balloon in which your words will appear to you and to other Chat users. You choose the style of the word balloon by clicking a button next to the compose pane, the text box at the bottom of the Chat window in which you type all your statements.

For example, for a particular statement, you can choose a think balloon so the words appear in the balloon style generally used in comics to represent what the character is thinking. (Snoopy, for example, can't actually speak, so all his words appear in thought balloons.)

Just a Minute

Keep in mind that while you're typing and editing your statements, no one sees them but you. A statement is sent to the chat only when you press Enter. That gives you a chance to choose your words carefully and correct typos before committing your statement to the chat.

18

To Do: Add Statements to a Chat

To add statements to a chat, follow these steps:

1. Enter a chat room that interests you, and follow the conversation until you understand what's being talked about.

2. When you are ready to contribute, begin typing. Anything you type while in a chat room appears automatically in the compose pane, the text box at the bottom of the Chat window. As you type, you can use the Backspace, Delete, Insert, and arrow keys to edit your statement and correct mistakes.

JUST A MINUTE

> When wording a statement, keep in mind that Chat automatically gives your character certain gestures based on words in the statement (see "Gesturing," later in this hour).
>
> Also, always observe the rules of netiquette (see Hour 15, "Reading and Posting to Newsgroups") when contributing—no flames, no sarcasm, and so on. Be prepared, however, because a chat room is the place you will see others breach netiquette the most.

3. When your statement is worded the way you want, press Enter. After a few moments, your statement appears as part of the scrolling conversation displayed in the chat window. It appears at the same spot in the list in the display of everyone else in the room.

   Those in the room using regular chat clients see your statement labeled with your nickname, so they know you said it. Those in the room using Microsoft Chat see your chosen comic character speaking the words in a *say balloon,* the type that surrounds words that comic characters say aloud. The say balloon is the default balloon style, the one Chat uses automatically when you don't select a different balloon style.

4. Type a statement that's more a thought than a statement—an opinion perhaps. Before pressing Enter to submit the statement, click the Think button (second from the left) in the compose pane. Then press Enter. Chat users see your character thinking the words in a thought balloon, the type that surrounds the thoughts of comic characters.

5. Think of a statement your character might whisper, rather than say aloud. Type the statement, click the Whisper button (third from the left), and then press Enter. Chat users see your character whispering the words in the type of balloon that surrounds the whispers of comic characters.

18

Showing Emotions

The emotion wheel in the lower-left corner of the Chat window lets you change the expression of your character's face when making a statement.

JUST A MINUTE

> Because some members in the room may not be using Chat and therefore can't see expressions, be sure your words alone carry your meaning.

To Do: Change Expressions

To change your character's expression, follow these steps:

1. Get into a chat.

2. Type a statement, but don't press Enter.

3. Select a face from the emotion wheel. The character in the self-view pane changes to show how your character will appear if you commit to using the selected expression. As long as you don't press Enter, you can choose a different expression until you find one you like.

TIME SAVER

> To choose your character's normal, *neutral* expression, click the + at the center of the emotion wheel.

4. When the self-view pane appears the way you want it to, press Enter to submit your statement.

Gesturing

If you watch a chat for awhile, you'll notice that the characters are not static. They change body position and gestures, panel to panel. The gesturing is selected automatically by Chat, based on words you use in your statements. For example, if a statement contains the word *I,* when speaking that statement your character will appear to point to himself or herself.

You can use other members' nicknames to control to whom the gesture is made. For example, if you say "Hi," your character appears to wave to the group. If you say "Hi, Eloise," your character appears to wave at the member using the nickname Eloise.

Table 18.1 describes the gestures that Chat applies. Observe that some gestures are based on words used to begin a statement and others are based on words within the statement.

18

JUST A MINUTE

When a statement both begins with a gesture word and contains a gesture word, Chat applies the gesture for the beginning word.

Table 18.1. Gestures used automatically by Chat characters.

Statement Begins With	Character's Action
I	Points to itself
You	Points to another member
Hello or Hi	Waves
Bye	Waves
Welcome	Waves
Howdy	Waves
Statement Contains	**Character's Action**
are you	Points to another member
will you	Points to another member
did you	Points to another member
aren't you	Points to another member
don't you	Points to another member
I'm	Points to itself
I am	Points to itself
I'll	Points to itself
I will	Points to itself

18

Switching Rooms

Often, you'll find that not much is going on in a chat room you enter, or that the conversation has taken a turn you don't care to follow. At such times, all you have to do is leave the room you're in and enter a different one.

JUST A MINUTE

When you leave the room, a message appears in the chat to inform everybody that you're gone. You can't "sneak out" without anybody knowing, as you can in life when a conversation turns ugly.

To Do: Switch to Another Room

To switch to another room, follow these steps:

1. While in a room, click the Leave Room button on Chat's toolbar.

2. Click the Enter Room button on the toolbar to open a dialog box that prompts for a password. Some chat rooms are set up for private conversations; to enter, you must type a password. Most chats are public, however, so you generally ignore the password box.

3. Type the name of the room. Be sure to include the pound sign (#) at the beginning of the room name, as in #Newbies.

4. Click OK.

TIME SAVER

If you don't know the name of the room you want to go to, click the Chat Room List button on Chat's toolbar to open the chat room list, and then choose a room from the list.

Summary

Chat is fun, as long as you stay among those whose reasons for chatting are the same as yours. Like a carnival or circus, chat is an entertaining place with a seedy underbelly, one to be enjoyed with caution. But if you're careful, you can have safe, interactive fun with chat.

Workshop

Q&A

Q Sometimes the sequence of statements in a chat looks all jumbled to me. Like, somebody asks a question, and then three unrelated statements appear, and then someone answers the question a few panels later. What's the deal?

A Often in a chat with three or more members, the conversation appears out-of-order, not following the logical order of a conversation. That jumbling happens because each member's words take a different amount of time to reach the server, and because some members take more time composing their statements than others.

After you've used chat for a while, you'll get used to the jumbling.

18

Quiz

Take the following quiz to see how much you've learned.

Questions

1. When you share a chat room with members using chat clients other than Microsoft Chat,

    a. Everyone sees the session as comics.

    b. Everyone sees the session as text.

    c. You see the session as comics (including statements made by non-Chat users), but they see it as text (including your statements).

    d. Chat users cannot share a room with non-Chat users.

2. To make a statement appear as a "thought" to other Chat users,

    a. Click the Think button before submitting the statement.

    b. Use the word *think* anywhere in the statement.

    c. Think really hard while typing it.

    d. Include the command [IDEA] in the statement.

3. Be careful what you include on your Personal Info tab, because

    a. Wrong information can crash Chat.

    b. The Internal Revenue Service monitors the tab, which is scary.

    c. Direct-marketing people at Microsoft monitor the tab, which is *really* scary.

    d. That information may be accessed by others you chat with.

Answers

1. (c) Remember that only you and other users of Microsoft Chat see the comics; all others just see the text.

2. (a) This choice is the only one that works.

3. (d) Don't give others the chance to learn more about you than you care to tell.

Activity

Open the chat room list, and spend some time scrolling through it and reading the names and descriptions of chats on the server. Make notes of the names of any chats you'd like to check out, and be sure to visit one or two new chats each time you go exploring.

18

Hour 19

Using Old-Fashioned Hacker's Tools: FTP, Gopher, and Telnet

People surfed the Internet for over a decade before there was a web. During those years, the principal tools for using the net—other than email and newsgroups—were good old Telnet and FTP and, in the final pre-web years, Gopher. One might call these "hacker's tools" because they were the primitive instruments of the earliest surfers, the net jocks and hackers immortalized in the film *War Games* and the book *The Cuckoo's Egg*.

None of these three tools is as easy or fun as the web, and frankly, so much is available on the web these days that most newcomers to the Internet never bother with FTP, Gopher, or Telnet; much of what used to be accessible only through these tools now resides on web pages. But not *everything* in the hacker tools' domain has yet made it to the web, so these remain an important part of your Internet toolset. To use *all* the Internet has to offer, you must be familiar with these powerful tools, which are easier to use than you might expect—you don't have to be a hacker to use them.

At the end of this hour, you'll be able to answer the following questions:

☐ What is FTP and how can I use it to download files?

☐ What is Gopher and how can I use it to browse for information?

☐ What is Telnet and how can I use it to explore and operate other people's computer systems?

☐ How can I use these tools from within their own client programs *and* from my web browser?

Downloading Files with FTP

You already know how to download files from the web. Some files you may want are stored not on web servers, but on *FTP servers*.

FTP stands for *File Transfer Protocol*, but you really don't need to know that; everybody uses just the abbreviation, like NBC or VCR. Still, the name says it all: FTP is for transferring files between computers. The files stored on FTP servers are waiting to be downloaded by an *FTP client*, a program on your computer that communicates with FTP servers through the Internet.

Many FTP servers are *password-protected* to limit access to only authorized users. If an FTP server is password-protected, you're prompted to enter a username and password when you access the server. If you don't have the correct username and password, you can't use the server.

Many FTP servers are called *anonymous* FTP servers, because they require no username and password at all, or they display instructions that enable you to enter a guest username and password (usually your email address) to use the server. When you access an anonymous FTP server through your web browser, you often do not have to log on (even with a guest password), because your browser automatically completes the logon with your email address, if required.

JUST A MINUTE

The kinds of files you can download from FTP servers are the same as those you download from web pages (.exe, .doc, .zip, and so on), and are subject to the same issues and considerations (such as whether a particular file can run on your type of computer). If you're not sure about file types, review Hour 11, "Finding Programs and Files."

19

Understanding FTP Addresses

As with any server, you access an FTP server by entering its address. FTP server addresses are made up of parts separated by periods (just like web addresses), and often—but not always—begin with ftp. For example, the following are FTP server addresses:

```
ftp.microsoft.com
ftp.mcp.com
```

Files for downloading are stored in particular directories on FTP servers, just as web page files are stored in particular web server directories (see Figure 19.1). The FTP address can point directly to a file or directory. For example, the address

```
ftp.mcp.com/samples/doc.txt
```

points directly to a file called doc.txt, in a directory called samples, on a server called ftp.mcp.com.

Figure 19.1.

FTP servers organize files into directories.

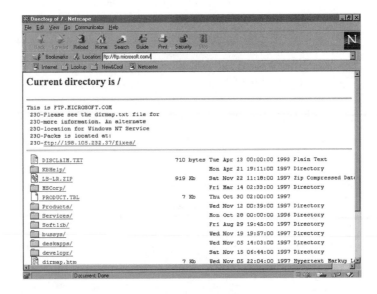

19

Downloading an FTP File with Your Web Browser

Many web browsers, as I pointed out earlier in this book, are multipurpose clients. At the very least, any web browser can act as a web client, communicating with web servers. Many web clients—including all versions of Netscape Navigator and Internet Explorer—can double as FTP clients (and triple as Gopher clients—but more about that later). If you have such a browser, you don't need a separate FTP client for downloading files from FTP servers.

From a browser, you may use FTP by entering an FTP URL in the address box, just as you would a web page URL. Remember that the URL of a web page begins with `http://` (even though you don't have to type that part in many browsers). An FTP URL is made up of `ftp://` followed by the FTP server address. For example, the URLs for the FTP addresses shown in the preceding section are

```
ftp://ftp.microsoft.com
ftp://ftp.mcp.com
ftp://ftp.mcp.com/samples/doc.txt
```

JUST A MINUTE

If your web browser allows you to omit the `http://` prefix when entering a web page URL, it probably also lets you omit the `ftp://` prefix in an FTP URL.

This feature, however, does not work as reliably with FTP URLs as it does with web URLs. When entering an FTP URL in any web browser, I recommend always including the complete `ftp://` prefix.

You can download a file either by entering the complete FTP address of the file, or by entering the address of the FTP server and then browsing through its directories to locate and select the file. When you view FTP directories through a browser, every directory name is a link. Click a directory name, and the contents of that directory appear.

Whichever way you get to an FTP file, after you select it, the download proceeds exactly like a regular web download (see Hour 11).

TIME SAVER

Because most web browsers do FTP, you'll often come across links in web pages that are FTP links—they point either to an FTP server or directory, or to a specific file on the server. In particular, the hits turned up by file searches (see Hour 11) often include links to files that reside on FTP servers.

If the link points to a file, clicking the link starts the download, just like any download—you may not even know you're doing an FTP download, unless you look closely at the download status message.

If the link points to an FTP server or directory, you'll need to browse through the directory listings to find and select a file—that's when knowing FTP comes in handy.

19

To Do: Use Your Browser to Get an FTP File

To use your browser to get an FTP file, follow these steps:

1. Begin in your browser, online and on any page. In your address box, enter the following URL to display the top-level directory on Microsoft's anonymous FTP server:

   ```
   ftp://ftp.microsoft.com
   ```

   The directory appears, showing folders and documents on Microsoft's FTP server. Each item in the list is a link.

   In many browsers, the links may be preceded by folder icons, indicating that they lead to directory listings, although other links show icons that represent the type of file the link downloads (such as a page for a document file).

2. Click any link preceded by a folder icon or labeled as a "Directory." A new directory listing appears.

3. Click Back to return to the top directory. In a browser, you move down through the FTP directory structure by clicking links, and back up by clicking your Back button.

4. Find the link for Ls-lr.zip. This file contains a complete index to the Microsoft FTP server, in a compressed ZIP file.

5. Click the link. A download commences, exactly as it would if you had begun downloading a ZIP file from a web page.

   Continue downloading the file or cancel the download.

TIME SAVER

For a variety of technical reasons, downloading a file from an FTP server often takes less time than downloading a file of the same size from a web server—even when you run the FTP download from a web browser.

If you know you can acquire the same file from a web server or an FTP server, you may cut the download time by choosing the FTP server, especially if it's a big file (larger than 1MB).

Using an FTP Client

For most people, the FTP capabilities of a web browser are all the FTP power they need. But FTP can do more than just download a file. Using FTP, you can send files—*upload* them— to an FTP server so others can download them, and control your uploading and downloading to a fine degree—such as downloading a whole family of files in one operation. Such advanced FTPing typically requires a real FTP client, not a web browser posing as one.

Why would you ever upload a file? Well, one common case is publishing a web page. After you create a web page on your computer, you must upload it to a web server to make it accessible to others.

However, you may not need to learn how to do an FTP upload to upload a web page. Many web authoring programs now include an easy-to-use facility that takes care of the uploading for you (see Hour 23, "Creating Web Pages and Multimedia Messages").

Windows 95 and the Mac have their own built-in FTP clients, but these remain true to FTP heritage as a hacker's tool: To use these clients, you must learn and use a family of FTP commands. Most casual Internet users don't use FTP often enough to justify learning to use these utilitarian FTP clients.

A better choice is an easy-to-use graphical FTP client, which combines the simplicity of a web browser with the full power of FTP.

A popular choice for Windows, WS_FTP (see Figure 19.2), which you can get from www.ipswitch.com, displays the directory of the FTP site you've accessed on the right side of the window and your PC's hard disk directory on the left. To download a file, you drag it from the right to the left. To upload, you drag a file from the left (your hard disk) to the right (the FTP server).

Remember that URLs are used only in web browsers. When accessing an FTP server through a real FTP client, you do not enter an FTP URL—such as ftp://ftp.microsoft.com—but only the FTP address itself—such as ftp.microsoft.com.

Figure 19.2.

Graphical FTP clients such as WS_FTP bring drag-and-drop simplicity to FTP tasks.

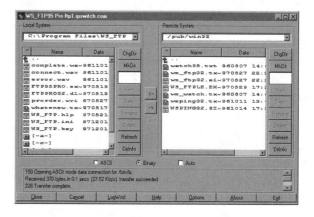

19

TIME SAVER

To find an FTP client for your computer, consult Yahoo!'s directory of them at

`www.yahoo.com/Computers_and_Internet/Software/Internet/FTP/`

Burrowing Through the Net with Gopher

Gopher was the first real crack at making the Internet easier to use, and it worked—but not as well as the web, which was developed hot on Gopher's heels.

Gopher introduced the idea that you could explore online information by navigating through an organized index of menu items—*links*, in effect (see Figure 19.3). You can explore all the information stored on Gopher servers the world over (most of which are in colleges and universities) by clicking your way through the menus and links in Gopherspace.

NEW TERM   *Gopherspace* is a term that collectively describes all the Gopher servers in the world and the information they contain. All the Gopher servers are interconnected so clicking a menu item on a menu displayed by one Gopher server may display a new menu or file that's stored on another Gopher server.

As on an FTP server, all the online information accessible through Gopher is organized like a table of contents or index.

You generally begin at a high-level directory. When you click an item in that directory, another more specific subdirectory of choices appears. You continue clicking down through the menu structure until you reach your goal—usually a document that displays to show you the information to which your choices have led.

Also like FTP, each item in a Gopher menu is preceded by an icon that indicates what the link leads to when viewed through a web browser (or graphical Gopher client). Items flagged by folder icons lead to other Gopher menus, items flagged by page icons lead to documents, and so on.

Browsing Gopherspace Through a Web Browser

Just as most web browsers can act as FTP clients, most—including, yet again, all versions of Netscape Navigator and Internet Explorer—can also be used as Gopher clients. So you probably already have your Gopher client ready to go.

In case you hadn't already guessed, you access Gopherspace through a web browser by entering a Gopher URL in the address box. A Gopher URL begins with the prefix `gopher://` followed by a server address. (This URL stuff gets pretty obvious after awhile, doesn't it?)

Figure 19.3.

Gopher provides a system of menus you can browse.

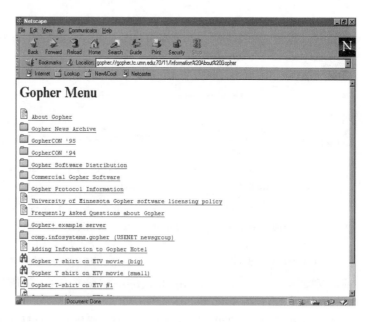

TIME SAVER

Unlike a real FTP client, a real Gopher client offers no advantage over using your web browser for Gopher. Just in case you use a browser that doesn't do Gopher, note that Gopher client programs are available for just about any system.

Your ISP can probably set you up with a Gopher client from among the programs it offers to subscribers. You may also find a Gopher client on your own, by exploring Yahoo!'s directory of Gopher clients at

www.yahoo.com/Computers_and_Internet/Internet/Gopher/Software/

To Do: Explore Gopherspace

Gopher was developed at the University of Minnesota. (In fact, Gopher borrows its name from the university's mascot, although the name also implies that you use it to "burrow" or "go for" information.) So the University of Minnesota Gopher—sometimes known affectionately as "Mother Gopher"—is a great place to begin exploring. Let's begin by following these steps:

1. Begin in your browser, online and on any page. In your address box, enter the following URL to display the top-level directory on Mother Gopher:

   gopher://gopher.micro.umn.edu/

   The top-level menu at Mother Gopher appears, showing a menu of links leading to other menus.

19

2. Click the top choice, Information About Gopher. Another menu appears. At the top of the menu is a link to a document about Gopher (About Gopher).

3. Click About Gopher. A document introducing you to Gopher opens.

4. Click Back once. The document closes, and you return to the menu.

5. Click Back again. You return to the top menu.

6. Now check out another great Gopher called Gopher Jewels at University of Southern California. Enter the URL:

   `gopher://cwis.usc.edu/`

7. On the menu that appears, choose Other Gophers and Information Resources.

8. On the next menu, choose Gopher-Jewels. A menu of fun and interesting Gophers appears.

9. Burrow!

Using Remote Computers Through Telnet

Using any web server is like using any other. Ditto FTP servers, news servers, and Gopher servers. Telnet, however, is the exception to the rule. Using Telnet, you access another computer out there on the Internet—known to Telnet as a *remote computer*—and use that computer as if you were there, as if you were using a terminal that was connected directly to that computer.

Understanding Telnet

For example, many libraries have a computerized card catalog system that visitors to the library use from terminals or PCs located at the library. If the library has configured the card catalog to support access via Telnet, you can use your Internet connection to use the card catalog system from thousands of miles away. What you'll see on your screen (see Figure 19.4) is exactly what you'd see if you went to the library in person and used one of the card catalog terminals.

The trick with Telnet is that all the computers you access work differently. Each has its own procedures for logging on, navigating menus, and more. In fact, accessing a remote computer through Telnet is the easy part. Getting logged on to that computer, and then figuring out how to operate it, is the challenge with Telnet.

NEW TERM   Actually, the term *log on* isn't so new; you've been logging on to the Internet—entering your username and password—since Hour 4, "Connecting to the Internet."

You must also log on (or log in, or sign in, or sign on—it's all the same thing) to most remote computers you access through Telnet, either using a private name and password you've been given for using that system or by entering a guest or visitor username and password.

19

When you start a Telnet session from a web link, instructions near the link usually describe what you need to know to log on. Some helpful Telnet systems actually tell you the guest username and password when you arrive.

Figure 19.4.

Telnet lets you access a remote computer and use it as if you were there.

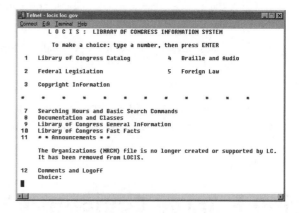

Getting a Telnet Client

Now, I know what you're expecting: You're expecting me to tell you that your web browser doubles as a Telnet client. Sorry, you can only use Telnet through a real Telnet client.

Fortunately, Windows 95 and the Mac both have built-in Telnet clients. Even better, most Windows and Mac web browsers know how to open the Telnet client automatically, as a *helper program* (see Hour 8, "Plug-ins, Helpers, and Other Ways to Do More Online"), when you click a link leading to a Telnet server. Although you must operate the remote computer through your Telnet client, you can navigate to the server and begin your Telnet session from within your browser.

TIME SAVER

If you use Windows 3.1 or another system that lacks a built-in Telnet client, ask your ISP for one or find your own using the search techniques from Hour 11.

To Do: Visit the Library of Congress Through Telnet

The U.S. Library of Congress has a great web page. But the whole card catalog (LOCIS—Library Of Congress Information System) has not yet been added to the web—it remains accessible only through Telnet. Give it a try.

1. Go to the Library of Congress web page at

   www.loc.gov

2. Click the link to SEARCH THE CATALOGS.

19

3. On the page that appears, scroll down to the COMMAND SEARCH portion.

4. Click the link TELNET to LOCIS. Your Telnet client opens, and the main menu of the LOCIS catalog opens.

   Observe that each menu item is preceded by a number. To choose an item, you type its number and then press Enter.

JUST A MINUTE

> Note that Telnet systems don't support your mouse, trackball, or other pointing device. You do everything in a Telnet session with your keyboard.

5. Press 1, and then Enter, to open the Catalog menu.

6. On the Catalog menu, type 12 (for Return to LOCIS MENU Screen), and press Enter. You return to the main menu.

7. Type 12 and press Enter again to log off LOCIS. Then close your Telnet client.

See how easy a Telnet session is? Just choose your menu items, follow any instructions you see onscreen, and you can't go wrong.

TIME SAVER

> Many Gopher links lead to Telnet sessions. A link that leads to Telnet is preceded by an icon that looks like a computer terminal. If you're browsing Gopher from within your web browser, clicking the link generally opens the Telnet client your web browser is configured to open.

19

Summary

Feel like a hacker yet? FTP, Gopher, and Telnet are a little more difficult than web browsing, but you'll only use them now and then, when no web page offers what you need. It's nice to have the keys to different doors, so you'll always have a place to go.

Workshop

Q&A

Q I noticed that the Library of Congress gave me two choices for accessing LOCIS: TELNET to LOCIS and TN3270 to LOCIS. What's that all about?

A When you use Telnet, you're making your computer perform something called *terminal emulation*; that is, it's pretending to be the kind of computer terminal that the remote system is designed to interact with. TN3270 is a common type of terminal; LOCIS lets you choose the type of terminal access (generic Telnet or TN3270), depending on the kind of terminal your Telnet program emulates.

If you start your Telnet sessions from web links and use the Telnet program your browser is configured to open, you can usually forget about terminal issues. If the screen images displayed by a Telnet session seem scrambled, however, it's likely that the remote computer wants your Telnet program to emulate a different terminal. Try changing the terminal emulation from the menus in your Telnet client until you hit one that works.

Quiz

Take the following quiz to see how much you've learned.

Questions

1. An FTP server that is not restricted to only users with a secret password is known as _____ FTP server.

    a. An open

    b. A loose

    c. A non–security-enabled

    d. An anonymous

2. When a Gopher menu item is preceded by a folder icon, clicking that item opens

    a. Another Gopher menu

    b. An FTP server directory

    c. A Telnet session

    d. A can of worms

3. True or False: You get around in a Telnet session by pointing to menu items and clicking them.

Answers

1. (d) Anonymous FTP lets anybody download.

2. (a) Folder items open menus.

3. False. Telnet sessions don't support point and click. You usually must type the number of a menu item, or a command of some sort, then press Enter.

Activity

If there's a file or program you've been looking for, do a search for it using the techniques from Hour 11, but add to your search term the word *ftp*. Doing so will bring to the top of the hit list files that are on FTP servers, from which you can now download the file, thanks to skills you picked up in this hour.

 19

Hour **20**

Making the Web Deliver Pages to You: Channels and NetCasting

Traditionally, to get information from the Internet you go out and get it. Each time you want to catch up with the latest information, you go out and get it again.

The idea behind *channels*, also known as *NetCasting*, is this: When you want to stay abreast of a particular kind of information, the information should be delivered to you, automatically, whenever there's news. If you use Navigator 4 or Internet Explorer 4, you can use the techniques in this hour to set up channels to bring the web to you. Depending on how you use a channel, all of a channel's new content can automatically be downloaded to your computer so you can read it offline, any time.

At the end of this hour, you'll be able to answer the following questions:

- ☐ How do I find channels?
- ☐ When I find a channel I like, how do I sign up for it in Internet Explorer?
- ☐ How do I subscribe to channels in Navigator?
- ☐ How do I update my channels with the latest information?

JUST A MINUTE

> Unlike most hours in this book, this one absolutely requires either Microsoft's Internet Explorer 4 or Netscape's Navigator 4 (Communicator)—for all practical purposes, only these two browsers support channel technology. (A service called Pointcast Network can supply the effect of channels to other browsers.)

Using Channels in Internet Explorer 4

If channels catch on, you won't need to go looking for them, you'll come across them. For example, when you first visit a web page about a topic that interests you, you may discover the buttons that enable you to subscribe to that page as a channel.

Because channels are new, Microsoft is trying to help you find and use them in two ways:

- ☐ Microsoft has created the Active Channel Guide, a channel for finding other channels. The Active Channel Guide contains links for subscribing to many of the channels currently available online.
- ☐ If you choose to install the web-integrated desktop or "Active Desktop," when installing Internet Explorer 4 (see Hour 24, "Moving Toward Web Integration"), a button bar called the Channel bar appears on your desktop. As you begin subscribing to channels, it will show those you've signed up for.

JUST A MINUTE

> Note that the initial group of buttons on the Channel bar really just contains shortcuts to web pages where you can subscribe to channels. As you subscribe to these and other channels, new buttons will appear on the bar.
>
> You can delete Microsoft's shortcuts or any other button from the bar by right-clicking the button and choosing Delete from the pop-up menu that appears.

20

In the Channel bar, there's a button labeled Active Channel Guide. Click it, and the Active Channel Guide opens, offering links to channels and general information about channels (see Figure 20.1). You can also open the Active Channel Guide from within Internet Explorer by clicking the Channels button on the toolbar, which opens a list of channels in the Explorer Bar panel on the left side of the window. At the top of the list is a link to the Channel Guide.

Observe in Figure 20.1 that Internet Explorer looks a little different when you view the Channel Guide; the toolbars look smaller and simpler, and the menu bar is gone. This is Internet Explorer's *Fullscreen* view, which kicks in automatically when you open most channels. You can switch back and forth between full screen and regular view by clicking the Fullscreen button on the toolbar.

Figure 20.1.

Microsoft's Active Channel Guide helps you find channels that may interest you.

Besides finding channels in the Channel Guide, you can also visit the Active Desktop Gallery to find new *active desktop items* (see Figure 20.2). To open the Active Desktop Gallery, go to

www.microsoft.com/ie/ie40/gallery

NEW TERM An *active desktop item* is a special kind of channel that displays not in the browser, but in its own little box or window right on your desktop. Desktop items are used most often to display a little box showing regularly updated weather reports, sports scores, or financial news.

Figure 20.2.

Microsoft's Active Desktop Gallery leads you to desktop items you may enjoy.

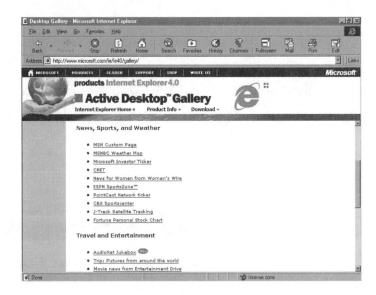

Subscribing to Channels

You subscribe to a channel by first navigating to a channel or a web page that contains a link for subscribing to the channel, such as Microsoft's Channel Guide.

Wherever you have the option to subscribe to a channel, you'll see a button labeled

- ☐ **Add Active Channel**—For a regular, full-screen channel
- ☐ **Add to Active Desktop**—For a desktop item

Some pages (such as Figure 20.3) offer both buttons, so you can choose the way you want the channel content to be displayed on your computer.

Click the button, and the Add Channel dialog box opens; just follow its prompts to complete the subscription. In the following To Do, I'll show you how to use that dialog box to subscribe to the *National Geographic Connection*. Feel free to substitute another channel, if one strikes your fancy as you go along.

Figure 20.3.

To subscribe to a channel, find a button or link with a label such as Add to Channels, Add Active Channel, or Subscribe.

20

JUST A MINUTE

Different channels may allow different subscription options, so the following dialog boxes and steps may not apply exactly for every channel you subscribe to. The general idea is always the same, however.

To Do: Subscribe to a Channel in IE4

To Do

To subscribe to a channel in IE4, follow these steps:

1. On the Channel bar (or in the Channel list in the Explorer bar), click the button labeled Lifestyle & Travel. IE4 opens in fullscreen view, and a list of Lifestyle & Travel channels appears.

2. Click National Geographic Connection to go to the channel. Wait for the page to finish downloading, which takes a while thanks to the multimedia content (animation and music—be sure your speakers are on).

3. After the page has fully arrived, click the button labeled Add Active Channel. The Modify Channel Usage dialog box opens as shown in Figure 20.4.

   The dialog box asks "Do you want to subscribe to this channel?" and offers three subscription options:

   ☐ **No, Just Keep It in My Channel Bar**—A button for this channel is added to (or kept in) your Channel bar so you can easily visit the channel online at any time. You are not subscribed to it, however.

   ☐ **Yes, but Only Tell Me When Updates Occur**—When you update channels (as described later in this hour), you'll be notified when this channel has new content, but the new content will not be downloaded automatically. You'll visit the channel online to see the new content.

   ☐ **Yes, Notify Me of Updates and Download the Channel for Offline Viewing**—When you update channels, you'll be notified when this channel has new content and that content will automatically be downloaded to your PC so you can view it anytime, even offline.

Figure 20.4.

Subscribing to a channel.

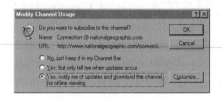

20

4. Choose a subscription option, and click OK to finish subscribing.

   Alternatively, you can customize the subscription by clicking the Customize button. The Customize button opens the Subscription Wizard, which leads you through a few simple dialog boxes on which you can choose when new content should be downloaded and whether you should be notified by email when new content is available.

After you subscribe to a channel, a button for it appears in the Channel bar, and an item for it appears in the Channels folder of your Favorites menu. You can use either to navigate to that channel at any time.

Subscribing to a Web Page

Besides subscribing to a channel, you can subscribe to any web page.

What's the difference? Well, a channel is smart. It's been specially designed to deliver to you only the new information, and only under certain conditions. It knows what you need to know, and when to tell you.

A web page isn't smart, so when you subscribe to a web page, the whole page is downloaded to your computer every time there's news, even if only a small part of the page has changed, or that change doesn't really amount to "news." Still, the overall effect is a lot like a channel.

To subscribe to a web page, you go to the page and choose Favorites | Add to Favorites (just as you would to add the page to your Favorites list). The Add Favorite dialog box offers three options much like those for a channel:

☐ **No, Just Add the Page to My Favorites**—This option creates a regular Favorite (see Hour 6, "Revisiting Places You Like").

☐ **Yes, but Only Tell Me When Updates Occur**—When you update channels, you'll be notified when this web page has new content.

☐ **Yes, Notify Me of Updates and Download the Page for Offline Viewing**— When you update channels, if this page has any new content, the page will be downloaded so you can read it offline.

After you choose any option, the page is added to your Favorites list. If you choose the second or third options, the page is updated along with your channels when you update channels.

Updating Channel Content

When and how channel content is updated depends on the choice you make for the Schedule option when subscribing. By default, most channels are updated automatically, according to a schedule set by the channel's publisher. You can use the Subscription Wizard to choose a different schedule.

On the final dialog box of the Subscription Wizard (see Figure 20.5), you'll see a drop-down list from which you can choose one of several predefined scheduling options. Alternatively, you can select the Manually option at the bottom of the dialog box to prevent all automatic updates and update only when you choose to.

20

Figure 20.5.

If you click the Customize button while subscribing, a wizard opens and leads you to this dialog box, on which you can set the schedule for updates.

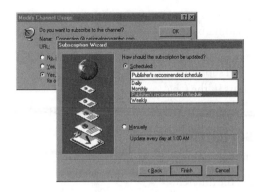

TIME SAVER

After subscribing, you can change the schedule and other options for a subscription from the Subscriptions list. Open the list from within IE4 by choosing Favorites | Manage Subscriptions. Point to the channel whose subscription options you want to change, and wait until the icon is selected. Then click the Properties button to open a dialog box on which you can change any of the options for that subscription.

If you choose the Manually option, you can update channels manually in a variety of ways:

☐ From the Internet Explorer menu bar, you can update all channels at once by choosing Favorites | Update All Subscriptions.

☐ From the Windows Start menu, you can update all channels at once by choosing Settings | Active Desktop | Update Now.

TIME SAVER

After a channel has been updated—regardless of how or when it was updated—you may disconnect from the Internet and read the channel content at your leisure, offline.

20

Removing Channels and Subscriptions

Adding channels, items, and subscribed web pages is all well and good, but eventually you'll decide it's time to separate the wheat from the chaff and blow away a few things.

You can delete channel and web page subscriptions from the Subscriptions list. But desktop items don't show up on the Subscriptions list, so you can't kill them from there. Instead, you can delete them from the Web tab of the Display Properties dialog box. You'll learn how to delete channels from the Subscriptions list and desktop items from the Web tab in the following To Do's.

If you ever delete a channel, a web page subscription, or a desktop item, and decide later that you want it back, subscribe again as you did the first time. Channels don't hold grudges.

To Do: Unsubscribe a Channel or Web Page Subscription

To unsubscribe to a channel or web page subscription, you use the Subscriptions list:

1. In Internet Explorer, choose Favorites | Manage Subscriptions. The Subscriptions list appears (see Figure 20.6).

2. To delete a subscription, click it once in the list to highlight it, and then press the Delete key. A warning appears, cautioning you that you're about to delete the channel or web page subscription permanently. (It's a paranoid warning. You can always resubscribe later.)

3. Click Yes to delete the subscription.

Figure 20.6.

Manage your channel and web page subscriptions from the Subscriptions list.

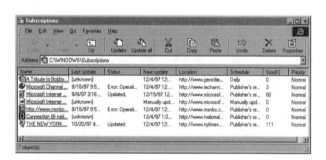

You don't have to actually delete a desktop item to get it off your desktop. You can simply disable it, which clears it from your desktop and prevents further updates. If you want to restore it later, you can reenable it and save the hassle of resubscribing.

To Do: Remove a Desktop Item

To remove a desktop item, complete these steps:

1. Right-click the desktop and choose Properties from the content menu. The Windows Display Properties dialog box opens.

2. Choose the Web tab (see Figure 20.7). The Web tab lists all items on your desktop.

3. Click the item to select it.

4. To disable the item, click its check box to remove the check mark. (If and when you want to restore the item, simply return to the Web tab and check the check box.) To delete it, click the Delete button.

Figure 20.7.

Delete desktop items from the Web tab of the Display Properties dialog box.

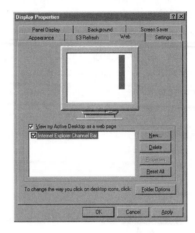

TIME SAVER

Clicking the Web tab's New button opens the Active Desktop Gallery so you can find and subscribe to a new desktop item.

Using Navigator 4's NetCaster

The channels capabilities in Navigator 4's NetCaster are similar in many ways to IE4's channels, as are the basic steps for using them. A few important differences exist, however:

☐ NetCaster is an optional component of Navigator 4. Today, it's included in most copies, but if you have an early release of Navigator 4 or Communicator, you may not have NetCaster. To learn how to download and install it, click the NetCaster button on the toolbar, or choose Help | Software Updates in Navigator.

☐ NetCaster's desktop items are called *Webtops*. Subscribing to a Webtop channel or one that displays in the browser window is identical; the channel generally decides itself whether it belongs on the desktop.

☐ NetCaster has its own family of channels; it is not compatible with channels designed for Internet Explorer 4. However, you can use NetCaster to schedule downloads of ordinary web pages, just as you can with IE4. You may use that capability to subscribe to web pages that contain IE4 channels, even though they will be handled by NetCaster as dumb web pages, not smart channels.

20

When NetCaster is installed, a tab labeled NetCaster appears on the right side of the Navigator window. Click it and NetCaster opens, showing its Channel Finder (a directory of available channels) and a toolbar for subscribing. You simply scroll through the list, pick a channel you want, and then click the Add button on the toolbar to subscribe. A channel properties window opens, on which you can choose options for the channel, such as an update schedule:

- [ ] To view content for channels you've subscribed to, click the NetCaster tab and choose My Channels, then choose one of your channels from the list.

- [ ] To manually update a channel, right-click it in the My Channels list, then choose Smart Update.

- [ ] To unsubscribe from a channel, right-click it in the My Channels list, then choose Delete.

Summary

Channels are a new idea, and the jury's still out. It's not clear yet whether they'll catch on, especially because they're really the most practical through full-time, rather than dial-up, connections. More importantly, the fact that Microsoft and Netscape have taken separate, mutually incompatible approaches may inhibit the growth of available channels.

Where a channel may work for you, give it a go. Keep your eye on developments as you go. Much about channels will change in the next few years.

Workshop

Q&A

Q Looking at the available channels, I see a few interesting ones. But mostly, they look like glorified commercials. Is that the way it's going to be with channels?

A At least for now, channels look more like a terrific new medium for advertising—a sophisticated form of junk mail—than a great new way to get information. After all, selling to you is the primary motivation for a company to spend the effort necessary to create and maintain a channel.

If you think about it, because channels are free (and will probably remain so), how else can companies recover the cost of supplying channel content if not through sales or advertising? True to their name—which derives from TV channels—channels will probably always supply a mix of valuable content and aggressive marketing.

20

Quiz

Take the following quiz to see how much you've learned.

Questions

1. A desktop item or Webtop is
   a. Any icon or folder on your Windows desktop
   b. A channel that displays regularly updated information on your desktop
   c. A news item relating to desktop technology
   d. A special pointer for opening channels

2. When a button on the Internet Explorer Channel bar gleams,
   a. The channel has been subscribed to
   b. There's new content for that channel you've not yet seen
   c. The channel is outdated and will soon be canceled
   d. The channel is happy

3. NetCaster can subscribe you to
   a. Channels set up to work with NetCaster
   b. Regular web pages
   c. Internet Explorer Channels (but only as regular web pages)
   d. All of the above

Answers

1. (b) The others look likely, but only (b) describes the real desktop item (in Internet Explorer) or Webtop (in NetCaster).
2. (b) The gleam is your signal that there's something new to see on a channel.
3. (d) All three top choices are potential input for NetCaster.

Activity

Look over the Favorites list or bookmarks you've accumulated since Hour 6. Do you visit any pages in the list daily? Several times a day? Do you visit some pages frequently, but find they don't often have new content? Do you spend long periods online reading some?

If you subscribe to these pages, you'll get the news automatically, you can read their content offline, and you won't waste time browsing to them when there's nothing new to see. Give it a try.

20

PART
VI

Getting the Most Out of the Internet

Hour

Hour **21**

Finding Safe Family Fun and Learning

Is cyberspace a family place? If you have kids, you may be wondering. One day, the media touts the Internet as the greatest thing since Gutenberg; the next, it's the harbinger of the Apocalypse, an instrument of pornographers, pedophiles, and disgruntled loners.

Actually, it's neither. It's a tool. Like any tool, it can be put to good and bad uses. A hammer can build shelter, or bash a finger. I think an adult has a right to use the Internet any way he or she wants to—within the law and without bothering anybody. But if you have kids who will use the Internet (and they should), you need to know how to insulate them from the net's racier regions.

More important, there have been cases of pedophiles and other such creeps starting online relationships with kids (and gullible grown-ups) that eventually lead to face-to-face meetings, and then to tragedy. In this hour, you learn commonsense rules for creep-proofing your kids.

At the end of the hour, you'll be able to answer the following questions:

☐ How can I get family surfing off to a fun, safe start?

☐ What steps can I take (and teach my kids) to keep them safe online?

☐ How can I use a utility or Internet Explorer's built-in censor to block out the smutty stuff?

Choosing a Family Starting Point

A good first step for family web surfing is to choose a good starting point, a "family home page" of sorts.

A good general-purpose family page provides a jumping off point from which all the links are family-friendly. Kids starting out should be taught to begin at that page, use only the links on that page, and to use Back to return to that page after visiting any of its links. That habit corrals a kid's surfing to a limited, appropriate range of sites.

You'll probably want to browse and search for a family page that best fits your family, but here are a few suggestions:

☐ **Yahooligans!** (www.yahooligans.com), a kids offshoot of the Yahoo! search tool containing links and a search engine that both lead only to good kid stuff (see Figure 21.1).

☐ **4Kids Treehouse** (www.4kids.com), a colorful site with great links and activities for kids, plus resources for parents.

☐ **Family.com** (www.family.com), an online family magazine.

☐ **Kids Avenue** (kidsavenue.home.mindspring.com), a fun collection of kids links and activities.

☐ The American Library Association's **Cool Sites for Kids** page (www.ala.org/alsc/children.links.html) has links for popular children's authors, games, and sports. It even has a homework help link!

After you pick the page, you may choose to make it your regular home page (see Hour 6, "Revisiting Places You Like"), or you may simply open that page at the beginning of any online session with your kids.

TIME SAVER

After you learn how to create web pages (Hour 23, "Creating Web Pages and Multimedia Messages"), you can create your own family home page, and fill it with links you'd like your kids to have easy access to.

21

Figure 21.1.

Yahooligans! makes a good starting point for family surfing.

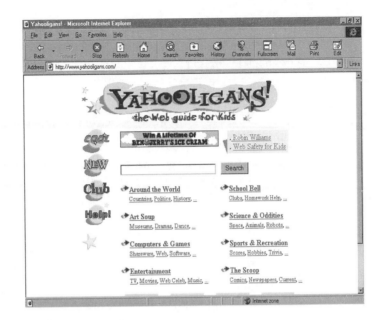

Important Family Safety Steps

Everybody's different and so is every family. It's not my place to say what's best for you or your kids. But in case you want some guidance about keeping your kids safe online, permit me to offer a few suggestions here. Then follow your own judgment.

Supervise!

This one's so obvious and so very difficult. As a parent I know that it simply isn't practical to supervise our kids every second of the day. To a tired parent of a preteen, the idea of the kid going off to his room for an hour to surf the net is appealing.

You must make your own choice about when to cut the cord, based not on what's convenient, but on your kid. Some kids are mature enough to surf responsibly at seven, others can't be trusted at seventeen. Only you know your kids.

If you're not sure whether your kid is ready to go solo, but you don't have time to supervise, keep him offline until either he's ready or you have the time. The Internet has lots to offer a kid, but your kid can live without it until the time is right for both of you.

TIME SAVER

I know it's not good to spy on your kids. But if your kid surfs unsupervised, and you want to know what he's been up to, open the browser's history file (see Hour 6) to see exactly where he's been.

21

Don't Defeat Passwords

Your Internet connection, email account, and a few other activities require you to enter a username and password to prevent unauthorized access.

Some software, particularly Internet connection programs, enables you to enter the password in a dialog box once, so you never have to type it again. That's a convenient feature, but it enables anyone who can flip a switch to use your computer to get online.

My advice is that you leave your computer configured so a password is required for both connecting to the Internet and retrieving email. Never tell your kids the passwords, and never log on or retrieve email in their sight. That ensures that you always know when your kids are online, and that they cannot receive email from anyone without your knowledge.

Resist Chat

It's a shame, because there's plenty of good clean fun to be had in chat rooms. But it must be said: Chat's the most dangerous place on the Internet. That's not because of all the sex-related chat rooms, although it's related to those.

On the web, the worst thing that can happen to a kid is that he or she gets exposed to *ideas*—words and pictures—you don't approve of. In chat, your kids can easily meet up with people who may hurt them. People are much more dangerous than ideas.

It works like this: A pedophile or other dangerous character—often posing as a kid—frequents chat rooms where kids hang out, and there establishes friendships, especially with lonely kids who are easy prey. As the friendship grows, the creep manipulates the kid into dropping the anonymous chat nicknames and exchanging email addresses, for private correspondence. Eventually, a private, face-to-face meeting is arranged.

There already have been numerous cases of kids abused this way, and the initial contact is almost always made in a chat room.

CAUTION

I pointed this out in Hour 18, "Chatting Live!" but it bears repeating. Most chat clients (including Microsoft Chat) include a dialog box in which you can create your chat nickname and also enter personal information, such as your name or email address.

Because this information is accessible to others online with whom you chat, I strongly recommend entering nothing in such dialog boxes except your nickname.

It's also a good idea to change your nickname from time to time, to keep chat friendships from getting too close.

Obviously, I recommend never allowing a child to use chat unsupervised, even if that child is trusted to surf the web unsupervised. Even supervised chatting is risky—by teaching a child how to chat, you increase the chances that the child may sneak a chat session unsupervised.

In fact, if you don't use chat yourself, I'd recommend simply not installing a chat client, so you needn't worry.

Online Rules for Kids

I know, my kids hate rules too. But these are pretty easy, and it's essential that you teach your kids these rules, even if you can't always be sure the rules will be followed. In particular, if you have older kids you will permit to use the Internet unsupervised, it's important that they know the rules for safe surfing. (Some folks suggest writing these up, having the kids sign them as a contract, and then posting the contract on the wall behind the computer.)

Tell your kids:

☐ Never reveal to anyone online your real name, email address, phone number, mailing address, school name, or username/password without a parent's involvement and consent. Any other personal information, such as birthday or Social Security number, is also best kept secret. Never, ever, ever send anyone a picture of yourself.

☐ Never reveal anything about your parents, siblings, teachers, or friends. Any such information can help a creep find you, and exposes family and friends to risks, too.

☐ Never arrange to meet in person any online friend unless a parent consents before the meeting is arranged, the parent will be present at that meeting, and that meeting will take place in a public setting, such as a restaurant or mall.

☐ Anytime you come across anything online that makes you uneasy, go elsewhere, or get offline. There's too much good stuff online to waste time looking at the bad.

☐ Never download or upload a file, or install any software on the computer, without a parent's okay.

Resources for Parents

Want to know more about protecting your kids online, teaching them to use the Internet smartly, finding great family sites, or just plain old parenting advice? You'll find all this and more online. Check out the following:

☐ **Parent Soup** at www.parentsoup.com (see Figure 21.2).

☐ **The Parents Place** at www.parentsplace.com.

21

☐ **Parent Time** at www.pathfinder.com/ParentTime/Welcome.

☐ **Kids Health** at www.kidshealth.org.

☐ *All About Kids* **magazine** at www2.aak.com/aak.

Figure 21.2.

Parent Soup, one of the best online resources for moms and dads.

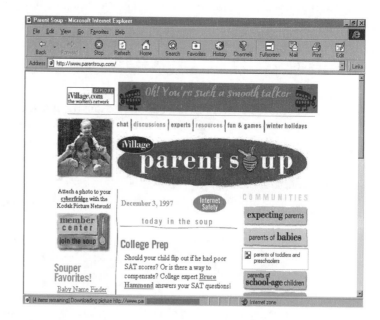

Censoring Web Content

You've probably heard of programs that can control what your kids see online. So why didn't I just mention those in the first place, and save you all this "online rules" crud?

Well, it's debatable how effective these programs are. First, most are really focused on the web, and aren't much protection elsewhere, such as chat or email. And, most censoring programs—erring on the side of caution, I suppose—inevitably censor out totally benign stuff that you or your kids may find valuable. (You'll see an example of that later, with Content Advisor.)

These programs may filter out sexual content, depictions of violence, and profanity, but what about ugly ideas? For example, the programs generally do not block out racist, sexist, or nationalist hatemongering, as long as those views are expressed without the use of profanity or epithets.

So even though these self-censoring tools are available, they're no replacement for supervision and safe-surfing practices. If you really do supervise, you probably don't *need* a censoring program. Still, you may find one or more of these programs useful, and they are getting better.

21

Getting a Safe-Surfing Program

Microsoft Internet Explorer has its own censoring program, which you'll learn about next. If you don't use Internet Explorer, or if you do but don't like Content Advisor, you'll want to check out the web pages of other popular self-censoring utilities.

From these pages, you can learn more about each product, and, in most cases, download a copy for your system.

- ☐ **Net Nanny** at www.netnanny.com.
- ☐ **SurfWatch** at www.surfwatch.com.
- ☐ **Cybersitter** at www.solidoak.com/cysitter.htm.
- ☐ **The Internet Filter** at turnercom.com/if.
- ☐ **CyberPatrol** at www.cyberpatrol.com.

Using Internet Explorer's Built-in Content Advisor

Internet Explorer (versions 3 and 4) has its own built-in system, Content Advisor, for controlling access to web sites and chat rooms. Content Advisor works much like the other safe-surfing programs (except it's a little harder to use than some), and it possesses many of the same strengths and drawbacks.

Understanding Content Advisor

Content Advisor works by relying on a rating system from the Recreational Software Advisory Council (RSAC), which also rates entertainment software and video games.

The RCSA ratings system assigns a score (0 to 4) to a web site or chat room for each of four criteria: Language, Nudity, Sex, and Violence. The higher the score in each category, the more intense the content that page or room contains.

For example, if a site has a score of 0 in the Language category, it contains nothing worse than "inoffensive slang." A Language score of 4, however, indicates "explicit or crude language" on the site. When a web site has been rated, the rating is built into the site, so Content Advisor can read the page's score before displaying anything.

Using the Content tab, you choose your own limit in each RSAC category. For example, suppose you are okay about violence up to level 3 but want to screen out all sexual content above a 2. After you set your limits and enable Content Advisor, Internet Explorer refuses to show you any page whose RSAC rating exceeds your limits in any category (see Figure 21.3).

21

Figure 21.3.

After you've enabled it, Content Advisor blocks Internet Explorer from displaying web pages whose RSAC rating exceeds your limits.

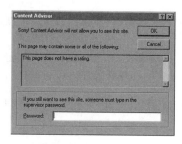

There's one problem: Only a tiny portion of sites online have been rated.

Therefore, enabling Content Advisor blocks not only rated pages you might find offensive but also *all* pages—offensive or not—that have not been rated, which means most of the web. For example, Content Advisor displayed the warning shown in Figure 21.3 when I was merely trying to access the Yahoo! search engine, which—like all search engines—is not rated.

As you may guess, blocking unrated pages severely cramps your surfing, and has little to do with protecting you from offensive content. As you'll see in the upcoming To Do section, you can choose an optional setting to allow unrated pages, but doing so defeats the purpose of Content Advisor because those pages will be permitted regardless of their content.

TIME SAVER

> Content Advisor works for both web browsing and Microsoft's Chat program (see Hour 18), blocking entrance to unsavory or unrated chat rooms.
>
> To use Content Advisor for Chat, replace step 1 of the following To Do by opening Chat and choosing View | Options, then choosing the Settings tab. Proceed with the remaining steps of the To Do section.

To Do: Enable and Configure Content Advisor

To enable and configure Content Advisor, follow these steps:

1. In Internet Explorer, open the Internet Options dialog box (choose View | Internet Options), then choose the Content tab.

2. In the tab's Content Advisor section, click the Enable button. A dialog box opens prompting for your Supervisor password. The Supervisor password prevents others from disabling Content Advisor or changing the settings.

3. Type a password, and then press Tab to jump down to the Confirm Password box. Type your password again, and then press Enter. The Ratings tab of the Content Advisor dialog box opens, as shown in Figure 21.4.

21

Figure 21.4.

On the Ratings tab, choose your personal limits for levels of Language, Sex, Violence, and Nudity.

4. Click the Language category. The Rating scale shows the current setting for Language.

5. Point to the slider (the rectangle) on the Rating scale, click and hold, and drag the slider along the scale. As the slider reaches each marker on the scale, a description appears below the scale, telling what type of language that setting permits. The farther to the right you pull the slider, the more lenient the setting. (Think of 0 as a G rating, 1 as PG, 2 as PG-13, 3 as R, and 4 as X.)

6. Release the slider at your preferred setting for Language.

7. Repeat steps 4, 5, and 6 for each of the other three categories: Nudity, Sex, and Violence.

8. When you have finished choosing ratings, click the General tab (see Figure 21.5). On the General tab, you can selectively check or uncheck the check box for two important options:

   ☐ **Users Can See Sites that Have No Rating**—Check this check box to allow the display of unrated pages. Content Advisor will continue to block rated pages that exceed your settings but will permit unrated pages, regardless of their content.

   ☐ **Supervisor Can Type a Password to Allow Users to View Restricted Content**—When someone tries to open a page Content Advisor would block, a dialog box pops up, prompting for the Supervisor password. If the password is typed, the page appears. This useful option gives your kids the opportunity to appeal to you for a temporary censorship waiver for a particular web site.

21

9. After selecting your options on the General tab, click OK. Content Advisor is enabled, and the Content tab of the Internet Options dialog box reappears.

Figure 21.5.

Choose Content Advisor options on the General tab.

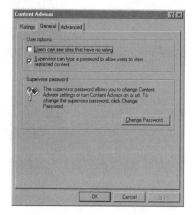

Summary

As you can see, no surefire way exists to protect unsupervised kids online. But there's no reason to worry, either. A few smart choices, and your supervision and guidance, will enable your family to enjoy the Internet's benefits while steering clear of its troubles.

I know I mentioned a lot of scary stuff here, but I do want you to relax and enjoy the net. Look at it this way: People get hit by cars everyday. Now, does that mean you should never leave the house, or lie awake worrying? No...it just means that you look both ways and hold your kid's hand when crossing.

Workshop

Q&A

Q I thought I heard they passed a law against online porn. If they did, why is it still there?

A The Telecommunications Reform Act of 1996 contained a highly controversial Communications Decency Amendment (CDA) that sought to impose penalties against anyone who made available online anything that was "harmful" to minors.

As everyone expected, the U.S. Supreme Court ruled the CDA unconstitutional in June of 1997, declaring that protecting freedom of speech demands protecting unpopular forms of expression.

21

So, for the time being, the Internet is a protected free-speech zone, which is probably best. But new censorship initiatives are already underway, as are the efforts to counter them. To learn more about the controversy, check out the Electronic Frontier Foundation (a free speech advocacy group) at www.eff.org.

Quiz

Take the following quiz to see how much you've learned.

Questions

1. Which of the following is safe for a kid to reveal online to others?

    a. Email address

    b. First name but not last

    c. School name

    d. Nothing

2. The most dangerous place on the Internet is

    a. The web

    b. A chat room

    c. A newsgroup

    d. A channel

3. Internet Explorer's Content Advisor can block the display of potentially offensive content found on

    a. The web, chat, and newsgroups

    b. Rated sites on the web and chat rooms

    c. All of the web

    d. A small portion of the web

Answers

1. (d) Kids should never reveal any identifying information online without your involvement and consent.

2. (b) Any place has risks to it, but among Internet locales, trouble starts most often in chat.

3. (b) Content Advisor can't control what you see anywhere but on the web and in chats, and really doesn't do much that's useful in those places, either.

Activity

If you have Internet Explorer, enable Content Advisor. Browse awhile, then disable it. Compare the two experiences. Do you feel safer when Content Advisor is on, or do you feel like the web suddenly got a lot smaller?

21

Hour 22

Buying and Selling on the Net

Only a few years ago, there was a huge hullabaloo about doing business online, about exploding interest in what we now call *e-commerce* (electronic commerce). But it was all talk—despite noises to the contrary, little real business was happening on the web. Most business web pages were mere e-advertising, not points of sale.

Someday, somebody may look back and call 1997 the "Year of E-Commerce," because last year e-commerce finally grew up and took off. You can buy or sell just about anything online these days, and companies are beginning to approach the web not just as an intriguing place to experiment, but as a market they mustn't miss.

In this hour, you'll get a taste of e-commerce from both sides of the e-counter. First, you'll expand upon what you picked up in Hour 7, "Protecting Your Privacy (and Other Security Stuff)," by learning how to shop and invest online safely. Next, you'll learn how to do business online and how to get started.

At the end of the hour, you'll be able to answer the following questions:

☐ How do I find and purchase products online?

☐ What's Microsoft Wallet, and how can it make shopping easier?

☐ Can I buy stocks and other financial stuff on the web?

☐ What are my options for doing business on the web, and how do I get started?

Shopping Till You Drop

Whattaya wanna buy? Whatever it is, you can probably buy it from a web page that sells, a *virtual storefront*.

NEW TERM *Virtual storefront* is just a fancy buzzword for a web page from which you can buy stuff. In coming years, you'll see the word *virtual* tacked onto all sorts of online activities to make them sound cooler: virtual jobs, virtual travel, virtual dentistry, and so on.

Using only the web-surfing skills you already possess, you can enjoy the benefits of online shopping:

☐ **24-hour, 365-day shopping**—Except for rare moments when the server is down for maintenance and repair, online stores are always open, such as many Denny's or Wal-Marts.

☐ **Access to product photos and specifications**—While browsing an online catalog, you often can click links to display product photos, lists of options, and even detailed measurements or other specifications. Such is the stuff of an informed buying decision.

☐ **Search tools**—Pages with extensive product listings often include a search tool you can use to find any product or type of product available from the merchant.

☐ **Web specials**—Some merchants offer discounts or other deals available only to those ordering online, and not to phone, mail-order, or in-person customers.

☐ **Custom ordering**—Some stores feature forms that let you specify exactly what you want. For example, PC sellers online such as Dell (see Figure 22.1) or Gateway let you choose each specification of a PC—processor, hard disk size, CD-ROM speed, and so on—from lists in a form. When you finish, the price for your system appears, along with a link for placing the order.

22

Figure 22.1.

*Forms in virtual
storefronts can help you
configure a custom order
or get a price quote on
one.*

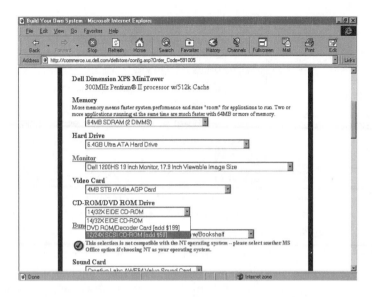

☐ **Mailing lists**—Many online merchants offer a form for subscribing to a mailing list that can keep you updated about new products and specials.

CAUTION

You know this already, but it bears repeating: Making an online purchase usually requires typing your credit card number and other sensitive information in a form. That's something you should never do on a site that's not secure (see Hour 7).

Explore virtual storefronts to your heart's content, comparing prices and other terms to make the best buy. But upon arriving at the page where you fill in your order form or open an account with the merchant, confirm that the page on which the form appears is secure. In most browsers, a secure site is indicated by a locked padlock icon or solid (unbroken) gold key near the bottom of the window.

If the order form is not on a secure page, buy elsewhere.

JUST A MINUTE

Buyer beware, online as anywhere else. As an online consumer, it'll behoove you to be an informed one. You can find reviews of products and merchants all over the web; one good way to find reviews is to use the product name and the word "review" together as a search term.

> You may also want to check out the web pages of consumer advocates, who help us beware by alerting us to schemes, scams, and duds. Two such sites can be found at
>
> ☐ **Consumer's Union** (publishers of *Consumer Reports* magazine) at www.ConsumerReports.org
>
> ☐ **Consumer World** at www.consumerworld.org

Using Accounts and Shopping Baskets

You already know how to fill out a form, and usually that's all there is to shopping. Many merchants also equip their storefronts with either or both of the following to make shopping more convenient:

☐ **Accounts**—When you set up an account with an online merchant, you give that merchant a record of your name and shipping address, and often your credit card information, too. After entering this information once, you can shop and buy anytime without having to enter it again. Just enter an account username and password, and the site knows who you are, how you pay, and where to ship your stuff.

☐ **Shopping baskets**—A shopping basket lets you conveniently choose multiple products, then place the order for all of it, instead of having to order each item as you select it. Shopping baskets also provide you with a chance to look over your list of selections and the total price, so you can change or delete items before committing to the order.

JUST A MINUTE

> Often, accounts and shopping baskets require the use of cookies on your computer (see Hour 7). If you have configured your browser to reject cookies, you may get a message when trying to set up an account or make a purchase, informing you that you must accept cookies to shop there.

In the following To Do section, you can get a feel for accounts, shopping baskets, and virtual storefronts by finding and ordering music CDs from CD Universe, a popular source for CDs, tapes, and videos. Note that you don't actually have to make a purchase; I'll show you how to cancel before committing.

22

To Do: Find Some CDs and Put Them in a Basket

Let's work with accounts, shopping baskets, and virtual storefronts. Follow these steps:

1. Go to CD Universe at www.cduniverse.com.

2. In the FIND form at the top of the page, choose Artist, then type the name of a recording artist in the box to the right of Artist.

3. Click the Go button. After a few moments, a list appears of titles available from that artist. (If CD Universe isn't sure which artist you want, a list of artists matching your search term appears first. Choose one to display the list of titles.)

4. From the list that appears, choose a CD or tape by clicking its price. The Shopping Basket screen appears, telling you that you've put that item in your basket (see Figure 22.2).

Figure 22.2.

A shopping basket lets you build a list of items to buy before placing the order.

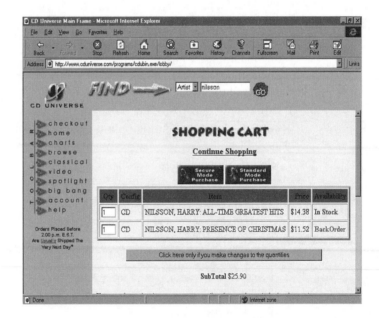

5. Click Continue Shopping. The list of titles reappears.

6. Choose another title by clicking its price. The Shopping Cart page reappears, showing both titles you've selected and the total price of your order so far.

7. Click Secure Mode Purchase to start the purchase process. A Purchase dialog box opens (see Figure 22.3) on which you may click Create a New Account (to open an account with CD Universe so you can complete the order) or enter the username and password of an existing account.

Figure 22.3.

Opening an account gives a merchant a record of your shipping address and payment information to make future orders easier.

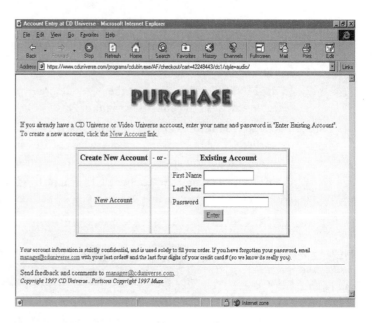

8. To quit without purchasing anything, just leave the site now. To order your selections, click Create New Account, complete the form that appears and follow any prompts.

JUST A MINUTE

Immediately after you place an order from an online store, some sort of confirmation of your order should appear. Many stores also email you a confirmation of your order.

Make a note of any information that appears in the confirmation—especially anything called an order number—and save any email message you receive. You'll need this information to query the merchant if your merchandise doesn't arrive within the time promised or if it isn't what you ordered.

Whipping Out Your Microsoft Wallet

Built into Internet Explorer 4, Microsoft Wallet is a little-known program that keeps track of the information you use for online purchases, such as shipping and billing addresses and credit card numbers.

It's a great idea—the only catch is that it only works when you're buying from a Wallet-enabled site, of which there are few now. A company called CyberCash, a major facilitator of online transactions technology, is working with Microsoft to promote Wallet, however,

22

so you may see more and more Wallet-enabled sites in coming months. Soon the CyberCash site may provide a directory of Wallet-enabled sites, so you might want to drop by www.cybercash.com if you plan to use Wallet.

TIME SAVER

For users of Navigator 3 or 4, a version of Wallet is available as a plug-in from Microsoft at

eu.microsoft.com/commerce/wallet/local/plginst.htm

You enter this information into Wallet only once. When making a purchase from a Wallet-enabled site, Wallet automatically presents you with lists of addresses and payment methods; to complete the purchase, you select the billing/shipping address and preferred credit card from the list.

JUST A MINUTE

All communications between Wallet and a Wallet-enabled web site are automatically secure, so your credit card information is safe from prying eyes.

To Do: Set Up Wallet in Internet Explorer 4

To set up Wallet in Internet Explorer 4, complete the following steps:

1. In Internet Explorer, choose View | Internet Options.

2. Choose the Content tab. At the bottom of the tab appear two buttons for setting up Wallet: Addresses and Payments.

3. Click Addresses. On the dialog box that opens, click Add. A dialog box opens on which you can enter your name, address, and phone number.

4. After entering the information, click OK to return to the Address Options dialog box. Observe that at this point you can click Add again, if you want, to add a second address.

5. Click Close to return to the Content tab.

6. Now click Payments. A dialog box like the one shown in Figure 22.4 opens.

7. Click Add, and a list of credit cards drops down.

8. Choose a card. A wizard opens to lead you step-by-step through entering the credit card information.

After you finish setting up Wallet, any time you initiate a purchase from a Wallet-enabled site, a dialog box will open on which you may choose the address and credit card to use.

Figure 22.4.

When you store your payment information in Wallet, it's easy to use when making a purchase from a Wallet-enabled site.

Buying Stocks and Such

The web makes a great place to sell intangible goods, such as stocks or securities—after all, if the product is intangible, why shouldn't the transaction be?

Obviously, such purchases carry the greatest risk among online shopping activities. They generally involve moving around large amounts of money and putting it at risk in investments. If that's your thing, however, you should know that trading online can be substantially cheaper than using a traditional broker, and in many cases your transactions are executed much more quickly—usually within minutes.

The steps for online investing are roughly the same as those for buying anything else online. Typically, you set up an account with an online brokerage, after which you may buy and sell at will.

Note, however, that opening an account with an online broker typically requires disclosing detailed information about yourself; you'll have to disclose your bank account numbers, Social Security number, and other private, sensitive information you would not have to reveal when making other kinds of purchases.

Investment Starting Points

To learn more about investing online, or to take the plunge and buy that 1,000 shares of Yugo, consult the sites described in the following sections.

For Financial Information and Advice

To learn more about online investing, read company profiles, and explore other money matters, check out

- [ ] **Stockpoint**—www.stockpoint.com
- [ ] **CNN's Financial News Network**—cnnfn.com
- [ ] *Wall Street Journal*—www.wsj.com
- [ ] **Dow Jones Business Information Services**—bis.dowjones.com
- [ ] **MoneyAdvisor**—www.moneyadvisor.com

22

- [ ] *Success* **Magazine**—www.successmagazine.com
- [ ] **Yahoo! Finance**—quote.yahoo.com
- [ ] **Finance Online**—www.finance-online.com
- [ ] **American Stock Exchange**—www.amex.com
- [ ] **NASDAQ**—www.nasdaq.com

For Making Investments

If you're ready to go ahead and put your money on the line (online!), visit these online brokers:

- [ ] **Yahoo!'s Online Trading directory**—www.yahoo.com/Business_and_Economy/ Companies/Financial_Services/Investment_Services/Brokerages/Online_Trading/
- [ ] **Mr. Stock**—www.mrstock.com
- [ ] **American Express Financial Services Direct**—www.americanexpress.com/direct
- [ ] **E*Trade**—www.etrade.com
- [ ] **Charles Schwab**—www.eschwab.com
- [ ] **Wall Street Electronica**—www.wallstreete.com

Selling on the Net

If you're interested in taking your own business into cyberspace, or if you've been put in charge of exploring that option for your employer, you already know that your research must consist of more than half an hour in this book. This is, however, a good place for you to begin considering what your company's web presence should be like.

 Web presence, sometimes also called *online presence*, describes the online identity and means of accessibility for a company; a company with a web page and email address has an online presence.

Other than learning about your options for establishing a web presence, you must also consider the laws and other issues related to expanding the scope of your business—online or offline.

Your business web page makes you an interstate (even international) business, one that must follow regulations pertaining to collection of sales tax, currency conversions, truth in advertising, and other laws of interstate and international commerce. Today, most of these laws are the same as those you'd follow if you did interstate/international business by mail order or telephone, although in coming years a distinct set of rules governing online commerce will evolve.

JUST A MINUTE

Why establish a web presence? Well, you probably already know the answer, but I'll offer the simplest, most compelling one: When a customer does a web search of companies carrying a particular product or service, do you want the hit list to include your competitors and not you?

To learn more about doing business online, check out these sites:

☐ The *Web Commerce Today* newsletter—www.wilsonweb.com/wct/

☐ BizWeb—www.bizweb.com

☐ AT&T's Business page—www.att.com/business

☐ U.S. Small Business Administration—www.sbaonline.sba.gov

☐ Dun & Bradstreet Small Business Services—www.dbisna.com/dbis/sbs/

Choosing a Degree of Presence

An important first step in taking a business online is choosing your initial degree of presence, the extent to which your company does business online. Many companies choose merely to promote themselves online, but don't actually sell there. Others are committed to offering online every product and service they have.

JUST A MINUTE

Each level of web presence requires a different level of commitment and resources from the company, in the form of time, money, and personnel.

Take care to choose a degree of online presence that you or your company can keep up with. Many companies overreach in their early forays online, deploying elaborate web sites that they fail to update regularly and keep working smoothly. To establish a good online reputation, it's generally better to field a modest—but well-maintained—web presence than to put up a state-of-the-art site and let it crumble.

Virtual Storefront

This is the Holy Grail of web presence, and for companies offering products or services that travel well, it's a great way to expand.

A real virtual storefront—including a catalog and ordering system—also requires the greatest commitment from the company. Above and beyond the demands of creating a web page— which anyone can do (see Hour 23, "Creating Web Pages and Multimedia Messages")—an online ordering system requires

22

☐ **Programming**—An ordering system requires scripts to process orders from what customers type in forms online. Writing those scripts demands programming experience and knowledge of a language such as Java, JavaScript, or CGI. Programmers with such skills are in high demand today, so they rarely come cheap (if they're good).

☐ **Security**—Processing orders demands creating and maintaining a secure web site, which takes the skills of a dedicated, full-time administrator. To ensure maximum security for transactions, most companies own and operate their own web servers—which dramatically increases the cost of web presence.

☐ **Customer Service**—A script can process orders, but dealing with customer questions and complaints requires experienced customer service personnel whom customers can contact via email or phone. Too often, companies expect existing personnel to also service web customers, forcing web customers to wait days or weeks for responses to queries. That's bad e-business.

☐ **Professional Design**—Sure, you can send some entry-level employee off in a corner with a computer and a web authoring book, and he or she will manage to produce a web page. If you take a look at what your competition is doing, however, you may notice that companies seeking a professional-looking online identity hire highly skilled, professional web designers.

JUST A MINUTE

An increasingly important part of having a web presence is having one's own *domain*, a unique Internet server address that identifies a company online. Sites such as www.toyota.com or www.kodak.com have domains that identify—and thus promote—their owners.

For example, I can set up a web page on an ISP's server (see Hour 23) without getting my own domain, but my page's URL would be something like www.isp.com/users/ned.htm. If I buy a domain, I can be www.nedsnell.com, which is much better for establishing my online identity.

If you set up and maintain your own web server, you get your own domain along with it. If you use space on another's server but want your own domain, you must apply for the domain and pay a fee (usually $100 to create the domain, and $75 a year thereafter to maintain it). The owner of the server will help you apply for the domain and pay the fee, which goes to InterNIC, the organization that controls Internet domains.

Informational/Advertising Page

For companies just starting out online, a full ordering system is prohibitive and unnecessary. Even today, most companies use the web not to sell directly, but to promote themselves and to provide customers (or investors) with company and product information. On such pages, you'll often find a toll-free number for placing orders. This approach is a great first step for a company that has a telephone sales or mail-order sales organization in place but is not yet ready to create and maintain an effective online ordering system.

A promotional page has another benefit: By offering web discounts a customer can take when calling, the company can easily track the amount of business generated by the web. This information is critical to evaluating whether and when the company should move up to a full virtual storefront.

JUST A MINUTE

> Any web programmer or ISP can add a *hit counter* to a web page to record the number of visitors to that page. A hit counter is a valuable tool, but it can be misleading. On most sites, a small proportion of the hits represent potential customers; the rest are just window-shoppers who happened to stroll by.

Selling Online but Off-Web

Finally, it's worth noting that the web is not the only medium for selling online.

A mailing list (see Hour 14, "Joining a Mailing List") can make an excellent sales tool. Many Internet programmers can set up and maintain a listserv for you, which you can promote to customers through a simple web page or your print and mail advertising. Because customers have the power to subscribe to and unsubscribe from the list, you know that those on the list at any given time are interested, well-qualified sales leads.

As an alternative to a listserv, you can broadcast email promotions to thousands of customers. As I hope the discussion of spam in Hour 16, "Putting a Stop to Junk Mail," showed you, however, sending unsolicited commercial email may win you more enemies than buyers. Limit your bulk emailing to customers who have explicitly expressed a desire to receive them. (Using a listserv can help you ensure this.)

JUST A MINUTE

> In general, do not attempt to advertise or sell in newsgroups.
>
> There's little to prevent you from doing so (although the moderators of some newsgroups delete commercial messages). The newsgroup culture is the heir to a time when much of the Internet operated under policies that barred commercial activity. Although the policies are gone, many newsgroup folks flame advertisers who invade their space. When you advertise in a newsgroup, you may antagonize the customers to whom you want to sell.

22

Some newsgroups are tolerant of advertisers. Watch carefully the groups in which you want to sell, and if you see no negative response to ads others have posted there, you may be able to post an occasional brief, non-pushy pitch without eliciting a backlash.

Publicizing Your Storefront

After establishing a web presence, you have to get the word out to let everybody know that cyberspace is your space, too.

Within a month or so after you put your company online, most of the search tools based on crawlers (see Hour 9, "Getting Started with Searching") will have found your page and added it to their databases. To ensure that customers find you, however, you should also visit such tools as Yahoo! and Excite and manually add your page to their databases.

For example, to add your site to Yahoo! (www.yahoo.com), browse to the category in which you want your site listed, then click the Add URL button at the top of the page. Follow the prompts, and you'll soon arrive at a form in which you can type your site's URL and descriptive information (see Figure 22.5). Phrase descriptive information carefully; the better you describe your site in such a form, the better the chances that your page will show up in the hit lists of customers looking for your kind of company.

Figure 22.5.

From links offered in search tools like Yahoo! and Excite, you can fill in a form to add your web page and description to the tool's database.

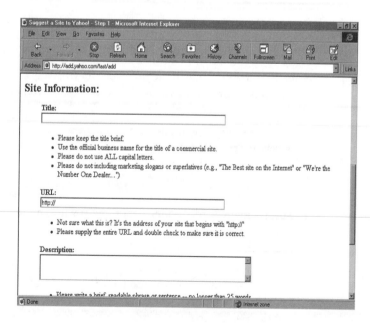

Besides adding your site to search tool databases, you can promote it through

☐ **Print/broadcast advertising**—Make sure your domain, web site address, and/or email address appears prominently in all your ads. A growing number of companies even incorporate their site addresses in store signs and company logos.

☐ **Company stationery**—Next time you print business cards or letterhead, add your URL. Put the web site URL on all employee business cards, along with the employee's email address.

☐ **Email**—Most email programs let you create a *signature*, a boilerplate block of text added automatically to the bottom of every message you send. If you use a signature, you can include the web site address in it.

Summary

By now you're ready to begin spending money online, making money online, or doing both (in which case you'll break even). I hope you've seen that actually buying or selling on the web is easy, but doing either *well*—taking into account all the risks and issues surrounding these activities—takes preparation, care, and practice.

Workshop

Q&A

Q **You say to buy only from shops I trust. I'm not sure who I can trust in my family. How am I supposed to know who to trust online?**

A Well, you don't—any more than you can trust any company until you've had some experience with it. The following are a few steps you can take to improve your chances of not getting stung:

When possible, deal online with companies you've already dealt with offline, such as mail-order companies whose print catalogs you've used or retailers whose stores you've visited. If the company was reliable on the phone or at the store, it probably will be okay online. When an online company is new to you, see whether it offers a toll-free number for phone orders. Try placing a phone order first, and if that works out well, order online next time. If you can't test the company that way, make your first order small and cheap, and make a second order only if the first goes well.

Finally, always try to make purchases with credit cards. I know that sounds funny, given my warnings about sending credit card numbers to unsecure sites. When a site is secure, however, using a credit card is safest. If a merchant lets you down, you can call the credit card company and dispute the charge.

22

Quiz

Take the following quiz to see how much you've learned.

22

Questions

1. True or false: You must be cautious to make Microsoft Wallet transactions only on secure sites.

2. Online shopping can be made easier by

    a. Shopping baskets

    b. Accounts

    c. Wallet

    d. All of the above

3. To best establish its online identity, a company needs its own Internet

    a. Personality

    b. Domain

    c. Attitude

    d. Programmer

Answers

1. False. All Wallet transactions are secure, so you needn't think about security when using Wallet to make a purchase.

2. (d) All three are techniques used to minimize the time and typing required to make purchases.

3. (b) The other three choices can all be useful, but it's the domain that gives a company its Internet name.

Activity

Look carefully at the next few print catalogs or brochures you get in the mail. Do you see a web or email address? If so, consider making your next purchase (or your next attempt to get more information) online.

Hour **23**

Creating Web Pages and Multimedia Messages

Got something to say or to sell? Want to offer your experiences or expertise to the world? There's no better way to do that today than by creating and publishing your own web page.

Building a web page is easier than you might think—if you know how to surf the web and to use any word processing program, you already possess the prerequisite skills for web authoring. This hour takes you the rest of the way, showing you several ways to create attractive web pages. The basic skills you'll learn here form a foundation upon which you can build later, on your own, to add scripts, multimedia, and other advanced techniques to your skill set. You'll also learn to create fancy, formatted email and newsgroup messages in this hour.

At the end of this hour, you'll be able to answer the following questions:

☐ What exactly is a web page, and what does it take to create one?

☐ How can I use a wizard or template to produce a simple page quickly?

☐ How can I compose and edit web pages in a web page editing program?

☐ How do I publish my pages on a web server?

☐ How can I apply my web authoring skills to create email and newsgroup messages adorned with fonts and pictures?

Understanding Web Authoring

Before you can dive into creating a web page, you need to pick up a more detailed understanding of how a web page works than you get by surfing the web.

What's in a Web Page?

A web page is actually a file in a format called HTML. An HTML file contains nothing but text (see Figure 23.1): the actual text you'll see online, and instructions for how that text is to appear.

Figure 23.1.

The actual text of an HTML file.

The text in an HTML file also includes the URLs where any links in the page lead, and the filenames, locations, and page positions of any pictures or other multimedia files, which are stored in their own, separate files.

When an HTML file is viewed through a browser, the browser interprets the instructions in the file. The browser formats the text onscreen as ordered, locates the picture files and displays them in their specified positions. The browser also reads and remembers the URLs the links point to, so it knows where to take a visitor who clicks one. Figure 23.2 shows the same file as 23.1, but now interpreted by a web browser.

Figure 23.2.

The same file as Figure 23.1, now interpreted by a browser.

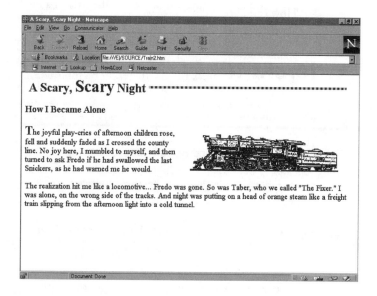

JUST A MINUTE

In general, the formatting instructions contained in an HTML file do not precisely control how the page will appear. Rather, the file provides a general idea of how the page is to appear, and each browser realizes those instructions slightly differently. That's why the same web page often looks different in two different browsers.

For example, the HTML file may specify that a particular line of text is to be displayed as a "heading." One browser follows that instruction by making the text big and bold, although another may follow it by underlining the text. This idea is often difficult to get used to for new authors accustomed to word processors that enable precise formatting control.

New, advanced web authoring techniques that give you greater control are available, but for most authors today (and certainly all beginners), formatting a web page is not about controlling *exactly* how the page will look, but rather about designating the *role* each element plays in the page: a heading, a normal paragraph, and so on.

A web page can be made up of many different parts, but most web pages contain most or all of the following core elements:

☐ **A title**—Browsers typically display titles in the title bar of the window in which the page appears. Note that the actual title does not appear within the layout of the page, although many authors repeat the title in a big heading near the top of the page layout.

☐ **Headings**—Browsers typically display headings in large, bold, or otherwise emphasized type. A web page can have many headings, and headings can be *nested* up to six levels deep; that is, there can be subheadings, and sub-subheadings, and so on.

JUST A MINUTE

> In HTML, there are six levels of headings, beginning with Heading 1 (the biggest and boldest, usually reserved for creating an on-page "title") and going down to Heading 6 (a very small, minor heading, indistinguishable from Normal text in many browsers).

☐ **Normal text**—Makes up the basic, general-purpose text of the page.

☐ **Horizontal lines** (sometimes called *rules*)—Dress up the page and separate it into logical sections.

☐ **Hyperlinks** (or simply *links*)—Links to many different things: other web pages, multimedia files (external images, animation, sound, video), document files, email addresses, and files or programs on other types of servers (such as Telnet, FTP, and Gopher). Links may also lead to specific spots within the current page.

☐ **Lists**—May be bulleted (like this one) or numbered.

☐ **Inline images**—Pictures that are incorporated into the layout of the page to jazz it up or make it more informative.

☐ **A background**—An inline image that, unlike a regular image, covers the entire background of the page so text and other images can be seen on top of it. Instead of an image, you can use a solid background color.

☐ **Tables**—Text and inline images organized in neat rows and columns.

What Tools Can I Use to Write a Page?

If you were skilled in HTML code, you could write a web page by typing the correct code in a text file, in any word processor or text editing program (such as Windows Notepad). Some folks do it that way, but doing so makes it hard to see what you're creating; you have to jump from the editor to a browser every time you want to see how the page will look online.

A better choice is a WYSIWYG web authoring program (see Figure 23.3). A WYSIWYG web authoring program shows you the page as it will look online, while you're working on it.

23

NEW TERM *WYSIWYG (What You See Is What You Get)* describes a program that shows you, as you create something, exactly how it will look in its finished form, on paper or online. For Windows and the Mac, most word processors, presentation programs, desktop publishers, and web authoring programs are WYSIWYG.

Figure 23.3.

A WYSIWYG web authoring program, such as Communicator's Page Composer, lets you use familiar word processing techniques to create a web page.

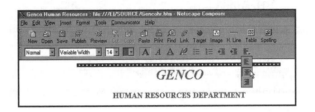

If you're careful to select and install the complete suite, you get a WYSIWYG editor with either of the Big Two:

☐ The full Communicator suite includes Page Composer, which you open from within Navigator by choosing Communicator | Page Composer.

☐ The full Internet Explorer 4 suite includes FrontPage Express, which you open from the same menu where you can open the browser (in Windows 95, choose Programs | Internet Explorer | FrontPage Express).

You can learn about other web authoring programs at

```
www.yahoo.com/Computers_and_Internet/Software/Internet/World_Wide_Web/
HTML_Editors/
```

JUST A MINUTE

Even when using a WYSIWYG editor, pages you create will look different when seen through different browsers: WYS is not always WYG.

Even when working in a WYSIWYG editor, it's a good idea to display the document in a browser now and then, to check its appearance. Composer and FrontPage Express each include a button for viewing the page you're editing in Navigator and Internet Explorer.

Where Do I Get the Pictures?

The pictures you'll use in your web pages can come from anywhere: You can draw them in a paint program (such as CorelDRAW! or Windows 95's Paint accessory), scan them from your own photos, or even use images captured by a digital camera.

What matters isn't the source of the pictures, but the image file format in which they're stored. The pictures you may include in a web page either as inline images or as background images must be in either the GIF (.gif) or JPEG (.jpg) file format. (GIF is usually preferable, because it is supported by all graphical browsers, although JPEG is also supported by most browsers and often produces better-looking results with photographs.) If the program you use to create images won't save in GIF or JPEG format, many paint programs (and some web authoring programs) can convert your files to GIF or JPEG.

If you want to use pictures, but don't want to create them, you can find libraries of commercial, shareware, and free clip art files in GIF and JPEG format at the software store and online. Good online starting places for getting clip art (and other media, such as sounds) include

- ☐ **Macmillan Computer Publishing's Design Resources Page**—www.mcp.com/resources/design
- ☐ **Yahoo!'s Clip Art Directory**—www.yahoo.com/Computers_and_Internet/Multimedia/Pictures/Clip_Art
- ☐ **Index to Multimedia Information Sources**—viswiz.gmd.de/MultimediaInfo/
- ☐ **Microsoft Site Builder Network Home**—www.microsoft.com/gallery
- ☐ **Netscape Page Starter Site**—home.netscape.com/assist/net_sites/starter/index.html
- ☐ **Free Graphics**—www.jgpublish.com/free.htm

Making Quick Pages with a Wizard

The quickest way to build a page is by running a *page wizard*. Both Composer and FrontPage Express have one of these wizards, which leads you through filling in a few quick dialog boxes and choosing some options. When you finish, the wizard spits out a finished page, ready for publishing.

A wizard doesn't give you as much control as composing the page in a web authoring program. Using a wizard is faster, however, and if the results aren't exactly what you want, you can always open your wizard-built page in your web authoring program and change it.

The following To Do section shows you how to use Page Composer's wizard, which is unusual because you must use it while online. If you'd rather try out FrontPage Express's wizard (which works offline), choose File | New to open a list of options for starting a new page, then choose Personal Home Page from the list.

23

To Do: Create a Page Fast with Composer's Wizard

To create a page quickly with Page Composer's wizard, follow these steps:

1. Open Navigator (not Composer) and connect to the Internet.

2. In Navigator, choose File | New | Page From Wizard. This instructs the browser to connect to the Page Wizard page at

   `home.netscape.com/home/gold4.0_wizard.html`

   You can also simply point the browser to that URL, although going through the menus is easier.

3. In the active frame (upper right), scroll down past Netscape's cheery introductory copy to display the START button.

4. Click the START button in the upper-right frame. The page appears as shown in Figure 23.4. The Wizard page is split into three frames:

   ☐ The upper-left frame, INSTRUCTIONS, describes each element you will create. Within each description are links that, when clicked, display a form or list of choices in the bottom frame.

   ☐ The bottom frame, CHOICES, is where you will type text in forms (to create page content) or choose aspects of the look of your page from lists of choices.

   ☐ The upper-right frame, PREVIEW, shows a preview of your page as you develop it.

Figure 23.4.

To compose a page in Netscape's wizard, you fill in choices in the bottom frame, according to instructions in the upper-left frame.

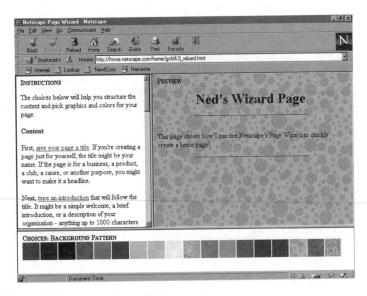

5. Scroll the INSTRUCTIONS frame until you see the link "give your page a title," and click that link. A form appears in the CHOICES frame.

6. Delete the descriptive text that appears in the form and type a title for your page. The Page Wizard uses this as the HTML document title *and* as a large, bold heading at the top of the page itself.

7. Click Apply. The new title appears in the PREVIEW frame (upper right), centered at the top of the page.

8. Scroll down the INSTRUCTIONS until you see another link to a page element you can create. Click it, then follow the instructions to complete the form in the bottom frame.

   Continue defining page elements until the PREVIEW frame shows a page to your liking. (Note that you can scroll the INSTRUCTIONS backward at any time to make changes.)

9. When done, scroll to the bottom of the INSTRUCTIONS frame, where you will see buttons labeled Build and Start Over.

10. Click Build. The finished page opens in Navigator.

11. From Navigator's menu bar, choose File | Edit Page. Composer opens, displaying your new home page.

12. Click the Save button on Composer's toolbar (or choose File | Save), select a folder and filename for your page, and save it. The page is given a default filename of Yourpage.html. You can change this name to anything you like, but make sure the file extension remains .htm or .html.

13. Click OK to save the file. Your page is ready to be published or to be edited further in your web authoring program.

Composing a Page in a WYSIWYG Editor

Composing a web page in a WYSIWYG editor is much like composing and formatting a document in any word processor. You type your text, then format it by selecting it with your mouse and applying formatting—such as bold, fonts, and so on—from toolbar buttons or menu items.

If you look at the toolbars in FrontPage Express or Composer, you'll probably recognize many of the tools, such as a drop-down list for choosing a font or a big **B** for applying Bold.

Although the web authoring programs present you with lots of formatting tools, it bears repeating here that precise formatting you apply—such as font selections—may not be supported by all browsers through which your work may be seen. The formatting that matters most is the application of *styles*, which you choose in either Composer or FrontPage Express

23

from a drop-down list on the toolbar (see step 10 of the upcoming To Do section). It's the style that really tells browsers how to handle a block of text.

TIME SAVER

Besides using a web authoring program or a wizard, there's one more way to create a page: your word processor. Increasingly, word processors have the capability to save files in HTML format, as the latest versions of both Microsoft Word and WordPerfect can.

A word processor is not as good for authoring as a real authoring program, but it will do in a pinch. More importantly, this program makes it easy for you to convert existing documents into web page files. For example, you can open your résumé in Word, then save it as an HTML file—now it's ready for the web.

To Do: Compose a Page in FrontPage Express

To compose a page in FrontPage Express, complete the following steps:

1. Open FrontPage Express. Opening FrontPage Express automatically starts a new page, but you can also start one by choosing File | New | Normal Page.

2. From the menu bar, choose File | Page Properties. The Page Properties dialog box opens, as shown in Figure 23.5.

Figure 23.5.

Use the Page Properties dialog box to give your page a title and background.

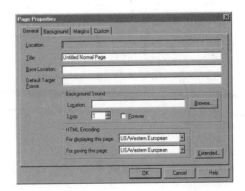

3. Click the General tab, if it is not already selected, then click in the Title box.

4. Delete the automatic title, and type one of your own. Then click OK to close the dialog box.

5. After giving your page a title is a good time to save it for the first time. Click the Save button in the toolbar or choose File | Save. A special Save dialog box opens.

6. In the dialog box, click the As File button.

7. Choose a location for the page file, and type a name for the file in the File name box. Then click the Save button to save the file. From now on, you can save the file at any time in one step, just by clicking the Save button on the toolbar.

8. Now type and edit the text of your page, just as you would in any word processor. Don't worry yet about formatting that text; just get the words down.

9. After your text is typed, you may format the text. Begin by selecting a paragraph to format.

10. Drop down the Change Style list (see Figure 23.6) from the toolbar, and choose a style (Normal, a heading, and so on) to apply to the selected text.

Figure 23.6.

Format text in a page by selecting it and then choosing a style from the Change Style list.

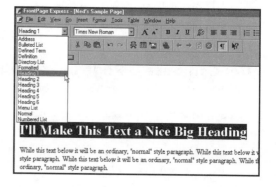

11. Now add a picture, if you happen to have an image file you want to use. Ideally, the file should be in GIF or JPEG format, but if it isn't, use it anyway—FrontPage Express can probably convert it for you.

12. In the page, click at the general spot within the text where you want the picture to go. Then click the Insert Image button on the toolbar to open the Image dialog box.

13. Click Browse, to browse for and select the image file.

    After the file appears in your page, you can reposition the picture by pointing to it, clicking and holding, and dragging to where you want the picture to appear. Note that you cannot precisely position a picture; "positioning" a web page picture means choosing its rough position within the text, and which side of the page it's on.

JUST A MINUTE

When you next save the page file, you may see a dialog box on which you click Yes to accomplish either (or both) of two important things: Convert the picture file to GIF format (if it was not already a GIF file) and save the picture file in the same folder as the HTML file (if it was originally stored elsewhere).

23

> It's always best to store all files that make up a web page—the HTML file, the image files, and so on—in the same folder or directory on your computer.

14. Now add a background. Open the Page Properties dialog box (File | Page Properties) and click the Background tab.

    ☐ To create an image background, check the check box next to Background Image, and then click Browse to browse for and select a GIF image file, just as you would when inserting a picture.

    ☐ To create a color background, choose a color from the Background drop-down list.

15. Finally, add a link. You can feature links that take your visitors to your favorite places on the web, or you can include a link to another page you've created, so your page can actually be made up of several pages linked together. Begin by selecting the text or picture that will serve as the link.

JUST A MINUTE

> If you use a picture as a link, always provide the same link elsewhere on the page (usually at the bottom) for use by visitors whose browsers don't display pictures.

16. Click the Create or Edit Hyperlink button on the toolbar. The Create Hyperlink dialog box opens.

    When you're creating a link to another web page, the Hyperlink Type box should read http://. If it does not, drop down the list and choose http://, which is the required type for a web page. (Observe, however, that the list lets you create links to resources other than web pages.)

17. In the URL box, type the URL of the web page to which this link should lead when clicked by a visitor. Be sure to leave the http:// prefix on the URL. Click OK to create the URL.

18. Save your page one last time. Now it's ready for publishing, or further editing and refinement.

Publishing Your Web Page

After your web page is finished, you must upload it to a web server so others on the Internet can see it. First, you need space on somebody's web server—enough to hold all the files that make up your page (the HTML file plus picture files). A typical web page with a picture or two usually requires less than 100KB (kilobytes) of space on a server. The larger and more picture-laden your page, the more server space you'll need.

Preparing to Publish

If your page is related to your job, you may be able to get permission to publish it on your company's server; talk to your company's network administrator or webmaster. Most colleges and universities also have web servers and often allow students and faculty to publish on them.

If you don't have permission to publish your web page on your company's or school's server and don't plan to create your own server (which is prohibitively expensive and technical for beginners), you need to acquire space on somebody else's web server, usually your ISP's web server.

After you know whose server will hold your web page files, you must upload the files from your PC to the server. The exact procedures for doing this differ by ISP; you must get complete uploading instructions directly from the company whose server you will use.

In particular, you need to know

- [ ] The server's address—for example, `http://www.server.com`
- [ ] The uploading protocol used by the server—for example, HTTP or FTP
- [ ] Any username and password that you are required to use to gain access to the server
- [ ] The posting command, which you give the server to gain access for uploading files
- [ ] The particular directory in which your files will be stored—for example, `http://www.server.com/ned/`

Using a Publishing Utility

After your ISP provides you with instructions for uploading your files, you can make uploading easier by supplying those instructions to a web publishing program like those built into FrontPage Express and Composer.

To use either of these utilities, first open in the editor the page you want to publish. Then, complete the following:

- [ ] In Composer, click the Publish button and follow the prompts.
- [ ] In FrontPage Express, choose File | Save As to open the Save dialog box. In Page Location, type the complete URL the page will have on the web. Click OK and follow the prompts.

23

The first time you use one of these publishing utilities, you need to spend a few minutes supplying information about the web server you'll use.

After you've done that, your uploads from then on will be quick and easy. These utilities remember all your server information so after you enter the information once, you don't need to fiddle with it again; just start the publishing procedure as before, and most of the steps happen automatically.

Creating Formatted Email and Newsgroup Messages

In Hour 13, "Sending and Receiving Email," you created email messages—wonderful, simple, flat email messages containing nothing but text. What you may not know is that you can put in an email message the same kinds of content and formatting you use in a web page (see Figure 23.7). You can send messages containing all kinds of fonts, colors, pictures, links—if it can be put in a web page, it can go in a message.

Figure 23.7.

In HTML-supporting messaging programs, you can create and display email and newsgroup messages with all the pizzazz of web pages.

There's one hitch to sending fancy messages like this: Your recipient may not be able to display them. Like a web page, a fancy message must be created in HTML format. To read the message, your recipient must use an email program—such as Messenger or Outlook Express—capable of displaying HTML-based messages in addition to regular email messages.

TIME SAVER

In Outlook Express and Messenger, it is not necessary to send an HTML message just to send links. Anytime you type a URL or email address in the body of a message, the email program detects it and formats it as a link.

While reading your message, your recipient can click the link to go where it leads, and you can click the links in messages from others.

The majority of those using Internet email today cannot display HTML messages, so unless you happen to know that your intended recipient has an email program that can show HTML messages, it's best to stick with plain text messages.

To create an HTML message, complete these steps:

☐ In Outlook Express—Open a new message window as you usually would. From the message window's menu bar, choose Format | Rich Text (HTML).

☐ In Messenger or Collabra—You must change the Preferences to send HTML messages. Choose Edit | Preferences, then choose the Messages subcategory under the Mail & Groups category. Check the By Default, Send HTML Messages check box near the top. Then close the Preferences dialog box and start a new message as usual.

When composing an HTML message in either program, you'll notice that the toolbar and menu bar show most of the tools and options available in the suite's web authoring program (refer to Figure 23.7). You compose and format an HTML message in Outlook Express exactly as you do a web page in FrontPage Express, and you compose and format an HTML message in Messenger exactly as you do a web page in Composer.

TIME SAVER

By default, most programs that can send HTML messages automatically send replies in the same format in which the message was received. In other words, if someone sends you an HTML message (which means the sender's email program can display HTML), and you click Reply to respond to it, the message you create is automatically in HTML format.

23

Summary

You don't have to create your own web page—it's not like there's a shortage. If you really do have something to say, however, you'll find creating and publishing a page fairly easy, especially if you rely on the tools in an Internet suite.

Workshop

23

Q&A

Q **What about Java? What about video clips, sound, forms, and frames? I want to be a web *author*!**

A Well, web authoring is a big topic. You've learned a huge part of it in just one hour, but there are 1,000-page books devoted to the subject, and even a thousand pages doesn't cover all of authoring.

Besides practicing and sharpening the skills you've already learned, your next step (other than learning frames, perhaps) should be to learn more about online multimedia—specifically, how to do more with pictures, and how to add sound, video, and animation to your pages. Many good books on this topic are available. Also, carefully study the design and layout of pages you see that impress you. Learn from what others are doing.

After multimedia, the next hurdle is scripting, and probably doing so with Java. Many good books are available about Java, too, but I'll tell you right now that many folks, upon meeting Java, suddenly decide that they already know enough about web authoring. Just about anybody can learn to create web pages and add multimedia to them, but learning Java takes thinking like a programmer, and that's a specialized talent.

You can also learn a lot about authoring online. A good way to start is by reading one of the web authoring books Macmillan often offers free on the web, or Macmillan's directory of web authoring resources:

☐ **Macmillan Computer Publishing's Personal Bookshelf (free online books)**—www.mcp.com/personal

☐ **Macmillan Computer Publishing's Web Authoring Resources page**—www.mcp.com/resources/webpub

Quiz

Take the following quiz to see how much you've learned.

Questions

1. The pictures you use in web pages must be in which formats?

    a. GIF or JPEG

    b. JIF or SKIPPY

    c. JEFF or MUTT

    d. All of the above

2. True or false: A carefully formatted page looks the same in all browsers.

3. The pictures or other multimedia files for a web page should be stored in

    a. Aluminum foil

    b. A safe place

    c. The same folder or directory where the HTML file is stored

    d. The same folder or directory where your web authoring program is stored

Answers

1. (a) GIF and JPEG are the web standards.

2. False. All browsers display the same page a little differently, no matter how carefully it's formatted.

3. (c) Both on your computer and on the web server, it's best to keep all of a page's files—HTML and media—in the same place.

Activity

Create a simple web page containing links to places you like to visit, and upload it to the web space provided by your ISP. Open the page online in your browser (like any other visitor) and test the links to be sure they work as designed.

23

Hour 24

Moving Toward Web Integration

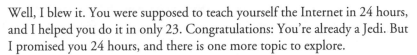

Well, I blew it. You were supposed to teach yourself the Internet in 24 hours, and I helped you do it in only 23. Congratulations: You're already a Jedi. But I promised you 24 hours, and there is one more topic to explore.

Now that you know how to use the Internet of today, it's a good idea to learn where the Internet is going—or rather, how the ways you use the Internet will evolve over the next few years. The most important change—the merging of web content and local content—has already begun, and will affect not just the way you use the Internet, but the way you use your computer overall.

This final hour offers a peek into what net-surfing is becoming, so you can anticipate and quickly exploit new developments as they arrive. It also shows the optional changes Internet Explorer 4 can make to your computer—changes that offer a preview of the way all computers will work one day. At the end of the hour, you'll be able to answer the following questions:

- [ ] How are the web and my computer merging and why?
- [ ] How can I use the web integration already built into some types of programs?

☐ How can I web-integrate my computer by installing Internet Explorer 4's "Active Desktop" component?

What's Web Integration?

Although you may not think of it this way, what you do on the web is not that different from what you do on your computer or local area network. The following table shows how online activities and local activities are really much the same.

On a Computer (Local Activities)	On the Web (Online Activities)
You navigate to programs and files by clicking folders or clicking through a directory.	You navigate to programs and files by clicking links in web pages and in directories of links.
Sometimes, you navigate to a file by specifying its location, for example, by entering a disk letter and path (such as `C:\file.txt`).	Sometimes, you navigate to a file by specifying its location, for example, by entering a URL (such as `www.web.com/file.htm`).
You open programs and files by double-clicking their file icons or names.	You open programs and files by clicking links, which may be pictures (icons) or text (names).

In light of this comparison, developers have wondered: Why do we treat online resources and local resources differently? Why not instead retool our computers so you can do everything the same way? Why learn two different ways to perform the same basic task, just because one file is on your computer and the other is on a web site in Vancouver? A file is a file—its physical location should be irrelevant.

That's the idea behind web integration. On a web-integrated system, you navigate among files and folders, and open files and programs, the same way whether the file is local or on the web. You needn't learn two different ways of getting around, and in many cases, you won't even have to think about whether the file or program you want to use is on the web or on your computer.

JUST A MINUTE

The linchpin of web integration today is the assignment of default programs for accessing online content.

When you install most browsers in Windows or the Mac, the browser is automatically assigned in the file Registry (see Hour 8, "Plug-ins, Helpers, and Other Ways to Do More Online") as the default program for displaying HTML files and dealing with URLs.

Anytime an HTML file icon is opened, or URL entered, the browser opens automatically to display it. On most systems, the browser also determines whether the requested file is online or offline, and connects to the Internet automatically, if necessary.

What's the Benefit?

When you get accustomed to web integration, you might find that you use your computer more productively and more intuitively.

Whenever your brain must jump back and forth between two skill sets (an activity called *code switching*), your productivity suffers. When you can do all things with one set of skills, your brain can focus on the task at hand, not on the techniques that accomplish it.

On a web-integrated computer, you'll deal with all files and programs the same way, whether they're online or local. This streamlined way of working may also make you more comfortable working with online resources, so you'll get more out of the web.

Where Will Integration Happen?

Web integration is already here—in a primitive form—in Internet Explorer 4 (see Figure 24.1), as you'll learn later in this hour.

Figure 24.1.

Internet Explorer 4's Active Desktop provides a preview of a web-integrated world.

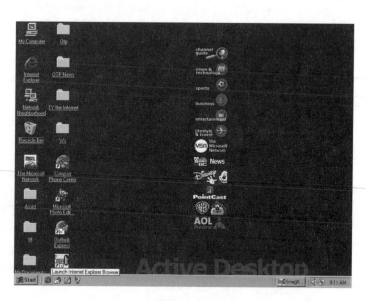

Very soon, however, a similar level of web integration will emerge as a standard feature of all personal computer operating systems, including any new versions of Windows, Mac OS, or UNIX to come along from now on.

Each time you buy a new computer or upgrade your present computer to a new operating system, you'll probably notice a tighter level of web integration and more built-in Internet software than before. Within two or three years from now, seamless web integration will be taken for granted on a personal computer.

But even sooner (now, actually), you'll see web integration manifesting itself in a variety of ways beyond the operating system. The following sections give descriptions of other ways you'll see the online and offline worlds mesh, now and in the near future.

Programs and Documents

A growing list of programs and file types are already designed to incorporate web-based content or integrate with web-based services.

Net-Smart Programs

Some items on the Help menu and within the help files of Internet Explorer, Navigator, and other programs lead to online content. For example, choose Help | Member Services in Navigator 4, and Navigator connects to the Internet and opens a Member Services page on Netscape's web site.

The interesting thing is that these menu items look just like any other menu items—you don't know that the item takes you online until you choose it. As far as the program is concerned, there's no difference between local and online resources.

It makes sense for a browser to assume that you have an Internet connection, but what about other kinds of programs, such as word processors or money managers? They also are beginning to incorporate online content, particularly in their Help menus and in menu items that lead to web pages for registering with the program's developer or downloading upgrades and accessories.

Many Microsoft products—even some unrelated to the Internet—have a "Microsoft on the Web" item on their Help menus. That item opens a submenu of choices, each of which leads to online content (see Figure 24.2). Microsoft's Cinemania—a movie reference CD-ROM—includes a Go Online button you can click to download the latest movie reviews and add them to your copy of Cinemania.

Also, many programs unrelated to the Internet are nonetheless built to integrate with related web-based services; for example, Intuit's popular Quicken financial management program can optionally interact with your bank's web site to provide you with online access to your accounts.

24

Figure 24.2.

In a growing list of programs, menu items may lead to online content, even when they look like any other menu item.

JUST A MINUTE

Before purchasing a program based on its capability to interact with the Internet, read the fine print. Some programs are designed to interact with the net only through a particular ISP or online service—you must use that provider to take advantage of any online features.

In such cases, the program developer is not really providing the benefit of web integration; rather, the developer is acting as a salesperson for an Internet provider.

As non–Internet-related programs rely increasingly on online content, users without Internet accounts may begin feeling a little left out. For the rest of us, however, this approach makes good sense.

Online content saves disk space on your computer. More importantly, it enables a program's developer to ensure that you can always get the latest, most complete information. For example, as users discover flaws (called *bugs*) in a program, instructions for dealing with the bugs can be added to the online help text, or a file for fixing the bug (called a *patch*) can be made available from a link in the help text.

Net-Smart Files

Recent versions of many document-producing programs enable you to put live, active links to online content within a document. For example, in Microsoft's Office 97 programs (Word, Excel, PowerPoint, Access, and Outlook), when you type an URL in any document (see Figure 24.3), that URL is automatically formatted as an actual, functioning link. (You can enable or disable this feature from each program's AutoCorrect dialog box.)

On paper, of course, the link is useless. Suppose you give someone that document as a file, however, either on a disk or attached to an email message? While reading the document on his or her computer, the reader can activate the link to access online content, if the reader's computer is Internet-equipped.

Figure 24.3.

*You can insert live links
to online content in
documents you create
with Word, PowerPoint,
and other web-integrated
programs.*

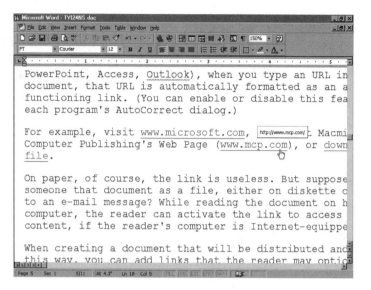

When creating a document that will be distributed and read in this way, you can add links
that the reader may optionally click to access online content that expands upon, reinforces,
or supports the content in your document. For example, when mentioning a particular
company, you might insert a link to that company's web page.

In fact, if I gave you this book as a set of Word files, you could click any web page I mention
to go straight to it.

Net-Smart Computers

The *Net PC* concept takes web integration one step further than a web-integrated operating
system. A Net PC is a PC with a sealed case—no floppy drive or CD-ROM drive. Files get
into or out of a Net PC only through a network it's connected to, such as the Internet.

JUST A MINUTE

> Despite its name, the new RCA Network Computer (mentioned later in this
> hour) is not a Net PC, but rather an Internet terminal like its cousin,
> WebTV.

In some Net PC scenarios (several are evolving), the programs you use would run on servers;
in others, programs are downloaded to your computer as needed. In either case, a Net PC
can be a smaller, cheaper box than the typical Mac or PC of today, and could be used
effectively to browse the Internet. A few Net PCs are on the market, and more on the way.

24

A team of heavy hitters—including Microsoft, Intel, Compaq, and IBM—is developing Net PCs.

The early models are aimed at corporate sales, but some foresee the Net PC as an affordable home Internet terminal. Most experts today, however, don't see the Net PC in homes. The cost of a Net PC is so close to that of a budget PC that a home user would always opt for a more flexible, full-function computer.

Net-Smart TV?

A computer and a television both need a screen, right? So why not make TVs that are also PCs, to save the cost of having two screens? That's the basic idea behind what some folks call *PCTVs*, televisions that are also computers (and maybe video phones, too). The PCTV hasn't arrived yet, but given the popularity of the Internet, any true PCTV to come to market will certainly be fully web-integrated.

Many experts believe that the PCTV idea won't catch on, because watching TV and computing are fundamentally different activities: One's a big-screen, group activity in the living room, the other is mostly a solitary, reading-intensive activity best done close to the screen, at a desk.

Still, many high-tech companies that believe in PCTV now offer products that could pave the road to PCTV:

☐ **WebTV** (see Hour 2, "What Hardware and Software Do You Need?")—The WebTV terminal box turns your TV into an Internet terminal (although not a full computer you may use for other applications). As I write this, new TVs with built-in WebTV capability (no terminal box required) are being readied for market. TV-maker RCA recently released its own version of the WebTV concept, the RCA Network Computer, which it plans ultimately to integrate with its satellite TV systems.

☐ **DVD**—The new home video format, Digital Versatile Disc (DVD) is an effort to establish a single standard for the discs used for movies, music, and computer software. With a DVD-ROM drive in your PC today, you can use DVD-based software, *and* play DVD movies and music. So the next step is to get your TV to use DVD-based games and other programs. DVD players are available now for showing movies on your TV, but newer models may soon show on your TV the DVD-based software designed for your computer.

☐ **DSS, DBS, and HDTV**—The popular new digital satellite TV services and the emerging High-Definition Television standard all carry television signals digitally—so eventually, all TVs will be capable of processing digital information. In other words, soon all TVs will *already* be computers, probably adaptable to other computing and communications tasks, such as the Internet.

24

☐ **Destination PC/TV**—Gateway 2000 Computers, a popular mail-order PC maker that recently opened a chain of retail stores, sells a product called a Destination PC/TV that's really a PC, a 31-inch or 35-inch TV, and home theater sound system packaged together. (Deluxe models include DVD.) It's not real, one-piece PCTV yet, but as an early attempt to sell the PCTV concept, it may prove or disprove the mass-market potential of PCTV.

How Is Internet Explorer 4 Web-Integrated?

Before Internet Explorer 4, Internet Explorer was only a web browser. It's still a browser, of course. But at your option (see Figure 24.4), Internet Explorer can add to Windows a feature called the Active Desktop, sometimes also called Web Integrated Desktop or Windows Desktop Update (Microsoft can't make up its mind).

Figure 24.4.

When installing Internet Explorer 4, you may optionally integrate your computer with the Internet by choosing the Windows Desktop Update option.

NEW TERM   The *Active Desktop* changes Windows 95 (or Windows NT) so accessing and opening files and programs on your own computer or local network is just like accessing and opening a web page on the Internet.

In effect, Internet Explorer makes all of Windows 95 behave a lot like the web, and it provides a preview of the way all computer systems will probably behave in the near future.

File Icons Become Links

The Active Desktop makes every file icon, program icon, or folder icon in a Windows folder, in Windows Explorer, and on the desktop into a link (peek back at Figure 24.1). The icon labels are underlined (just the way a link is underlined in a web page), and the pointer turns into a pointing finger when on the icon, just as it does on a link.

Because of this link formatting, you don't have to double-click the icon to open a file, folder, or program, as you have always had to do in Windows. Instead, you point to the link-like file

24

icon and click once, just as you do to activate a link online. Also, you no longer have to click at all to select a file icon when moving, copying, or performing another such operation on it. Just point to the icon and wait a second, and the icon is selected.

The Channel Bar Appears on the Desktop

As you learned in Hour 20, "Making the Web Deliver Pages to You: Channels and NetCasting," Internet Explorer puts the Channel bar on your desktop when the Active Desktop is installed. By putting one-click access to Internet resources right on the desktop, the Channel bar is both an important tool for, and symbol of, web integration.

Your Folders Turn Webby

The appearance and behavior of all your Windows folders changes on the Active Desktop. As mentioned earlier, file and folder icons become links, but there's even more webbiness than that. You can now get from place to place in a folder just as you get around the web, by using the browser-like toolbars on every folder window (see Figure 24.5).

Figure 24.5.

All Windows folder windows change so using them is just like using a web page.

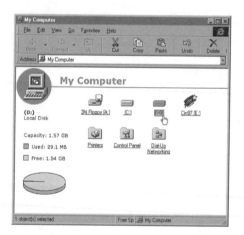

Folders on the Active Desktop also work like a web page in other ways. They may show inline images or have backgrounds. When you point to an icon (selecting it), information about that icon is displayed on the left side of the window. Sometimes, a preview may appear automatically; point to an image file, and a rough view of the image appears automatically on the left side of the folder window.

Windows Explorer Turns Webby

People often get confused when I talk about Windows Explorer—the file management system built into Windows 95—because they think I'm talking about Internet Explorer, the browser.

Perhaps in part to eliminate the confusion (or to increase it?), Microsoft has more or less merged Internet Explorer 4 with Windows Explorer. You now use a browser-like window (see Figure 24.6) to do all the stuff you used to do in Windows Explorer: display and navigate among disks, folders, and file lists; create, copy, move, and delete files; and open files and programs.

Figure 24.6.

The Windows Explorer after Internet Explorer 4: It's webby!

TIME SAVER

If you install the Active Desktop, and later decide you don't like it, you can easily remove it, whole or in part:

☐ To turn on or off the display of the Channel bar and Active Desktop wallpaper, from the Start menu choose Settings | Active Desktop | View as web page.

☐ To customize the way you click and other ways the Active Desktop works, choose Settings | Folders & Icons.

☐ To completely delete the Active Desktop, open Control Panel, choose Add/Remove Programs, select Internet Explorer 4 from the list, and click the Add/Remove button. On the dialog box that appears, choose Remove the Windows Desktop Update component, but keep the Internet Explorer web browser.

24

The Programs Menu Sprouts Favorites

The Active Desktop puts your Favorites (your list of pages you like to visit; see Hour 6, "Revisiting Places You Like") right into your Windows Start menu, as shown in Figure 24.7. Choose a Favorite, and Internet Explorer 4 opens automatically to take you there.

Figure 24.7.

Internet Explorer 4 puts your Favorites menu right in the Windows 95 Start menu.

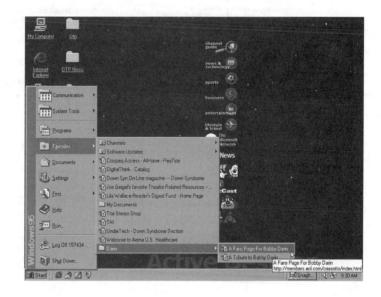

TIME SAVER

Besides opening the Favorites list from the Programs menu, you can open it in any folder window or in Windows Explorer, just by choosing Favorites from the menu bar.

Summary

I hate long goodbyes. So I'll just say thanks for spending these 24 hours with me. I hope you got what you came for.

See you on the Internet.

Workshop

Q&A

Q **My computer is not connected to the Internet 24 hours a day. So when accessing an online resource, it must first dial the net and open my browser. With that extra step added, getting to online resources is still different from using local ones, even with the web integration, right?**

A True, true. But two things are erasing that difference. First, the popularity of the Internet has resulted in the availability of local access numbers almost anywhere and in unlimited accounts being the norm. When the call is local and the ISP account unlimited, people connect to the Internet more freely and spontaneously; they no longer must consider the cost before connecting.

Second, Internet Explorer 4's enhancements to your connect dialog box and other changes make connecting to the Internet more automatic than before. In most configurations, you can access Internet resources with one click from anywhere in Windows. True, when Internet Explorer 4 must dial the net to access a resource, getting that resource takes more time than opening a file on your computer. But the effort on your part is identical; you click and go.

As the underlying hardware—modems, phone lines, and so on—evolves, the delay will continue to shorten, soon reaching a point where you'll perceive little or no difference between accessing local and online files.

Quiz

Take the following quiz to see how much you've learned.

Questions

1. True or false: To use the Internet Explorer 4 web browser, you must also use the Active Desktop.

2. Web integration may improve the productivity of computer users because

   a. They'll be grateful, and therefore motivated.

   b. They needn't learn or use different skills for local and online activities.

   c. They'll find it easier to email questions to others who can help them.

   d. Their computers will run faster.

3. Experts give the Net PC little chance of catching on as a home Internet terminal because

    a. A Net PC costs almost as much as a cheap PC, but can't do as much.

    b. A Net PC's "sealed case" prevents its use as a place to hide jewelry.

    c. "A Net PC" sounds too much like "Annette Peicie," a cheerleader nobody liked in high school.

    d. Anything collectively supported by Microsoft, IBM, and Intel can't be good for us.

Answers

1. False. The Active Desktop is optional.

2. (b) Choices (a), (c), and (d) are silly.

3. (a) The main reason is (a), but I have a feeling (d) isn't that far wrong.

Activity

Now that you're done, do you have an opinion about your experience with this book (good or bad)? If so, let the folks at Macmillan Computer Publishing know. They're always working to make their books better, and feedback from readers is the most important input to that effort.

You can email comments about this book to support@mcp.com. (Be sure to include the title, so they know you're not commenting on *Teach Yourself Java* or *Teach Yourself Tire Rotation*.)

24

Appendix A

When Things Go Wrong: Troubleshooting

The information listed in this appendix is designed to help you through some potential trouble spots you might—I repeat, *might*—encounter on the Internet. Remember, just because you see warnings here on some potential trouble spots doesn't mean you will experience any of these problems.

Q I installed an Internet suite, but I can't find some of its components—such as its conferencing or web authoring component. Is there another way to open them?

A If the components aren't accessible, you may not have included them when you installed the suite. For example, when you install Internet Explorer 4, you have the option of selecting Minimal, Standard, or Full installation; only Full installs all components. Try reinstalling (and perhaps redownloading) the suite, being sure to choose options for full installation.

Q I have a 33.6Kbps modem, but my Internet connection dialog box says I'm connected at 28.8Kbps.

A The speed at which a connection runs is determined by the slowest of the modems involved. If your ISP does not support 33.6Kbps access, you'll run at the ISP's modem speed (probably 28.8Kbps), no matter how fast your modem is. Some ISPs use different dial-in numbers for different speeds; contact your ISP and ask how to get 33.6Kbps access.

If you're already connecting through a 33.6Kbps modem at your ISP, your modem may be configured for 28.8Kbps operation. Double-click the Modems icon in Control Panel, and reconfigure your modem for its top speed. Consult your modem's manual for configuration details.

Also, note that a poor phone connection or a "noisy" phone line makes accurate modem communications more difficult. To compensate, most modems automatically slow down to a speed at which they can communicate reliably over the line. If you've eliminated the other potential causes, and you still see your modem communicating below its rated speed, you may have a noisy phone line. Contact your local telephone company to find out what can be done about the problem.

Q I have a really fast modem, but I've noticed that downloads often happen much slower than the rated speed of my modem and connection. How can I download at full speed?

A When a web server sends you a file, it generally cannot do so all at once, at full speed. The server must split its attention between sending you the file and taking care of other tasks for other users. Often, a download even pauses from time to time, and the speed of transfer is constantly going up and down. You can control the speed of your own connection, but there's nothing you can do about a slow server.

If it's a server you download from often, try accessing it at different days and times, to find the time or day that it seems least busy—that's the day to download. FTP transfers don't pause like web downloads, and therefore may be quicker and smoother, so see if you can find the file you want on an FTP server, and then use an FTP client (see Hour 19, "Using Old-Fashioned Hacker's Tools: FTP, Gopher, and Telnet") to get it fast.

Q I know that some programs, such as Internet Explorer 4 and its components, are integrated with my computer's autoconnect capabilities so they can connect to the Internet automatically, when necessary. But sometimes, I get messages that I'm offline when I know I'm online.

A Autoconnect works fairly well, but not perfectly—it's quirky. Sometimes while you're online, an Internet program may think you're offline. You cannot do much

A

to correct it, other than keeping up with new releases of your Internet software, in case the problem gets fixed.

If you're online when a program thinks you're off, when you try to do something that requires a connection, it asks whether you want to go online. Even though you're already online, just humor the program and click Yes. The program then immediately detects that you're online, and continues the operation you started.

Q Before I installed my browser, my graphics editing program opened whenever I opened an image file icon. Now my browser opens instead.

A When you install most browsers, the installation program edits your file types Registry to make the browser the default program for lots of different file types, including web page (HTML) files and most image file types. This is so the browser can display most types of files you encounter on the web quickly, without having to open another program first.

If you want a certain image file type to always open in your graphics program instead of your browser, you can open your file types Registry and change the program used for opening that file from your browser to your graphics program. Alternatively, you can simply reinstall your graphics program, which may automatically update the file types Registry to make the graphics program the default for opening images.

If you do change the file types Registry, note that images that are part of a web page layout—*inline* images—will still display in the web page, in the browser. If you click a link that opens an image file of a type registered to your graphics program, however, the image will not appear in the browser. Instead, your graphics program opens to display the image.

Q Sometimes when I enter a URL, use a Favorite (or Bookmark), or click a link, I get a message saying that my browser couldn't find the server, or that it couldn't find the file.

A When a browser reports that it can't find a file, it has successfully reached the server but can't find the specific file (page) the address points to. The file may have been deleted, renamed, or moved, or you may have typed the part of the URL that comes after the server address incorrectly. Try entering just the server portion of the URL—everything up to and including the first single, forward slash (/)—to access the server's top page, and then see whether you can navigate to what you want by clicking through links from there.

When a browser reports that it can't find the *server*, you may have typed the server address portion of the URL incorrectly, or the server may have changed its address or gone out of business. When you get this message, however, the server may just be experiencing temporary technical problems. Double-check the URL, and if you still can't get through, try again in a few hours, by which time the server may be back in action.

A

Q **About half of a web page or only certain parts appeared, and then everything just quit. My connection is still open—how do I display the rest of the page?**

A Sometimes, a web page quits transferring to your computer midway through; it gets hung up somehow and quits. Most browsers feature a button labeled Reload (or Refresh) that you can click to get the whole page all over again, from scratch. When a page seems incomplete or is acting quirky, Reload is often the best, first thing to try.

Q **When I click the Back button, nothing happens.**

A Is the Back button grayed out? If so, you've already reached the page at which your current session began. Back no longer works because there's nowhere to go back to.

If the Back button is not grayed out but seems to do nothing when you click it, you're probably looking at a page that uses frames. Remember, when you view a frames page, Back and Forward move you among the frames. If you keep clicking Back, however, you'll eventually move to the page you visited before the frames page.

Q **I've noticed that most web server addresses begin with www.-. Is this a universal naming convention?**

A No hard and fast rule exists concerning the use of www. You've probably already noticed web sites that vary, such as the AltaVista search tool (altavista.digital.com) or Netscape's home page (home.netscape.com).

Some web pages have *aliases* so a wrong URL leads to the right one. For example, many sites that don't begin with "www" nonetheless have an alias to an address that *does* begin with www. If you enter www.netscape.com, an alias at that address redirects you to the real page: home.netscape.com. Aliases can bail you out when you enter an old or near-miss URL, but don't count on them; at Microsoft, www.microsoft.com and home.microsoft.com lead to two different pages.

Q **If I choose to send someone an HTML email message, and the recipient is not using an email client capable of displaying HTML (such as Messenger or Outlook Express), won't the recipient's email program just spit out the part it can't read?**

A Yes, that is true. If you receive a message containing HTML and your email client can't read HTML, the program ignores the part it can't understand.

That means you can send HTML email to anyone. But it also means that you must be sure that all important information in the message is contained within the text itself and is not dependent on any images, text formatting, or other HTML features the reader will not see if his or her email program is not HTML-compatible.

A

Q My friend told me about this great newsgroup, but when I try to subscribe to it, I get a message that it's not on the server.

A Does your friend use a different ISP or online service than you do? Not all newsgroups are available on all servers. Some newsgroups are private and are maintained on servers accessible only to those with permission to use the newsgroup.

Also, each ISP maintains its own news server. Although most ISPs keep all 14,000+ newsgroups on their servers, some do not. For example, some attempt to minimize sexual traffic by not including the alt. groups on their servers. Others try to save space by including only newsgroups their members have requested. In case that's the reason you can't get through to the newsgroup, try sending an email to your ISP, requesting that the newsgroup be added to the server.

Q I instructed my service provider's news server to display all newsgroups; I've been waiting for several minutes, and nothing seems to be happening.

A Because of the sheer number of newsgroups on the typical news server, it may take more than several minutes to display all newsgroup names, so don't panic if it appears that nothing is happening. Just be patient. Also keep in mind that the speed of your Internet connection also affects how long it takes to display all those newsgroups.

Q My friend called me up and said he visited my home page, and said it looks sloppy. The text colors make it hard to read, he said, and the placement of graphics and text looks haphazard. The page looks okay to me in my web authoring program, so what gives?

A The same web page looks different through different browsers. Some browsers handle certain kinds of formatting instructions differently than others, and some don't support certain kinds of formatting. For example, some browsers don't support backgrounds, text alignment, or most image-positioning options. When you've applied these techniques in your page, it will look dramatically different to someone using that browser than it does to you. Variations in the viewer's equipment—such as different monitor resolutions (640×480, 800×600, and so on) or color depths (16 colors, 256 colors, and so on) might also play a role in making a page look different.

When you work on your page in a WYSIWYG (What You See Is What You Get) authoring program such as Page Composer or FrontPage Express, what you see is generally what you'd see if you viewed the page online through Internet Explorer (version 3 or 4) or any recent version of Netscape Navigator. Most folks online who use a graphical browser use either of these two browsers. Your tactless (but reliably frank) friend must be using a different browser. If you want to make sure your page looks great through any browser, keep the formatting simple and test the page by viewing it through as many different browsers as you can get your hands on.

Q Since I started subscribing to channels and web pages, browsing the rest of the web has become deadly slow. What's wrong?

A Channel technology offers the greatest benefit to folks who have full-time, dedicated Internet connections. Channels can be updated on and off throughout the day, often when the user isn't doing anything else on the Internet.

But for those who browse through a dial-up connection that's open only for a short time each day, channels present something of a problem. Each time you go online, your browser has a ton of catching up to do. It has to send its web crawler out to check for new content on your subscribed web pages. If the scheduled time for channel updates has passed, the browser has to check for new channel content as well as download that content if you use the Download Content option.

All this activity drains resources from your computer and your Internet connection that would otherwise be dedicated to your browsing activities. The problem gets worse when you add more subscriptions, when you schedule them to be updated often, when those subscriptions tend to have lots of new content often, and when you're not online often. Also, browsers must work harder with web page subscriptions than with channels, so web page subscriptions affect your system more heavily, in general.

You can't do much about it, except to restrain yourself. Don't subscribe to more than you need to, and keep scheduled updates to a reasonable minimum. You might also want to connect to the Internet each day for five minutes or so before actually doing any browsing, to give your browser a chance to get its daily updating and downloading out of the way.

A

Appendix B

New Riders Yellow Pages Preview

JUST A MINUTE

In versions 3.0 and above of Netscape Navigator or Internet Explorer, you can enter any of the URLs in this appendix exactly as shown (see Hour 5).

In other browsers, you may be required to precede each of the URLs shown here with the standard prefix for web pages:

http://

Adventure Travel

Above All Travel

www.aboveall.com/AAT.html

A full-scale travel agency specializing in exotic and unusual travel destinations. Links include destinations to Tahiti, Antarctica, French waterways, European skiing, and tropical scuba diving adventures.

Adrift Adventures

www.netpub.com/adrift/

Adrift Adventures is a travel agency and outfitter specializing in white-water rafting adventures on the Colorado River, Moab, UT, and the Green River. You have to use a telephone to actually book your trip.

Antiques

Antiques Road Show

www.pbs.org/wgbh/pages/roadshow/

Even if you're an inexperienced antiquer, PBS's *Antiques Road Show* is a great show and web site to visit to get into it. The show visits antique conventions all around the country where they have experts appraise items that regular people bring in and are clueless about.

Famous Furniture

famous-furniture.com/

We all have a little antiquer within us, yearning to grasp the old and rare. Famous Furniture imports antiques from all over the world and presents them well in this information-rich site.

Architecture

Design Basics Home Online Planbook

www.designbasics.com/feat06.htm

Design Basics, Inc. provides single family home plans with available technical support and custom design options. Build your dream home with plans that are also marketed through catalogs, newsstand magazines, and home building industry trade publications.

The Pritzker Architecture Prize

www.pritzkerprize.com/

The Pritzker Architecture Prize is sponsored by the Hyatt Foundation, and is the world's most prestigious architecture award. Learn about its Laureates and about their international traveling exhibition, "The Art of Architecture."

Astronomy

Astronomy-Related Web Sites

www.skypub.com/links/astroweb.html

Offers an extensive listing of astronomy-related web sites and includes brief descriptions.

NASA World Wide Web Information Services

www.gsfc.nasa.gov/NASA_homepage.html

Contains news and resources of value to a variety of people. Provides scientific information for professionals as well as educational information for teachers and students.

Automotive Clubs & Organizations

AAA Online

www.aaa.com/

Go directly to your state's "Triple A" office by entering your zip code. You already know about their famous Triptiks and the 24/365 road service that offers car lockout help, jump starts, and fixed flats.

The National Motorists Association

www.motorists.com/

The NMA exists to protect your rights as a driving citizen. Among their many services, the NMA lobbies for sensible road traffic laws and engineering, argues for your right to drive whatever you want, helps you fight tickets, and opposes camera-based enforcement, as well as speed traps designed only to generate revenue.

Bookstores

Amazon.com

www.amazon.com/

Touted as the "Earth's Biggest Bookstore," Amazon.com maintains and sells over one million titles. With a well-developed search engine, you can search by just about anything you know about a book or author—even if it is just one word.

B

Macmillan Publishing USA (The Information SuperLibrary)

www.mcp.com/

The Information SuperLibrary is chock full of interesting and useful information about computer-related titles, including a link to the online version of this book, *New Riders' Official Internet and World Wide Web Yellow Pages.*

Camping

Basecamp

www.intx.net/basecamp/

The people at Basecamp manage to communicate the joy of camping. This is a lively site with lots to do and see. The staff actually takes you with them on a hike through several different places.

GORP—Great Outdoor Recreation Pages

www.gorp.com/default.htm

So what do people actually *do* when they camp? Learn about all the great outdoor activities here—fishing, hiking, canoeing, bicycling, and more. Learn about little known and uncrowded camping places in National Parks and Forests and some State Parks and Forests.

Cooking

Cookbooks On/Line Recipe Database

www.cookbooks.com/reg.htm

Cookbooks On/line recipe database is the largest recipe database on the web. If you are looking for any recipes, this is the place to start!

Good Cooking

www.goodcooking.com

Good Cooking features food, wine, and cooking with professional recipes, submitted recipes, recipe links, good cooking information, nutritional links, consumer information, fish/shellfish recipes, culinary schools links, and much more.

Dieting & Weight Loss

The Calorie Control Council

www.caloriecontrol.org/

Contains sections that discuss everything from low calorie sweeteners to trends and statistics. Use the calorie counter calculator to determine the fat grams and calories in what you eat.

CyberDiet

www.cyberdiet.com/

Contains pages on food facts, menus and meal plans, recipes, and exercise. Search the database of foods, use the daily food planner, or assess your nutritional profile.

Domestic Violence, Child Abuse, & Missing Children

C.A.P.A.—The Child Abuse Prevention Association

www.childabuseprevention.org/

Child abuse prevention tips and responsibilities, calendar of events, programs, and ways to get involved in prevention methods are all highlighted at this informative site.

Child Quest International

www.childquest.org/

Site dedicated to the recovery of missing, abused, and exploited children. Offers safety tips to keep your kids safe, lists of other resources that can answer questions you may have, and links to other important sites dedicated to the safety of children.

Families

All About Kids Online

www2.aak.com/aak/

Way cool site that is about families and parenting. Features great articles about hot topics such as choosing prenatal care, education in the United States, Attention Deficit Disorder, and so on. Also offers a "virtual community," calendar of family events, and a parents' forum.

Childbirth.org

www.childbirth.org/

This award-winning site provides a wealth of information on every aspect of childbirth, from the pros and cons of episiotomies to the history of Cesarean deliveries. Pages are both informational and personal, aiming to educate consumers on the many facets of childbirth while helping expectant mothers secure the best possible care.

family.com

www.family.com/

Super cool site that offers information on the following topics: activities, computing, education, travel, entertainment, and finance sections are just for starters. These sections are then broken down into sections of the United States.

Financial Aid

fastWEB! (Financial Aid Search Through the Web)

www.fastweb.com/

Set up a personalized profile that will match your skills, abilities, and interests to fastWEB's database of more than 275,000 scholarships. Then check your fastWEB mailbox for updates and new awards. Come back regularly for info on hot new awards and updates on current scholarships.

Student Services, Incorporated

web.studentservices.com/

Student Services has a database of more than 180,000 scholarships, grants, fellowships, and loans representing billions of dollars in private-sector funding for college students living in the U.S. Enter your major into the search engine to look up scholarships in that area.

Gardening

The Flower Link

www.flowerlink.com/

Enables you to order from budding flower shops across the U.S. and Canada. Many of these florists even provide same day delivery. What distinguishes this service is that that there are no accompanying service or transfer charges, saving you as much as 30 percent.

The Tree Doctor

www.1stresource.com/t/treedoc/

This is the place to go to find answers to your urban tree questions. Find out about tree diseases and pests, tree topping, and organic bio-stimulants. There is also a directory of professional arborists. The Tree Care Doctor will gladly answer your questions.

Government Offices & Agencies

FedWorld Information Network

www.fedworld.gov/

FedWorld links to every federal government Web site there is. It is pretty easy to get around in and has some of the most valuable links listed on the main page, including listings of all federal job openings and a way to download all tax forms.

The House of Representatives WWW Service

www.house.gov

Students needing information on the legislative process for school could not find a better source. All the committees, legislation and of course, the congressional members are accessible here.

The White House Home Page

www2.whitehouse.gov/WH/Welcome.html

This site takes a while to load if you have a slower modem, but it's worth it. Besides looking great, it's full of resources. It's an excellent historical site and provides access to all the most recent White House press briefings. You can even send e-mail to the president, vice president, and first lady.

Health & Fitness

American Heart Association National Center

www.amhrt.org/

The American association that fights heart disease and stroke. They maintain an extensive heart and stroke guide that contains over 300 articles from the association on various subjects such as aspirin, cigarette smoking, and exercise.

Healthtouch

www.healthtouch.com/

Provides updates on health, diseases, wellness and illness, a resource directory guide to organizations and government agencies, access to pharmacies in your community, and a drug search program that enables you to find information about prescription and over-the-counter drugs.

Medicine OnLine

meds.com

Serves as a commercial online medical information service. Provides health care professionals and consumers a convenient place to obtain medical information. Serves as a gateway to access other health information services on the Internet. Currently focuses on cancer information.

History

African-American History

www.msstate.edu/Archives/History/USA/Afro-Amer/afro.html

A page devoted to the history of African Americans, with text and documents relating to Buffalo soldiers, the history of slavery in the United States, African-American scientists, writers, musicians, and much more. Links to related sites.

The Historical Text Archive

www.msstate.edu/Archives/History

Award-winning site that contains links to East and West European history topics. Historical information, images, and documents relating to many countries, including Estonia, Iceland, France, the Netherlands, and more.

Home Improvement

The Construction Zone

www.construction-zone.com/

Provides a resource for your home improvement needs. Their growing service offers listings of contractors and related businesses specializing in home repair, home improvement, remodeling and other related services covering the U.S. Visit their free handy hints forum or join their monthly online newsletter for ideas and tips.

B

The Home Team

www.hometeam.com/

Contains information on intelligent home design, lighting controls, standards, security systems, communication systems, and more. Involves many industries and numerous members who represent a wide range, from manufacturing to service providers.

Libraries

Internet Public Library

www.ipl.org/

Includes resources for children, teenagers, and adults. The reference center allows one to ask questions of a live librarian (not a computer).

The Library of Congress

www.loc.gov/

Provides access to the Library of Congress online catalog through Telnet searches of LOCIS, Gopher searches of LC MARVEL, the Library of Congress FTP site, and the Library of Congress Z39.50 Gateway.

Library Resource List

www.state.wi.us/agencies/dpi/www/lib_res.html

This site contains lists of links to other sites, arranged into the categories of Reference Resources, New Sites and Search Engines, Government Resources, Library Sites, Professional Information, and Libraries, the Net, and the NII (National Information Infrastructure).

B

Movies & Videos

The Academy of Motion Picture Arts and Sciences

www.ampas.org/ampas/

Check out the latest press releases and new web features by the Academy. This site also includes the Interactive Guide to the Academy Awards, the winners of the latest Academy Awards, and information on the Academy itself.

The Internet Movie Database

www.msstate.edu/Movies/

The Internet movie resource provides information on over 65,000 movies and TV shows. Search for a film of interest to learn about the cast, production company, and staff on the film. This site also includes stills from films, sound clips, and synopses of the films.

Movies.Com

www.movies.com/

Maybe you were looking for information on movies and hit on this site, and to your chagrin found that it was a movie studio. Hollywood Pictures puts out plenty of titles you'll recognize. If you decide to stay, it's worth the visit.

Museums

Metropolitan Museum of Art, New York

www.metmuseum.org/

One of the largest art museums in the world, its collections include more than two million works of art—several hundred thousand of which are on view at any given time—spanning more than 5,000 years of world culture, from prehistory to the present.

The Smithsonian Institution

www.si.edu/newstart.htm

The 150-year-old Smithsonian Institute comprises the National Portrait Gallery, the National Museum of American Art, the National Air and Space Museum, the Sackler Gallery, the Cooper-Hewitt Museum of Design, the National Museum of American History, the National Museum of Natural History, and more. This site defies categorization, as it has a lot of everything.

Personals & Dating

The Internet Computer-Dating Service ™

computer-dating.com/

This service is free for now, although the site says there will be a low fee in the future. It is a matchmaking service that compares your questionnaire answers to others and notifies you of your matches.

SOLO Lifestyles for Singles

www.solosingles.com/

This site lives up to its claim of being "as current as a newspaper but as thorough as a magazine." It is extremely detailed and offers a wide range of topics of interest to today's singles. Covers everything from tips on looking good, self-improvement, coping with being "suddenly single" as the result of death or divorce. Also offers personal ads and matchmaking services.

Pet Care

The AVMA Network American Veterinary Medical Association

www.avma.org/

This site is an excellent source for info on caring for your pet. The Health section includes pictures you can print out and let your kids color, and each picture includes an activity or advice on feeding, training, or basic care. Submit a photo or story here about your pet.

Pet Care Corner

www.pet-vet.com/index.htm

Authored by Lowell Ackermann, a board-certified veterinary dermatologist and author of 34 books on animal health, this site provides answers to owners' questions about their pets' health.

Real Estate

HomeBuyer's Fair

www.homefair.com/homepage.html

Contains classified listings of homes for sale. Provides information on buying, selling, relocating, getting a mortgage, and apartments. Includes a special section for first-time buyers.

Internet Real Estate Network

www.iren.com/

Free Web pages for real estate properties, professionals, and organizations. Fully searchable database. HTML/CGI authoring and other custom services are also available. Provides answers to frequently asked questions and links to other related sites.

B

Religion & Philosophy

Finding God in Cyberspace

users.ox.ac.uk/~mikef/durham/gresham.html

A guide to religious studies resources on the Internet. Takes you to print, people, digital, gateway resources, starting points for further exploration, e-texts, and so on.

Islam's Home Page

www.utexas.edu/students/amso/

A valuable Islamic resource containing articles about various Islamic issues including the Renaissance of Islam, women in Islam, and Jesus in Islam. An English translation of the Holy Qur'an and several Islamic prayers can be found at this site, as well as a collection of Islamic images.

Jewishnet

jewishnet.net/

Offers a list of Jewish-related sites. Offers links to Gopher sites, home pages, libraries, ftp sites, and provides information on Jewish newsgroups and mailing lists.

Taxes

Forms and Publications

www.irs.ustreas.gov/prod/forms_pubs/forms.html

This site contains every tax form and pub imaginable. Choose from many formats, including PDF, and you'll never have to drive to the library in the rain to find files they may not have for some reason.

Taxpayer Help and Education

www.irs.gov/prod/tax_edu/teletax/tc101.html

This site coincides with volunteer-based programs the Service provides to help citizens drudge their way through murky roads.

Television Resources

CineMedia/Television Sites

www.afionline.org/CineMedia/tele.html

B

This page is filled with links to TV-related sites including shows, networks, organizations, schools, research, and production. Also links to audio clips, video clips, and photos of different shows and performers.

TV Guide Entertainment Network

www.tvguide.com/

Links to TV Guide Online, FOX Sports, FOX News, and more. Enter your ZIP code to get TV listings specific to your area. Also contains feature articles on your favorite stars.

Travel & Vacation

Airlines Online

airlines-online.com/airlines/

Airlines-Online is your one-stop web directory for every airline, airport and other aviation site that is on the World Wide Web today. This site is the source for aviation links. Airlines-Online is a free service and the site is updated weekly on Monday mornings.

Rental Agencies

www.yahoo.com/Business/Corporations/Automotive/Rentals/

Yahoo!'s lengthy list of rental agencies is located here, which include over fifty rental agency home page links. Also recreational vehicle links are situated here.

Traveling in the USA

www.travelingusa.com/a1/assistance/youhere.html

These pages will help the U.S. traveler find information on parks, campgrounds, resorts, and recreation. From relief maps to kiddie activities, you'll probably satisfy your travel needs here.

Women's Studies

The National Organization for Women (NOW)

www.now.org/

This home page for NOW offers press releases and articles, issues NOW is currently involved in, information on joining (with email or web addresses for many local chapters), and the history of NOW. Also provided is a search form if you're looking for a specific topic at NOW's site.

B

Resources for Women's Studies on the Web

www.middlebury.edu/~jaj/women.html

An impressive list of links broken down into several major categories, including journals, databases, and history.

Zoos

National Zoological Park Home Page

www.si.edu/natzoo

Web site of the National Zoo. Includes a user questionnaire, news, and information, as well as a photo library. Also includes links to the Smithsonian Institution and educational games that complement the information found on the site. Includes downloadable files that contain press coverage of the zoo. Coffee drinkers, take note: The site contains an interesting legend about Lewak coffee.

ZooNet

www.mindspring.com/~zoonet/

Attempts to provide information about every zoo in the world. Includes the ZooLinks page, which offers jumps to hundreds of zoos and zoo-related information. Offers the ZooNet Image Archives, which features numerous jumps to online zoos and animal pictures.

B

Appendix C

Internet Business Guide Preview

JUST A MINUTE

In versions 3.0 and later of Netscape Navigator or Internet Explorer, you can enter any of the URLs in this appendix exactly as shown (see Hour 5).

In other browsers, you may be required to precede each of the URLs shown here with the standard prefix for web pages:

http://

Business Startup and Planning

BizTalk

www.biztalk.com/

BizTalk is an electronic magazine devoted to small business. Departments include news, finance, law, politics, technology, and more. *BizTalk* runs contests to provide seed money for start-ups.

Business Plan Resource File

www.aifr.com/startup.html

Sponsored by the American Institute for Financial Research, this site is designed to help emerging business with their first business plan. A full compendium of general advice is offered in addition to having information on interactive business plan software.

Marketing Resource Center

www.marketingsource.com/

A free service of Concept Marketing Group, Inc., the Marketing Resource Center has an extensive articles library on planning your business, marketing tools and contacts, a database of industry associations, and links to online business magazines.

Small Business Advisor

www.isquare.com/

A terrific collection of articles for the new businessperson forms the core of this site. Example titles include "Don't Make These Business Mistakes," "Getting Paid," and "Government Small Business Resources." You'll also find tax advice and a glossary of business terms.

U.S. Small Business Administration

www.sbaonline.sba.gov/

SBA Online is your online resource to government assistance for the small businessman. The site is organized into special areas on Starting, Financing, and Expanding Your Business, as well as other information on SCORE, PRONET, and local SBA links.

Business Financing

America Business Funding Directory

www.businessfinance.com/

America Business Funding Directory is the first search engine dedicated to finding business capital. You can search categories ranging from venture capital to equipment lending to real estate, as well as a private capital network of accredited investors.

Computer Loan Network

www.clnet.com/

Borrowers can use this web site to add a loan Request for Proposal (RFP) directly to the CLN MortgageNet mortgage multiple listing service. Mortgage brokers, lenders, banks, and

C

secondary marketers will search the system, locate your RFP, and then find ways to offer you a lower note rate than your currently quoted rate, if possible.

FinanceNet

www.financenet.gov/

FinanceNet was established by Vice President Al Gore's National Performance Review in Washington, D.C. in 1994 and is operated by the National Science Foundation. This site features a list of government asset sales including a subscription to daily sales.

Financial Women International

www.fwi.org/

Founded in 1921, Financial Women International serves women in the financial services industry who seek to expand their personal and professional capabilities through self-directed growth in a supportive environment. FWI's vision is to empower women in the financial services industry to attain their professional, economic, and personal goals, and to influence the future shape of the industry.

Securities and Exchange Commission

www.sec.gov/smbus1.htm

This page of the SEC site opens its small business area where you can find information on taking your small business public. In addition to a complete Q&A, you'll also find current and pending initiatives of interest.

Job Opportunities and Labor Resources

America's Job Bank

www.ajb.dni.us/

A multi-state project of the public Employment Service, America's Job Bank is for both employers and employees. A section on Occupational Employment trends offers in interactive outlook handbook and answers to many surveys such as, "What's the fastest growing occupation?"

CareerPath.com

www.careerpath.com/

CareerPath.com posts more than 400,000 new jobs on the Internet every month, and is updated daily by newspapers across the U.S. You can search their help wanted database by category, newspaper, and keyword.

JobWeb

www.jobweb.org/

Run by the National Associations of Colleges and Employers, JobWeb lists jobs, employer profiles, and career planning resources. One resource, the Catapult, offers a variety of career assessment tools.

Telecommuting, Teleworking, and Alternative Officing

www.gilgordon.com/

This site features telecommuting information from around the world—and from many different perspectives—on the subjects of telecommuting, teleworking, the virtual office, and related topics. Includes a FAQ section and a list of upcoming events.

Legal and Regulatory

American Law Source Online (ALSO)

www.lawsource.com/also/

This site is notable because it has links to all American online legal systems, including the Federal judiciary and all 50 states and territories. ALSO has equally far-reaching coverage of Canadian and Mexican law.

Business Law Site

members.aol.com/bmethven/index.html

Sponsored by Methven & Associates, the Business Law Site covers federal and state statutes, as well as legal research sites for both business and high-tech law. You can also find a full compendium of tax forms, information on international law, and a list of legal research sites.

Corporate Counselor

www.ljx.com/corpcounselor/index.html

The Corporate Counselor has resources including daily news columns and articles on employment law, securities, antitrust, and other business issues.

Magazines Online

Advertising Age

www.adage.com/

All the information you could ever need about the movers and shakers of advertising. The site features a section called NetMarketing that covers getting the most out of your web site, and a section called DataPlace that features industry reports and statistics.

BusinessWeek

www.businessweek.com/

BusinessWeek's online-only content includes Maven (the interactive computer shopper) and BW Plus (lists of the best business schools, business book reviews, and articles on the computer industry and the Information Age). You can also access BW Radio, hourly market reports in RealAudio format.

Fast Company

www.fastcompany.com/

A new edge business magazine with a host of "how-to" articles: how to make a group decision like a tribe, how to deal with the issues of dating and sexual harassment on the job, how to choose a career counselor, how to disagree (without being disagreeable), and more.

Hispanic Business Magazine

www.hispanstar.com/

This site covers information for business owners and professionals with a Hispanic interest. There is also a national résumé referral service, a market research area focusing on the U.S. Hispanic economic market, and a special events department that provides a calendar of events.

Inc. Online

www.inc.com/

Self-described as the "Web site for Growing Companies," *Inc. Online* is actually several minisites, including Inc. itself, which offers articles and archives; Business & Technology, which contains statistics to benchmark your business; and Local Business News, where you can choose from more than 25 U.S. cities for local business news and resources.

Marketing and Market Research

American Demographics/Marketing Tools

www.marketingtools.com/

At the American Demographics/Marketing Tools web site, you can check out consumer trends, tactics and techniques for information marketers, or access *Forecast*, a newsletter of demographic trends and market forecasts.

Business Wire

www.businesswire.com/

Business Wire is a leading source of news on major U.S. corporations, including Fortune 1000 and NASDAQ companies. You can look up a company, category, keyword, or region and find all the pertinent business news. You can sign up for their service online.

Marketing Resource Center

www.marketingsource.com/

Sponsored by the Concept Marketing Group, the Marketing Resource Center maintains an articles archive with more than 250 business-related articles. Their Tools of the Trade section links to an association database and software for general business and project management.

Sales Leads USA

www.abii.com/

This site is run by American Business Information, Inc., which specializes in generating company profiles. Free services include searching for businesses or people by name with American Directory Assistance or searching by type of business with American Yellow Pages.

Nonprofit Information

Council of Foundations

www.cof.org/index.html

The Council of Foundations is an association of foundations and corporations gathered to promote responsible and effective philanthropy. You'll find information on the various types of foundations as well as a Community Foundation Locator service.

The Grantsmanship Center

www.tgci.com/

The Grantsmanship Center specializes in training for grant-writing and fundraising. Much of the site is designed to support their courses around the country. The site also contains a cross-referenced database of state and federal funding.

Nonprofit Resources Catalog

www.clark.net/pub/pwalker/

A personal project by the head of United Way Online, this site features meta-links (links to pages of links) dedicated to Interlink sites that benefit nonprofits. Categories include Fundraising and Giving, General Nonprofit Resources, and United Ways on the Internet.

C

Procurement and Contracting

BidCast

www.bidcast.com/

BidCast is a subscription service that allows you to browse and search thousands of U.S. federal government bids. You can sign up for the email service for personal notification. There is a free trial section that allows you to look at Commerce Business Daily listings.

Electronic Commerce Resource Center

www.ecrc.ctc.com/

The ECRC Program promotes awareness and implementation of Electronic Commerce and related technologies into the U.S.-integrated civil-military industrial base. Downloadable products can be found in the Electronic Commerce Testbed.

Environmental Protection Agency Procurement

www.epa.gov/epahome/Contracts.html

Visit this site for a full listing of business opportunities and EPA acquisition resources. In addition to covering policy and procedure, you can also find an acquisition forecast and a special section devoted to small business opportunities.

General Services Agency

www.gsa.gov/

The GSA's mission is to provide expertly managed space, supplies, services, and solutions at the best value to Federal employees. In addition to full information on buying practices, you can also visit its online shopping service, GAO Advantage.

State and Local Procurement Jumpstation

www.fedmarket.com/statejump.html

This invaluable web page gives you links to procurement sources for all 50 states, not to mention Washington, D.C. and Guam. Most states also have some local listings for specific cities as well as economic development links supplying market data.

Small Office/Home Office

America's Small Business Finance Center

www.netearnings.com/

Sponsored by Net Earnings, Inc., this one-stop shop offers business advice on insurance policies and prices, and on applying for loans and credit cards. You can also sign up for online payroll service here.

BizResource.com

www.bizresource.com/

Dedicated to encouraging small businesses and entrepreneurs, BizResource offers an on-going series of business tips (both via email and archived online), a business chat area, and a series of audio, video, and computer resources.

Business@Home

www.gohome.com/

An electronic magazine dedicated to the working-from-home community, Business@Home includes articles on opportunity, marketing, and technology. Its Cool Tools department reviews recent hardware and software important to the general home office worker, while the Consultant's Corner focuses on the consultants work experience.

Home Office Association of America

www.hoaa.com/

There's power in numbers—even if you're working alone. The Home Office Association of America offers group health insurance, a long-distance calling plan, a debt collection service, home business and equipment insurance, and more. Be sure to visit their 50 Great Home Office Startup Ideas page.

Home Office Links

www.ro.com/small_business/homebased.html

Home Office Links is a full compendium of web links for small and home-based offices including franchises, business opportunities, reference material, newsgroups, searching tools, and services for small business. It includes links to just about anything related to small- and home-based business.

U.S. Chamber of Commerce Small Business Institute

www.uschamber.org/programs/sbi/index.html

The U.S. Chamber of Commerce runs a Small Business Institute with a variety of resources both for free and for sale. There are self-study programs on Mastering Your Business on the Internet and the Small Business Institute Series, as well as information on the SOHO Conference.

Trade Shows and Conferences

EXPOguide

www.expoguide.com/

If you're thinking about selling your product through a trade show, stop by this site first. It has a full list of trade shows, conferences, and exhibitions as well as comprehensive coverage of show services and associations. Although primarily intended for trade show managers, it also offers plenty of information for exhibiting companies.

Trade Show Central

www.tscentral.com/

Sponsored by the International Association for Exhibition Management, Trade Show Central gives you easy access to information on more than 30,000 trade shows. Its searchable database links to an e-mail notification service where you can request more information. Its AudioNet connection broadcasts and archives keynote speeches from major events.

EventWeb

www.eventweb.com/

A free mailing list service for meeting, conference, and trade show promoters. Sample articles include "How to Exhibit at a Virtual Trade Show," "Expanding Educational Horizons in the Online World," and "Promote Your Speakers—Inexpensively!"

C

INDEX

Complete and Return This Card
for a *FREE* Computer Book Catalog

Thank you for purchasing this book! You have purchased a superior computer book written expressly for your needs. To continue to provide the kind of up-to-date, pertinent coverage you've come to expect from us, we need to hear from you. Please take a minute to complete and return this self-addressed, postage-paid form. In return, we'll send you a free catalog of all our computer books on topics ranging from word processing to programming and the Internet.

Mr. ☐ Mrs. ☐ Ms. ☐ Dr. ☐

Name (first) ☐☐☐☐☐☐☐☐☐☐☐☐ (M.I.) ☐ (last) ☐☐☐☐☐☐☐☐☐☐☐☐☐☐☐☐☐☐☐

Address ☐☐☐☐☐☐☐☐☐☐☐☐☐☐☐☐☐☐☐☐☐☐☐☐☐☐☐☐☐☐☐☐☐☐

City ☐☐☐☐☐☐☐☐☐☐☐☐☐☐☐☐☐☐ State ☐☐ Zip ☐☐☐☐☐ ☐☐☐☐

Phone ☐☐☐ ☐☐☐ ☐☐☐☐ Fax ☐☐☐ ☐☐☐ ☐☐☐☐

Company Name ☐☐☐☐☐☐☐☐☐☐☐☐☐☐☐☐☐☐☐☐☐☐☐☐☐☐☐☐☐

E-mail address ☐☐☐☐☐☐☐☐☐☐☐☐☐☐☐☐☐☐☐☐☐☐☐☐☐☐☐☐☐

1. Please check at least three (3) influencing factors for purchasing this book.

Front or back cover information on book ☐
Special approach to the content ☐
Completeness of content ☐
Author's reputation ☐
Publisher's reputation ☐
Book cover design or layout ☐
Index or table of contents of book ☐
Price of book ☐
Special effects, graphics, illustrations ☐
Other (Please specify): _____ ☐

2. How did you first learn about this book?

Saw in Macmillan Computer Publishing catalog ☐
Recommended by store personnel ☐
Saw the book on bookshelf at store ☐
Recommended by a friend ☐
Received advertisement in the mail ☐
Saw an advertisement in: _____ ☐
Read book review in: _____ ☐
Other (Please specify): _____ ☐

3. How many computer books have you purchased in the last six months?

This book only ☐   3 to 5 books ☐
2 books ☐   More than 5 ☐

4. Where did you purchase this book?

Bookstore ☐
Computer Store ☐
Consumer Electronics Store ☐
Department Store ☐
Office Club ☐
Warehouse Club ☐
Mail Order ☐
Direct from Publisher ☐
Internet site ☐
Other (Please specify): _____ ☐

5. How long have you been using a computer?

☐ Less than 6 months   ☐ 6 months to a year
☐ 1 to 3 years   ☐ More than 3 years

6. What is your level of experience with personal computers and with the subject of this book?

	With PCs	With subject of book
New	☐	☐
Casual	☐	☐
Accomplished	☐	☐
Expert	☐	☐

Source Code ISBN: 1-57251-393-1

7. Which of the following best describes your job title?

Administrative Assistant .... ☐
Coordinator .... ☐
Manager/Supervisor .... ☐
Director .... ☐
Vice President .... ☐
President/CEO/COO .... ☐
Lawyer/Doctor/Medical Professional .... ☐
Teacher/Educator/Trainer .... ☐
Engineer/Technician .... ☐
Consultant .... ☐
Not employed/Student/Retired .... ☐
Other (Please specify): _____ ☐

8. Which of the following best describes the area of the company your job title falls under?

Accounting .... ☐
Engineering .... ☐
Manufacturing .... ☐
Operations .... ☐
Marketing .... ☐
Sales .... ☐
Other (Please specify): _____ ☐

9. What is your age?

Under 20 .... ☐
21-29 .... ☐
30-39 .... ☐
40-49 .... ☐
50-59 .... ☐
60-over .... ☐

10. Are you:

Male .... ☐
Female .... ☐

11. Which computer publications do you read regularly? (Please list)

_____
_____
_____
_____
_____
_____
_____
_____
_____

Comments: _____
_____
_____

Fold here and scotch-tape to mail.

MACMILLAN COMPUTER PUBLISHING USA

A VIACOM COMPANY

Technical ---- Support

If you need assistance with the information provided by Macmillan Computer Publishing, please access the information available on our web site at **http://www.mcp.com/feedback**. Our most Frequently Asked Questions are answered there. If you do not find the answers to your questions on our web site, you may contact Macmillan User Services at **(317) 581-3833** or email us at **support@mcp.com**.

Using the CD-ROM

The companion CD-ROM contains a wide variety of software, services, and resources that enable you to connect to the Internet and start surfing. All of the contents of the CD-ROM can be viewed with a frame-enabled web browser. If you do not have a web browser installed, follow the instructions to install either EarthLink's Internet access software or stand-alone browsers from Netscape and Microsoft. The contents of the CD-ROM include the following:

- [ ] EarthLink's Internet Connection Software Package
- [ ] Microsoft Internet Explorer 4.0 and Netscape Navigator 4.0
- [ ] Hyperlinked version of New Riders' 1998 World Wide Web Directory
- [ ] NetTaxi's multimedia-based Internet tour (Windows 95 version)
- [ ] Software and demos for online gaming, banking, investing, and shopping
- [ ] A large collection of Internet tools and utilities including FTP, email programs, newsreaders, graphic viewers, and more

To view the contents of the CD-ROM, open the START.HTM file in your web browser. If you haven't installed a browser yet, see the following steps for installing either the Internet Explorer or Netscape browser on a PC or Macintosh.

Windows Installation

EarthLink's Internet Access Software

This CD-ROM contains EarthLink's TotalAccess software to enable you to sign up and get connected to the Internet. Follow the directions below to install TotalAccess.

1. Insert the CD-ROM into your CD-ROM drive.
2. Use Windows Explorer or File Manager to view the files on the CD-ROM.
3. Open the ELINK directory.
4. Open the WIN31 directory if you are running Windows 3.1 or the WIN95 directory if you are running Windows 95 or NT 4.0.
5. Double-click on the SETUP.EXE file.
6. Follow the installation wizard's instructions to finish.

Installing Web Browsers Only

If you only need to install a web browser or would like to update your web browser, you should follow the directions on the next page. We have provided both Internet Explorer 4.0 and Netscape 4.0 for your convenience. You only need to install one browser to view the

CD-ROM content. However, once you are comfortable with using one browser, we suggest that you install the second and become comfortable using both. Each browser has its strengths and weaknesses.

1. Insert the CD-ROM into your CD-ROM drive.
2. Use Windows Explorer or File Manager to view the files on the CD-ROM.
3. Open the NAVIGATE directory to install Netscape Navigator 4.0 or the EXPLORE directory to install Microsoft's Internet Explorer.
4. Double-click the SETUP.EXE file.
5. Follow the installation wizard's instructions to finish.

Macintosh Installation

EarthLink's Internet Access Software

The CD-ROM contains EarthLink's TotalAccess software to enable you to sign up and get connected to the Internet. Follow the directions below to install TotalAccess.

1. Insert the CD-ROM into your CD-ROM drive.
2. Double-click on the CD-ROM icon on the desktop.
3. Double-click on the ELINK directory.
4. Double-click on the SETUP file.
5. Follow the installation wizard's instructions to finish.

Installing Web Browsers Only

If you only need to install a web browser or would like to update your web browser, you should follow the directions below. We have provided both Internet Explorer 4.0 and Netscape 4.0 for your convenience. You only need to install one browser to view the CD-ROM content. However, once you are comfortable with using one browser, we suggest that you install the second and become comfortable using both. Each browser has its strengths and weaknesses.

1. Insert the CD-ROM into your CD-ROM drive.
2. Double-click on the CD-ROM icon on the desktop.
3. Open the NAVIGATE directory to install Netscape Navigator 4.0 or the EXPLORE directory to install Microsoft's Internet Explorer.
4. Double-click the SETUP file.
5. Follow the installation wizard's instructions to finish.

Additional instructions and a complete file listing can be found in the README file on the CD-ROM.